"With rich insight, practical guidance, and a light touch, Dan Pontefract shows how to design workplaces where everyone can thrive—at every age."

CARL HONORÉ, international bestselling author of *Bolder*

"*The Future of Work Is Grey* reveals pragmatic, forward-looking strategies for doing better business in our aging society. Insightful, energizing, and unexpectedly fun—complete with pop-music references that tie it all together—this book is an excellent guide to find opportunity in our changing world."

LEANNE CLARK-SHIRLEY, PhD, president and CEO of the American Society on Aging

"Dan Pontefract masterfully shows how longer lives can lead to better work. He provides clear practices for age-diverse teams. A needed guide for leaders ready to ride the age wave."

KEN DYCHTWALD, PhD, bestselling author of 19 books, including *Radical Curiosity* and *What Retirees Want*

"Dan Pontefract brilliantly shows how broadening our longevity lens to the twenty-first-century's new talent and market realities can contribute to innovation, resilience, and growth. This is a playbook for any leader ready to build a truly all-age, all-stage workforce and market. Plus, it's a great read."

AVIVAH WITTENBERG-COX, longevity strategist, speaker, and podcast host of *4-Quarter Lives*

"This is not a dry exercise in age-related data and workforce planning; rather, it is a timely call to harness the wisdom and intelligence inherent in every demographic now present in our workplaces."

TONY BINGHAM, president and CEO of the Association for Talent Development

the future of work

DAN PONTEFRACT

The Untapped Value
of Age in the Workforce

is
grey

Cataloguing in publication information is
available from Library and Archives Canada.
ISBN 978-1-77458-644-0 (hardcover)
ISBN 978-1-77458-730-0 (ebook)

Page Two
pagetwo.com

Page Two™ is a trademark owned by
Page Two Strategies Inc., and is used
under licence by authorized licensees

Cover, interior design, and illustrations by Taysia Louie
Printed and bound in Canada by Friesens
Distributed in Canada by Raincoast Books
Distributed in the US and internationally by Macmillan

26 27 28 29 30   5 4 3 2 1

danpontefract.com

To Steven Hill, Lorna Shapiro, and
Brian Reid, three beautiful Canadian
Rubies who showed me the way.

OF THE ERAS

I begin as a stream, naive,
a rivulet brimming with intent,
buoyed by promise, curiosity, zeal,
pushing relentlessly towards uncertainty.

These currents help shape my eventual shine,
eddies sculpting subtle destiny,
guiding imperceptibly, softly, insistently,
my youthful ardour formed by my fluidity.

My path is now halfway. I am settling, hardening,
gaining resilience shaped by issues and ideas.
The middle is messy, mercurial, at times melodious,
face etched fervently by lessons manifold.

Custodian of the stone, I have become steadfast yet introspective,
patience calcifying beneath my deepening insight,
crystallizing through the lessons, the failures, the wins;
a sharp bulwark, unyielding, maturing.

Coda? Denouement? Neither, as now my gem forms radiantly,
a polished brilliance emerging, sublime, seasoned, rich,
irony sparkling amongst the grey facets,
a wheel of wisdom shimmering, roaring, calm.

An epiphany, of the eras, humbling revelation:
A Ruby, I am,
cut from a weathered Rock, gently shaped, unhurriedly,
by the persistent cadence of my River's unending flow.

DAN PONTEFRACT, 2025

TRACK LISTING

Side A

Age
Debt

Drop the (Age) Needle

How old are you?

It's a question that's both personal and loaded—and whether you're prepared to deal with it or not, it is already reshaping the future of work.

Society is aging. Fast. We are entering a massive demographic change that will forever alter the workplace. Indeed, we're teetering on the precipice of an era-defining shift. As a leader, adopting a new perspective on age to tackle this issue will become crucial, just as saving for your retirement is crucial. And this is not just a human resources issue—it's geared at leaders at every level of the organization. Like you!

You may not realize it, but you are suffering from what I call "Age Debt." You're not yet aware of the looming age-related challenges that will significantly impact your team and organization. Those challenges are bursting at the age seams.

So, I'm going to ask the question again. But with added emphasis.

How old are you?

Go ahead. Say it out loud. I'll wait. (I'm not going anywhere.)

How did that feel? For some, easy. "I'm X years old," you said, no problem. For others, intrusive. "What gives you the right,

Mr. Author?" And some of you stayed quiet, terrified someone might overhear. "No way I'm sharing my age!" Because you're young. Or middle-aged. Or old. Whatever that means.

I'll let you know my age in a minute. But first, a story. The first of many.

A few months after I turned 50 (spoiler alert: I'm now older than that), I received a rather blunt yet alarming email from the founder and CEO of a US-based speakers bureau. Let's call him Michael. It went something like this:

"Hi, Dan. We are refreshing our speaker roster. Thanks."

I'm paraphrasing, but basically, I got fired.

After years of featuring on the bureau's roster and delivering many keynotes for them, I was tossed to the curbside without so much as an explanation. My follow-up email for rationale was answered with vague and ambiguous platitudes.

Was it my hair?

After all, wasn't that what happened to Lisa LaFlamme? Canada's iconic news anchor was famously and suddenly fired in the summer of 2022 after 35 years at CTV, with two years left on her contract. When she let her hair go grey during the pandemic, her boss at Bell Media, the parent company, reportedly took issue. And then—just like that—she was out. Too old!

Maybe the speakers bureau had too many MAWGs—middle-aged white guys—and was trimming that persona on their roster. (I discovered that acronym in 2009 and laughed hysterically.)

It's possible that a client from the speakers bureau submitted a complaint, criticizing my hyper-kinetic keynote style.

No, it must have been my hair.

And then it hit me. I'm 50. I'm "old."

I was "old" even before LaFlamme. I received that email in 2021, a few weeks after I had just finished social-distance-celebrating my first half century. Fifty! It was a grand party, devoid of any hugs, because, you know, COVID. However, there *was* cake. And something about the way I felt prompted me to start seriously exploring the subject matter in this book.

I couldn't have published what you're about to read when I was 20, 30, or heck, even in my mid-40s. The follow-up email I received from Michael was the proverbial icing on the 50-year-old birthday cake, marking the beginning of a full-scale investigation into the topic of *age*.

By the time I finish writing, editing, marketing, and cajoling people to read and rate this sixth book of mine—*The Future of Work Is Grey*—I will be very close to my 55th birthday.

Who cares? What's the big deal about 55? A minute ago, you were 50.

I grew up in Hamilton, Ontario, Canada. It's a former industrial town, similar to Pittsburgh, Pennsylvania; Bilbao, Spain; or Essen, Germany. When people listened to the radio, they often heard a jingle from a financial services company. The message focused on retiring at the age of 55: "Freedom 55," they would sing. I frequently think about that phrase.

Let me make something abundantly clear: What you are about to read is the polar opposite of Freedom 55.

I am 53 as I write these introductory words—there, I revealed my age. I will be 54 or older by the time you read this, but freedom is not something we should aspire to at 55. Organizations should also avoid basing their talent planning on that number. The idea of Freedom 55 is misguided for a whole slew of reasons, as you will soon discover.

I must be absolutely clear, however: This is neither a retirement book nor a self-help book. So, what is it?

This book is an emergency siren because the future of work demands that we face what lies ahead differently. It's equally a signal to alter how you should lead going forward.

Look around and you'll see there are far more organizations and leaders acting and behaving like Michael at the speakers bureau than not. And that's only the beginning. Michael might have acted with a touch of ageism, but that's merely a sliver of the problem we will unpack.

My years of research on this topic have taught me that a multitude of challenges are associated with age in the workplace. A disastrous future awaits those who do not confront them.

The challenge is as big as it gets. But we will look at ways to turn it—this gigantic Age Debt, as I call it—into a dividend. An Experience Dividend.

This book is about you and the future of work. As the title suggests, it may be "grey," but I am not a pessimist. There is hope! I have written it to protect your organization's future. It is about your leadership on the important yet almost wholly overlooked issue of age. There are massive problems to face, but don't worry; I will provide an array of solutions for you to consider.

Oh, and you may even want to turn the lens on yourself as a human being. You may be a leader, but you're also an individual—and like me, you may want to prepare for the day when Age Debt catches up to you, personally.

Are You a River, a Rock, or a Ruby?

Where are you right now on life's racecourse? Cicero, the Roman statesman and philosopher, once said, "Life's racecourse is fixed; Nature has only a single path and that path is run but once, and to each stage of existence has been allotted its own appropriate quality."

Your organization will soon begin to wrestle with an invisible but potent unintended conflict on the racecourse, if it isn't already doing so: an Age Debt imbalance that concerns intelligence. And not just any type of intelligence. The two competing forces are known as fluid intelligence and crystallized intelligence, thought of as follows:

Fluid intelligence: The capacity to adapt, innovate, and think quickly, unaffected by the past.

Crystallized intelligence: A form of deep expertise built over time and through various and different forms of experience.

Both are critical. Employees of any age can demonstrate both, but studies have shown that older workers possess more—and arguably better—crystallized intelligence than younger workers.

The flip side can also be true. Younger employees tend to excel in fluid intelligence, uninhibited by the long careers of experiences and outcomes. They tend not to be set in their ways. However, when an organization has to deal with a lack of harmony between the two—when team members of any age fail to recognize both types of intelligence and their importance—the consequences can be staggering. War ensues. And not the friendly card game of War.

Psychologist Raymond Cattell first conceptualized the duality of fluid and crystallized intelligence in 1963. Later researchers described fluid intelligence as "the capacity to think logically and solve novel problems independently of prior knowledge"—a cognitive flexibility that typically peaks in early adulthood.

In contrast, they defined crystallized intelligence as the accumulated knowledge, skills, and expertise acquired over a lifetime, often growing more potent with age as individuals draw upon their educational and professional experiences. You can clearly see how both are important to an organization, particularly as it ages and younger workers become less common.

Subsequent research further emphasized the importance of these two intelligences in organizational settings. As the researchers noted, "Fluid intelligence declines earlier in adulthood, whereas crystallized intelligence continues to grow and remains stable as individuals gain more experience." Even more reason to balance the intelligences and not create artificial wars.

Studies have demonstrated that organizations thrive when they harness the complementarity of both intelligences. Researchers Christian Grund and Niels Westergaard-Nielsen observed in 2008, "Young employees bring adaptability and technological skills, while older employees offer institutional knowledge and strategic insights. Usually, both kinds of human capital are necessary for firm productivity."

In this book, I want to challenge these two types of intelligence. Through my research, observations, and direct involvement with leaders and individual contributors at all levels, I have found that most organizations have three intelligence personas, not two.

Take a moment to think about the following:

- Are you a River flowing with youthful energy and ambition, eager to carve new paths?

- Are you a Rock, firmly grounded; someone others depend upon for stability and strength, with on-demand fluid thinking still available?

- Or perhaps you're a Ruby, polished by time, gleaming with wisdom, and offering solid brilliance shaped by experience?

Team Member Age Eras

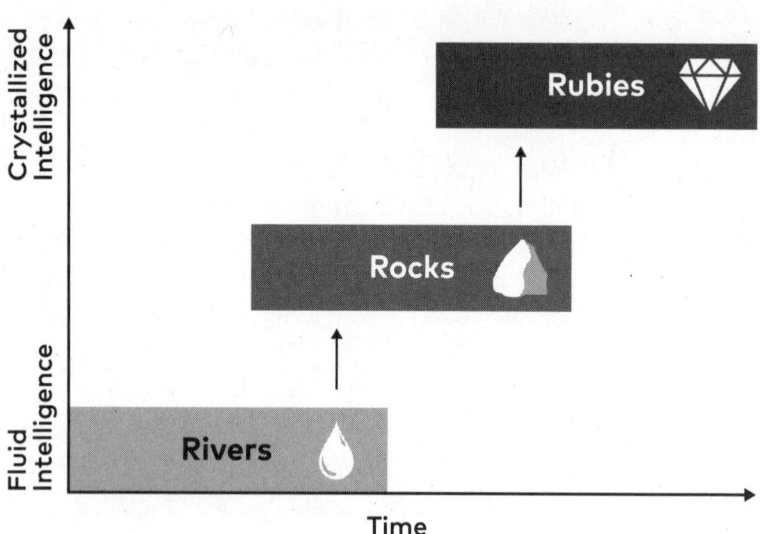

Throughout the book—and like with Taylor Swift's popular Eras Tour—I will pay homage to each of these three crucial age eras: Rivers, Rocks, and Rubies, which correspond to young, middle-aged, and older personas. I'm firmly in my Ruby era. Which are you?

- **If you're a Ruby,** you've moved beyond the impetuosity of youth. Your edges have been smoothed and your wisdom honed through years of learning and contributing, yet you're still open to ideas.

- **If you're a Rock,** you're no longer carving out brand new paths like a River—you've settled, standing firm and steady in the currents. But you still have a strong source of fluid creativity.

- **If you're a River,** you're not yet grounded by the core of middle-life experience or refined by time's hand. You're free-flowing, gushing, and almost infinitely curious.

Each stage brings its own unique power, and, just as Cicero reminds us, "The weakness of childhood, the impetuosity of youth, the seriousness of middle life, the maturity of old age—each bears some of Nature's fruit, which must be garnered in its own season." Each of us runs life's racecourse, carrying strengths and contributions unique to our age and stage. Yet, workplaces often fail to recognize the full extent of these contributions. They overlook the River's insatiable drive, the Rock's durability and dependability, and, especially, the radiant potential that Rubies bring to light the way forward.

This book challenges the notion of only two types of intelligence. And it challenges—if not burns to the ground—the misconception of generations. As tropes and memes go, labelling me as brooding, latchkey, Nirvana-loving GenX may be cute, but in the workplace, generational branding like this is destructive. Research has shown that generational differences at work are largely exaggerated and, more concerning, that focusing on them can be harmful to effective organizational decision-making.

The Future of Work Is Grey offers a way to see yourself—and others—as part of a larger whole, where every era matters. Whether you're a River, a Rock, or a Ruby, your persona holds an untapped value. Together, these three eras are the foundation for workplaces that will thrive in the future. And all of us go through the three eras in our careers. You may be part of a generation outside of work, but from now on, you must think of yourself and your team members as Rivers, Rocks, and Rubies.

And yet, it is the Ruby—the culmination of experience, reflection, and wisdom—that stands out as both a problem *and* the beacon for that future. In a world so quick to move forward, we often forget to look back, to treasure what's been built, and to lean on those who can guide us towards what's next.

So, who are you? And who are the Rivers, Rocks, and Rubies around you, in your management group and teams? As you move through these pages, you'll discover how embracing the contributions of every era can transform how we lead, work, and grow—individually and collectively.

And what's getting in the way of this epic transformation is quite simple: Age Debt.

Introducing Age Debt: A New Reality

I started the book by asking you how old you were. It was cheeky, but that was the point.

Whether you are a River, Rock, or Ruby, we need to have a very different conversation about age. Much like Swedish scientist Svante Arrhenius's first-known acknowledgement of climate change in 1896, many people and organizations remain in denial. An age crisis is ahead, but you are essentially rejecting its reality. You're an unknowing age denialist. This is also why we must define and discuss a new term: Age Debt. I define it as follows:

> **Age Debt:** The organizational failure to plan for and value age, resulting in capability loss and a weakened workforce.

In broader terms, Age Debt is the cumulative burden organizations face as our populations age, birth rates plummet, the internal skills gap widens, multi-generational issues grow, and various economic structures fail to keep pace. Think of it as a demographic time bomb—a workforce model hollowed out by dwindling younger generations and inflamed by an untapped reservoir of seasoned workers sidelined by outdated policies and biases.

Paying homage to Arrhenius, Age Debt is the workplace equivalent of the climate crisis. I could even call it the "clim*age* crisis." It's slow-moving, but when the storm breaks, the costs become astronomical, and the impacts are unavoidable, overwhelming everyone. Think of the 2004 Boxing Day Tsunami in Thailand, New Orleans' 2005 Hurricane Katrina, the 2011 Horn of Africa drought and the 2025 LA fires, all striking at the same time in your organization.

Age Debt is more than just a demographic and financial oversight; it's a missed opportunity. Age diversity could be your greatest asset, yet many organizations treat age as a liability. Imagine a workplace where age isn't a limitation but a foundation for collective wisdom. This gets at the very point of this book.

The lack of leadership concerning Age Debt triggers a crisis of productivity, adaptability, and lost potential. Age Debt strains an organization's resources, stifles innovation, and impedes growth. Sadly, as I have discovered, a leader's unwillingness to rethink what aging means in the workplace and for its future is the root cause of the issue.

To bring just a few snippets of the Age Debt problem into focus for you, let me introduce projected population dynamics across several global regions:

- **Canada:** By 2030, one in five Canadians will be over 65—whereas it was one in seven in 2010. The 2024 birth rate plummeted to 1.26 children born per woman, down from 1.68 in 2010. Where I live in British Columbia, the birth rate is the lowest in Canada, below 1.0. Net new immigration into Canada is the only factor saving the population from collapse, but it brings its own issues, as you will discover. (Fun fact: The replacement birth rate for any region is 2.1 children born per woman. You'll see me mention this at various points in the book.)

- **United States:** By 2032, Americans aged 65 and older will make up 8.6 percent of the workforce, a 31 percent increase from 2022. This group is projected to drive 57 percent of overall labour force growth during this period. The participation rate for older adults is one of the few expected to rise, with 21 percent of those aged 65 and over projected to be in the labour force by 2032—up from 19 percent in 2022. And what is the only other group expected to increase its participation rate by 2032? Those aged 55 to 64, swelling to nearly 70 percent.

- **Europe:** Europe's working-age population is projected to decline by nearly 10 percent by 2030, with countries like Germany, France, and Italy already experiencing labour shortages. To put this in perspective, by 2030, almost 7 percent fewer people will be working compared to 2005. Without leadership adjustments, these declines will inevitably lead to reduced organizational productivity and increased costs for companies across the entire EU zone.

- **United Kingdom:** By 2030, 22 percent of the UK population will be 65 or older—up from 19 percent just ten years earlier—with birth rates remaining (and falling) below replacement levels at 1.6 children per woman. As in Canada and the United States, immigration has become one of the few stabilizers for the population, yet the demand for social services and healthcare continues to escalate, intensifying labour shortages and productivity challenges.

- **Japan:** Japan faces one of the most urgent Age Debt scenarios worldwide. With a birth rate of only 1.2 children born per woman, the Japanese workforce continues to shrink rapidly. By 2030, more than one-third of Japan's population will be over 65, placing an extraordinary strain on all sectors. Rising participation among older workers has been essential but insufficient to counterbalance the steep productivity drop across many industries due to labour shortages.

- **South Korea:** But if there was ever a demographic decline leader, it's South Korea. The country faces one of the world's most extreme population shifts. With a birth rate of 0.75 children per woman—one of the lowest globally—the country is headed for a sharp workforce population decline. By 2030, 25 percent of South Korea's population will be over the age of 65.

Together, these projections illustrate a stark reality: The age crisis isn't looming—it's here, just like climate change. Regions around the world will continue to face their own unique demographic ticking clocks, but the overall trend is clear: We're all facing declining birth rates and aging populations, placing steady pressure on organizations and economies alike.

Living longer is a positive development, but as illustrated in the following graphics, the G7 countries (and others) face a significant demographic challenge in the years to come. That's why the future of work is *grey*—it's both aging and murky.

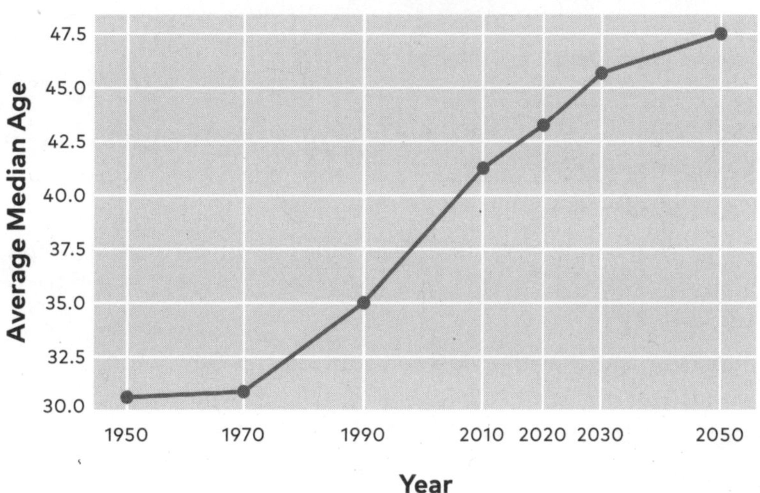

Average Median Age of G7 Countries (1950–2050)

Source: United Nations Department of Economic and Social Affairs, Population Division, *World Population Prospects 2022: Summary of Results* (United Nations, 2022), un.org/development/desa/pd/content/World-Population-Prospects-2022.

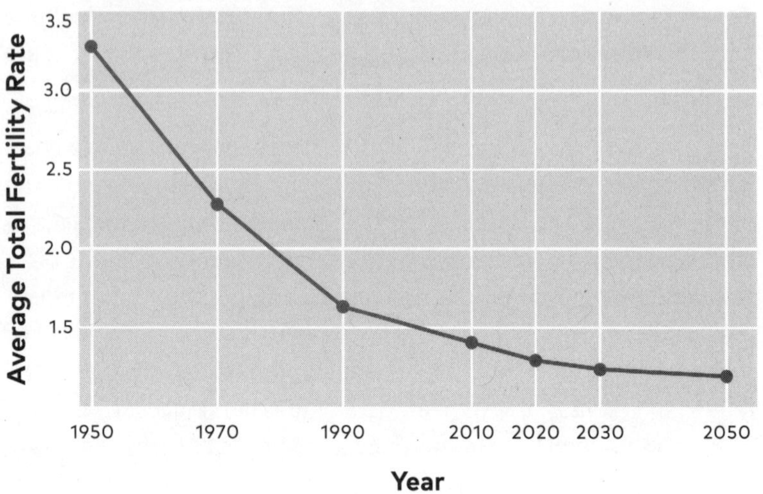

Source: OECD, *Society at a Glance 2024: OECD Social Indicators* (OECD Publishing, 2024), doi.org/10.1787/918d8db3-en.

More Age Debt to Worry About

Unfortunately, Age Debt extends beyond the demographic time bomb. Three additional factors must be considered, which I will detail further throughout the first half of the book: longevity, the talent paradox, and ageism. Consider the following a mere appetizer.

Longevity

Age Debt comes with a dash of irony. In this newfound, greying world, debt can lead to credit. Specifically, as mentioned, we are living longer. Hooray! Who doesn't love a little life credit? In 2025, even Goldman Sachs wrote, "Living longer really is a good thing."

However, the challenges created by longevity will reshape the workforce. As people live longer, they'll need to work longer. It turns out that living costs money, and those people are nowhere near prepared for the costs associated with living longer. In other words, employee financial security and insecurity are additional issues that all leaders will need to consider for their team members and themselves.

In the United States, for example, the average 401(k) retirement savings balance for people aged 55 to 64 in 2024 was just under $250,000. That may seem like a lot of money, but not if you think you will retire at 65 and live to 90. The median for all retirement savings is worse; it's a paltry $185,000.

You can probably guess what will happen if we live longer and have insufficient retirement savings.

While social security and various government pension plans *might* help, there is no guarantee these programs will survive, since fewer people contribute to government coffers as taxpayers each year. The savings gap is real, right across the world, and underscores a lack of preparedness for large swaths of the population.

Bottom line? Many people will need to work longer.

The Older Worker Talent Paradox

The next layer of the Age Debt challenge is the talent paradox regarding older workers. While organizations claim to desperately need experience and skills, they often overlook the very individuals who possess these qualifications. Leaders may not be creative enough to rethink how older workers can make significant contributions to the organization, or, regrettably, they may mistakenly view them as too expensive.

This organizational blind spot results in valuable institutional knowledge being ignored, leading to a potential "talent vacuum."

Without strategic workforce planning that incorporates mentorship, knowledge capture and transfer, and innovative ways of integrating workers of all ages, organizations forgo the continuity and opportunities that experienced employees can provide. It's like *Star Wars* without Yoda or Obi-Wan Kenobi.

Age Debt problem

Canada: By 2030, one in five Canadians will be over 65.

United States: By 2032, Americans aged 65 and older will make up 8.6 percent of the workforce.

Europe: Europe's working-age population is projected to decline by nearly 10 percent by 2030.

United Kingdom: By 2030, 22 percent of the UK population will be 65 or older.

Japan: By 2030, more than one-third of Japan's population will be over 65, placing an extraordinary strain on all sectors.

South Korea: By 2030, 25 percent of South Korea's population will be over the age of 65.

Ageism

Then there is the often overlooked and frequently invisible bias that silently corrodes workplace culture: ageism. Perhaps the last of the "isms." Hello, Dan's former speakers bureau!

This bias batters individuals and hinders various organizational functions, such as knowledge transfer, storytelling, innovation, and overall collaboration. What's worse is that ageism is even more pronounced for women, minorities, and Indigenous people.

Ageism appears in hiring, promotions, project assignments, and daily interactions. Organizations must challenge and eliminate these outdated beliefs about age and foster a culture that appreciates contributions at every career stage to remain competitive and prepared for the future. And as I will show, ageism doesn't just harm older workers. This prejudice can be found across all age spectrums, including against younger workers.

What are the risks if you don't address the rather large issue of Age Debt and its four components: demographic apocalypse, longevity, older worker talent paradox, and ageism? I am so glad you asked.

The Risks of Ignoring Age Debt: MapleCo 

I'd like you to consider the following scenario, which will unfold throughout the entire book. It's hypothetical, but it's also a very real situation in today's organizations. Maybe yours.

MapleCo CareNet (MapleCo for short) has been in business for over 50 years and is deeply rooted in its purpose. It strives to ensure its clients feel constantly supported. The company launched its popular telehealth platform a decade ago, transforming how its customers access various aspects of healthcare insurance and related wellness services.

These days, the conversations within MapleCo's leadership team have begun to shift. Leaders are no longer solely focused on expanding telehealth or streamlining claims processes. There is something far more pressing: the 3,750 people who have made it all possible; the Rivers, Rocks, and Rubies working at MapleCo.

At a recent senior leadership retreat, CEO Marla Benson brought the issue into sharp focus. "Our success has always come from our people. They built the systems, created the relationships, and earned the trust that defines MapleCo. If we don't rethink how we attract, retain, and develop talent, we risk losing the essence of what makes us who we are."

Her words are grounded in a stark reality. Nearly 40 percent of MapleCo's most experienced employees—almost 1,500 Rubies—have the opportunity to retire within the next three years. As you might expect, these individuals carry decades of institutional wisdom. For years, they have been the ones building the systems to navigate complex claims and adapting to shifting regulations, all the while helping to build the culture of care that MapleCo's clients expect. Replacing them is a matter of preserving the company's current, future, and past DNA.

Meanwhile, MapleCo's efforts to attract younger professionals—the Rivers—are falling short. Many of today's graduates, particularly those skilled in AI and data analytics, are drawn to roles in fast-moving industries with bold cultures. MapleCo, by comparison, seems too tied to tradition. Even as the company invests in an AI task force to modernize claims processing and member services, its ability to recruit the talent needed for that transformation remains in question.

The gaps are already showing. Teams at MapleCo are severely stretched. Meeting deadlines has become increasingly challenging. Mid-level managers—the Rocks—who often act as bridges between senior leaders and junior team members, are burning out under mounting workloads. Younger Rivers are struggling to grow without the time for mentorship that only seasoned colleagues can provide.

Senior leaders are grappling with some fundamental questions:

- How can MapleCo honour the contributions of those who built its success while creating an environment that excites the next batch of Rivers and Rocks?

- How does MapleCo balance the stability of experience with the energy of innovation?

- Should the company consider hiring Rubies?

Age Debt doesn't announce itself in dramatic ways. It creeps in like an unsuspected fog. The after-effects can be brutal. However, when leaders act with intention, the situation can become a net-positive advantage. When you value the wisdom of older workers and build systems that bring all three eras together, companies like MapleCo can move forward with strength.

MapleCo may be a fictional company that I patched together from many of my experiences, but let me assure you that this scenario is unfolding worldwide in real time. For example, focusing solely on the United States, let's investigate four real-life industry scenarios:

- **Manufacturing:** By 2030, the manufacturing sector may face a shortage of 2.1 million skilled workers due to retirements and an ongoing skills gap, as nearly 25 percent of the workforce is already over the age of 55.

- **Nursing:** The United States is projected to need more than 1.1 million new nurses by 2026 to fill the roles vacated by over 900,000 retiring nurses. Significant shortages are expected in Pennsylvania, Illinois, and North Carolina.

- **Energy:** As of 2024, nearly half of all utility workers were over the age of 50, and many are expected to retire by 2030. This trend poses a risk of significant skills gaps in a sector where specialized knowledge is essential.

- **Trucking:** The US trucking industry is projected to face a shortage of up to 160,000 drivers by 2028. Currently, only 12 percent of drivers are under 25 years old. The industry continues to struggle to attract younger workers due to high training costs and challenging working conditions. The average age of a truck driver in the United States is 46, five years older than the average age of the broader workforce.

In terms of future risks, here's what MapleCo—and countless organizations—will face if Age Debt continues to be ignored:

- **Productivity decline:** Organizational productivity will suffer as more people leave the workforce without being replaced. According to McKinsey, by 2030, global GDP growth could drop by 40 percent, and much of that decline is due to a shrinking labour pool. The Organisation for Economic Co-operation and Development (OECD) reports that an aging population may reduce per capita income by 8 percent over the next three decades, with fewer workers to sustain productivity levels. Whole industries will feel the pull as experience drains away and fresh talent is unable or slow to fill the gap.

- **Increased organizational costs:** Costs will skyrocket in response to the skilled labour shortage. In Canada, by 2030, wage growth in key sectors is projected at 4 to 5 percent each year. As the pool of experienced workers decreases each year, wage demands will soar. Great news if you are an employee—bad news if you're an employer having to pay the wage bill.

- **Institutional knowledge decay:** When experienced employees leave, they carry decades of knowledge with them. OECD countries could lose $5.4 trillion in productivity by 2030 due to this loss of expertise. The manufacturing and natural resources sectors will be severely impacted as the deep expertise that drives operations suddenly becomes scarce.

- **Innovation decrease:** According to BCG, companies with management teams scoring above the median for age diversity generate 38 percent more of their revenue from innovative products and services compared to less age-diverse companies. With a lopsided age workforce—too few Rubies—companies risk falling into routines that limit agility while their competitors find new ways forward.

- **Talent planning nightmare:** Companies lacking a strong talent plan will be at risk. Researchers discovered that sectors facing labour shortages saw productivity growth decline by up to 8 percent over two years, with turnover and mismatches further exacerbating these gaps. Overlooking Age Debt puts organizations in a perpetual state of talent instability.

Whether you work at an organization like MapleCo or not, Age Debt is here, and its impact will only grow. The question you must ask yourself as a leader is whether your organization or team will ignore this inevitable crisis or confront it head-on.

In my home province of British Columbia, more than 30 emergency departments closed in 2022 alone, primarily in remote, rural communities, not because of infrastructure issues, but due to a critical shortage of healthcare staff, many of whom had retired or left with no succession plan in place. Similar crises have emerged in other sectors. For example, in Ontario, school boards have struggled to staff classrooms, relying on underqualified substitutes as veteran educators retire and leave a shortage in their ranks. In Germany, labour shortages are beginning to disrupt core industries. For example, in April 2025, more than a quarter of construction firms and nearly half of architecture and engineering firms reported their operations hindered by a lack of skilled workers, a challenge compounded by the reality that roughly one in four construction employees is already aged 55 or older.

These are structural talent collapses tied to decades of slow demographic change. Organizations and public services are buckling under the weight of unaddressed Age Debt, with productivity, quality, and service continuity all being impacted by the fallout. Have you considered this potential scenario for you and your team? And please don't say, "Don't worry, AI will solve it."

Well, there is good news ahead!

Marla Benson and her team at MapleCo have decided to rise to the challenge. Can they do so with positivity, determination, and, ultimately, success? Throughout this book, we'll follow their efforts

If Age Debt continues to be ignored, there will be...

Productivity decline: Organizational productivity will suffer as more people leave the workforce without being replaced.

Increased organizational costs: Costs will skyrocket in response to the skilled labour shortage.

Institutional knowledge decay: When experienced employees leave, they carry decades of knowledge with them.

Innovation decrease: Companies with management teams scoring above the median for age diversity generate 38 percent more of their revenue from innovative products compared to less age-diverse companies.

Talent planning nightmare: Companies lacking a strong talent plan will be at risk.

at the company as they tackle the complex realities of Age Debt. You will hear from Benson, her direct reports, and other Rivers, Rocks, and Rubies at the organization to see if they can turn Age Debt into something more fruitful.

Now, I need you to take a deep breath. At least ditch the idea of drinking an entire bottle of whisky. There is hope on the horizon. There is always hope in my books.

How do you pay down Age Debt? I call it the "Experience Dividend."

Hope on the Age Horizon: The Experience Dividend

Amid today's formidable demographic shifts and the four components of Age Debt, a major advantage is hiding in plain sight: the Experience Dividend. Embracing age as an asset turns debt into a steady source of insight, continuity, and strength rather than a liability. The Experience Dividend is what organizations gain by integrating the skills, insights, and wisdom of Ruby employees into their strategy. It's what occurs when you inculcate an all-ages era culture that includes your Rivers and Rocks as well. It is era-balanced, not generation-biased.

The Experience Dividend takes organizations well beyond the mindset of succession planning and retirement support, antiquated relics from yesteryear. The Experience Dividend harnesses age diversity as a calculated advantage. I define it as follows:

> **Experience Dividend: The payoff that arrives when organizations leverage age as an asset rather than a liability.**

The Experience Dividend reflects the accumulated value that organizations gain by integrating the skills, insights, and mentorship of seasoned employees (those Rubies) into their workforce strategy, rather than cutting them loose because they're old, expensive, or some combination of the two. It ensures that all three age eras—Rivers, Rocks, and Rubies—are thoughtfully integrated into an improved talent plan and organizational culture.

Forward-thinking organizations will tap into the experience of older workers to unlock a level of value that fuels innovation, stability, learning, mentorship, and growth. As a leader, this is where you come in. What will you do to tap into the wisdom and experience of your older workers?

BMW is an excellent example to highlight as an organization that is already profiting from the Experience Dividend. Recognizing the invaluable expertise held by senior employees, BMW introduced the Senior Expert Program that transitions long-standing leaders into Ruby roles. When I met BMW design director Tom Allemeier during an author dinner in Vienna, he filled me in on the framework of BMW's thinking. He was speaking from first-hand experience because Tom was in the middle of the transition.

Rather than stepping out entirely or retiring from the company, experienced professionals like Tom can shift from their existing leadership positions to roles as individual contributors. They remain at the company, where they're dedicated to mentoring up-and-coming leaders while also continuing with their non-leader responsibilities. In Tom's case, he gets to continue his passion for automobile design while contributing to the development of the next-in-line leader for his unit.

A Ruby is polishing a Rock to eventually become another Ruby while helping Rivers along the way.

The model enables BMW to retain and share its deep institutional knowledge and unique design insights—those "crystallized" aspects of intelligence that can only be gained through years of experience in the field. It enables BMW Ruby experts to share hands-on guidance with Rock mentees while allowing newer employees to apply and develop their skills independently. It permits the company to seamlessly transition invaluable assets, such as Tom, not out of the organization but into new and important roles. I discussed the program in detail with BMW's Konstanze Carreras-Solé, director of diversity, equity, and inclusion. Her wonderful insights will surface in Track 8: Wisdom Wheel.

This BMW Experience Dividend example transforms age from a looming challenge into a workplace culture must-have, ensuring the organization thrives on intergenerational collaboration, diverse perspectives, robust knowledge sharing, and business continuity. For both BMW *and* Tom, it's a win–win outcome.

Organizations (and you) face a choice: continue to operate as you have for decades or, instead, unlock the inherent value that Ruby workers bring to the workplace while rethinking how to treat your Rivers and Rocks.

There are three key components to the Experience Dividend that I will introduce briefly. Later in the book, I'll provide a full account of various tactics related to each component.

Career Canvas

This is a new line of thinking that reimagines how work can be structured to accommodate team members in their various eras. Age should not dictate an employee's value. The Career Canvas emphasizes the need for workers to contribute meaningfully throughout their careers, depending on their age era. Careers are no longer vertical but have become multidirectional.

The Career Canvas provides an enhanced framework for workers to develop, perform, and excel across all ages and stages, regardless of experience level. It offers a refreshed approach to incorporating Rubies at various points in the revised talent timeline, in addition to rethinking how Rocks and Rivers can develop in different, nonlinear ways.

Wisdom Wheel

As a leader, you will also need to focus on creating formal systems for multi-directional knowledge transfer across the River, Rock, and Ruby eras. This concept comes to fruition in the form of the Wisdom Wheel, an assortment of knowledge capture, transfer, mentorship, apprenticeship, and learning models. The framework is designed to make sure that institutional wisdom is captured, preserved, and passed on. The Wisdom Wheel emphasizes the importance of both lifelong learning and continuous growth within your organization.

Longevity Lens

I predict that by 2030, the concept of retirement will have undergone a complete transformation. The Longevity Lens is a framework that supports a work environment where team members' physical, mental, financial, and emotional well-being are prioritized. This revised organizational approach will provide the people you lead with the resources they need to maintain their well-being and sense of purpose throughout their careers, particularly as they age and work well past their sixties.

What to Expect: Grey Goodness

I like music. You might even call me a music junkie. Along with cycling, it's a big passion and hobby of mine. You may have noticed that this opening chapter is titled "Track 1: Drop the (Age) Needle." Why?

I want you to imagine listening to an album while reading this book. (Unless you are listening to the book, which makes this part of the first track awkward.) As with any physical album, you have a musical choice between the two sides. You might not have realized it, but you've just listened to the opening track on Side A of the album *The Future of Work Is Grey*. (I sure hope you liked it.) There are four more tracks on Side A: Age Debt. The rest of Side A is as follows:

- **Track 2:** The Demographic Tidal Wave
- **Track 3:** The Experience Conundrum

- **Track 4:** The Pressure Points of Longevity
- **Track 5:** The Silent Saboteur of Ageism

As you may have guessed from the song titles, Side A lays out the vexing problems you must contemplate. Perhaps they are *tracks* to overcome. Side A sets the stage. It explores the tidal wave of demographic shifts, the talent missteps we repeat, the tensions of longevity, and the quiet yet ugly weight of ageism. These tracks will provoke, inform, and challenge your thinking, preparing you for the solutions waiting on Side B.

If you feel the night is long and seek the warmth of a new musical day, you can easily skip to Side B. You may not want to slog through the problems of Side A but instead choose to hurtle towards the ideas that solve this inevitable mess. I wouldn't blame you.

Once you flip (or skip) to the book's second side, you will be met with a geyser of hope and valuable consideration. There are five tracks on Side B, curated by DJ Dan and called the Experience Dividend, as follows:

- **Track 6:** Plot Twist
- **Track 7:** Career Canvas
- **Track 8:** Wisdom Wheel
- **Track 9:** Longevity Lens
- **Track 10:** The Encore

The Experience Dividend reveals what happens when wisdom, energy, experience, age diversity, and curiosity converge. It's time to transform Age Debt into a future we can all look forward to.

Each track on Side A ends with a summary of the chapter's main points. Think of them as "Greyaways," not takeaways. On Side B, the Greyaways become "Golden Nuggets." (It will make sense, trust me.)

The future of work may be grey—perhaps it already *is* grey—and it demands something from you: leadership that finds opportunity in every corner of the workforce. Organizations that view age as an asset gain a new kind of musical advantage.

So, what happens next? Step up to the phonograph. It's time to really drop the needle. Next up? Track 2: The Demographic Tidal Wave.

The Demographic Tidal Wave

magine for a minute that you're in the CEO's chair. Or maybe you *are* the CEO.

The team is gathered, the usual updates are rolling in, and you're seated at the head of the table. Recruitment is steady, retirements are being managed, and the workforce strategy appears to be decent enough. At first glance, everything seems fine.

But you feel it—there is a strong undertow pulling at the foundation of your organization.

Decisions are taking longer. Productivity feels like it's mired in some newfound quicksand. Teams that once ran like clockwork need help to keep up. Some require a lesson on what "clockwork" means, while others are having trouble deciphering the latest Fibonacci sequence of emojis in their DMs. Young employees, while eager, often require more depth of experience to effectively step into complex roles. Knowledge is slipping away with each retirement party. Of course, there are the "we-pay-them-too-much-and-thus-we-have-to-reduce-our-costs" termination exits.

In sum, the once-steady rhythm of your workforce is beginning to act off-kilter.

This is *Age Debt*.

As I suggested in Track 1: Drop the (Age) Needle, organizations have relied on a comfortable narrative for decades: Young workers replace older ones, and the workforce system regenerates itself. Growth—be it in new employees, revenues, or profits—is a given.

But that story is unravelling. Fast!

Worldwide birth rates are declining—if not plummeting—and life expectancy is increasing. This is the crux of the demographic tidal wave. As a result, the future snapshot of the employee population map vastly differs from what most systems were designed for.

Age Debt is here, now. Failing to address it will erode your organization's productivity, morale, and, eventually, its existence.

The Slow Crisis That's Already at Your Door

Age Debt doesn't shout. It whispers, slipping through the cracks in your strategy until its effects are impossible to ignore. Every time an experienced employee retires without sharing their knowledge, Age Debt silently accumulates. It increases whenever systems fail to support older workers, alienating them rather than leveraging their strengths. Every day a leader dismisses the aging of their workforce as a "later" issue, Age Debt grows and accrues mutely.

This is why Age Debt is similar to the climate crisis. You know it's been growing for a while, but only when you're displaced from your house by a flood, fire, or hurricane do you finally believe it's actually happening. Just ask anyone from the 2023 catastrophic fires in Lahaina, Hawai'i, or the 2025 infernos in Southern California.

The consequences are subtle at first. Decisions take longer because institutional memory has evaporated. Young employees struggle to fill roles (or complete tasks) they weren't trained for. Leaders delay change because they're overwhelmed by more visible crises. But Age Debt becomes impossible to ignore over time, mainly because your house has caught fire.

Let me introduce the concept further with a positive story about Age Debt. There is such a thing.

With over 150 years of corporate history and total assets under management of US$350 billion, Zurich Insurance Group faced a challenge that epitomizes the reality of Age Debt. Their workforce, rich with experience and institutional wisdom, was beginning to age, as is the case with many global organizations. Decades of expertise were at risk of vanishing into thin air as retirements loomed across their 60,000 employees. Compounding the challenge was Zurich's simultaneous push to modernize and embrace a digital-first approach while ensuring continuity in their core competencies like underwriting and risk assessment.

Zurich's head of talent and learning, Sally Henderson, reflected on the stakes in a Harvard Business School podcast: "Our skills today aren't necessarily the ones we'll need in five years, even a year. Future-proofing our people is about creating an environment where they can grow and thrive."

The solution required more than incremental adjustments; it demanded a bold reimagining of how Zurich approached talent. Their rethinking included introducing flexible working arrangements and enabling older workers to retire at their own pace while mentoring their successors. The company introduced job-sharing roles that allowed retiring team members to remain engaged without the full weight of their usual job tasks. Older employees' less taxing workload helped ensure that institutional knowledge was handed down systematically, rather than being lost the day they walked out the door.

Steve Collinson, chief HR officer at Zurich UK, described their approach to leveraging the wisdom of experience in an interview: "Age is just a number and we recognize the benefits of a multi-generational workforce."

Zurich didn't stop there. The company introduced significant ergonomic improvements to its workspaces, ensuring that employees of all ages could remain physically comfortable and productive. They also introduced a clever career development platform called "MyJourney" to reinforce these efforts. The technology released via MyJourney empowered employees of all ages to map their skills against future roles, identify areas for growth, and access targeted learning opportunities. By providing options that emphasize career ownership, Zurich has evolved its talent strategy into a thriving eco-system of continuous learning and adaptability, regardless of age.

Zurich leaders anticipated Age Debt and addressed it proactively. Their strategy demonstrates what is possible when leaders treat Age Debt as an opportunity rather than a threat. By valuing the collaboration between generations, Zurich created a workplace where experience and innovation meet—employees were empowered to contribute at every stage of their careers.

Now, think about your organization or team and the following questions:

- How often do you prepare for your pending retirements as carefully as you plan for recruitment?

- How many critical roles rely on undocumented knowledge, that invisible "this is how we've always done it" cadence?

- What systems have you built to capture and transfer expertise—not simply job descriptions, but the "how" of success?

Age Debt grows when organizations treat experience as replaceable, as though one employee's decades of insight can be handed off in a two-week transition period. Zurich Insurance Group chose not to go bankrupt due to Age Debt. Will you?

What Age Debt Reveals About Leadership

Age Debt isn't solely about knowledge gaps or retirements, either. It's a mirror. It shows us how our organizations were designed for a world that will no longer exist—a world where growth still seems infinite, younger workers arrive in steady numbers, and older employees quietly step aside.

Let me be crystal clear—that world is gone. Kaput! It will never return.

This moment demands more than incremental adjustments from you as a leader. It requires you to rethink the assumptions underlying your workforce strategy. Maybe it's your team. Perhaps you're in charge of an entire unit. You may even be a member of the C-suite. Age Debt asks whether you're prepared to lead in an era where age diversity is no longer a "nice to have" but an organizational necessity.

Consider these questions as you further reflect on your current leadership:

- Are you redesigning roles and processes to unlock the potential of experienced employees?

- How will you retain and transfer critical knowledge before the next wave of retirements?

- What steps are you taking to foster a culture where employees of every age and era thrive?

The answers are the foundation of your organization's ability to adapt or fall behind further.

While many will feel its weight and crumble, leaders who act decisively can turn Age Debt into their most significant advantage. Older workers possess insights, networks, and expertise that are impossible to replicate. Middle-aged workers are often the glue that binds the organizational productivity book together. Younger workers—while diminishing in number—have ideas and creativity that are necessary. Organizations unlock resilience when systems are designed to amplify these River, Rock, and Ruby contributions, rather than sidelining them.

What Is the Demographic Tidal Wave?

Life looks young. Wherever you look, the illusion of youth is right in front of your eyes.

Tokyo's Shibuya Scramble Crossing, New York's Times Square, Berlin's Alexanderplatz, Manchester's Piccadilly Gardens, Montreal's

Mont Royal—when you walk these streets and parks, you can't see a problem at all. They're teeming with young people. And yet beneath the surface, birth rates are plummeting and populations are shrinking.

How can this be? We read that global and country populations are increasing, and the daily papers call urgently for more housing. Yes, but two things can be true at the same time. And right now, you're only paying attention to the headlines and not the trendlines. There is another truth staring you in the face.

Since 2003, my wife, Denise, and I have been parenting our three children, whom we refer to as "goats." They will be 23, 21, and 19 years old in 2026, so in fairness, they are no longer children, but I will always refer to them as goats despite their adultness. (If you're questioning my sanity, goats = billy goats = kids = children = goats, not "greatest of all time.")

Why am I mentioning the goats?

It is highly unlikely that any of them will have three children, like Denise and I did. In fact, looking across the globe, I would argue that, for the first time in history, children are an endangered species. They are the Sunda tiger or Bornean orangutan of humans.

This track on the album is titled "The Demographic Tidal Wave," but a more appropriate title might be "The Demographic Apocalypse." Oh, and it's a loud one.

Speaking of loud, when Denise and I decided to have three kids, it felt like a natural extension of the world we grew up in. Our parents, and their parents before them, lived in an era where having children wasn't simply a choice—it was a rhythm of life. You settled down, built a family, and the world kept turning. Denise and I have five siblings between us. And our four parents? Thirteen. But my goats are entering adulthood in a world that looks nothing like the one I grew up in.

Today, across the globe, we're witnessing what some refer to as the "great demographic reversal." Birth rates have plummeted, with many countries struggling to reach even the replacement rate of 2.1 children born per woman. It may look young out there, but it most definitely is getting older.

My hunch about my family's shrinking generational footprint mirrors a global phenomenon: the demographic tidal wave quietly reshaping societies' rhythm everywhere. For example, South Korea has an astonishingly low birth rate of 0.75—one of the lowest anywhere in the world. Put differently, for every 100 South Korean women, only 75 children are born. Fast-forward to some date in the near future and you start to see a society folding in on itself.

I don't want you to think for a second that this is a localized issue in one country or region. Japan, Italy, Germany, the United Kingdom, and Canada grapple with similar trends, as do many other countries. Even the United States, once seen as somewhat immune to these challenges, is inching closer to demographic inertia. Children are no longer the natural replenishment of our societies; they're becoming a rarity. As rare as finding a Cabbage Patch Kid doll during the Christmas 1983 buying frenzy or during the Tamagotchi-mania era of Christmas 1997.

The consequences of this demographic shift are already rippling across our workplaces and economies. If birth rates are the supply chain of humanity, we're facing an inventory crisis of epic proportions. And like any good supply chain issue, the signs were there long before anyone chose to act—or even noticed.

Birth rates are dropping *and* reshaping the foundation of society. As the demographic bell bends, the workplace consequences are becoming impossible to ignore. This is why I think we are facing a "demographic tidal wave." It's not an asteroid racing towards Earth or a zombie uprising as depicted in HBO's *The Last of Us*, but rather a gradual, sneaky, and unavoidable recalibration of society's core element: *people*.

Unlike other crises, this one is stealth. It doesn't appear as a CNN breaking news alert or a viral social media meme. No one is holding a sign about the coming demographic apocalypse as you enter the subway. It creeps in quietly until entire industries, organizations, and economies suddenly struggle. Maybe even to stay afloat. Perhaps yours already does.

From Bell to Bulb

Since time immemorial, our society has followed a rhythm as predictable as three chords and the truth. Generations arrived, grew, and contributed to society, each replenishing the one before. It was normal—as normal as a bell curve distribution.

Now, picture a different bell, a regular church bell—a shape wide at its middle, a bit wider at its base, and narrowing towards the top. This shape reflected the natural order of things. A broad foundation of children—people procreating as per the norm—a robust middle of working-age adults, and a manageable, smaller top of retirees until people died. The bell defined how economies functioned, anchored our institutions, and shaped our assumptions about the future.

Today, society is evolving into the demographic shape of a light bulb. We are shifting from bell-shaped to bulb-shaped.

Demographic Change: Bell to Bulb

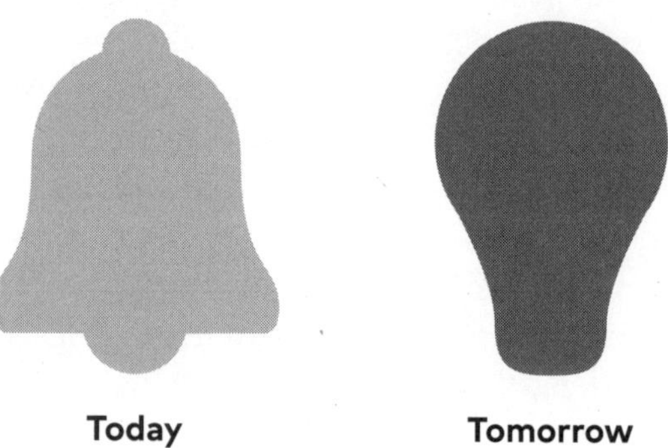

The bulb tells a very different story.

The bulb's narrow base reflects plummeting birth rates, leaving fewer hands to carry the load forward. Its constricting middle—the working-age population—stretches thin under rising pressures and shrinking cohorts. The top of the bulb inadvertently swells. People are living longer—hooray—but with unintended consequences.

Healthier lifestyles have transformed retirement from a quiet exit into an extended, active phase of life—but this transformation hasn't yet extended to work itself. This reimagining signals a recalibration of humanity's entire structure, and society remains woefully unprepared for what lies ahead.

The bell is no longer ringing.

Japan is perhaps the clearest example, the demographic canary in the coal mine. There, the shift is so dramatic that adult diapers now outsell those made for infants. Nearly 30 percent of Japan's population is over 65, a demographic reality already straining healthcare systems, pension funds, and the very fabric of Japanese society. Even more pronounced, Japanese workers 55 and older will approach 40 percent of the workforce by 2031. There is no relief in sight either. In 2025, the country's national fertility rate fell to 1.15, the lowest in its history.

As I pointed out earlier, South Korea faces a potentially starker challenge: with a birth rate of just 0.75, it is a country literally running out of children to sustain its future. Remarkably, by 2030, South Korea's population aged 55 and over is expected to make up approximately 55 percent of the total population, surpassing even Japan's.

Across Europe, pension systems built for a bell-shaped society are cracking under the weight of the bulb as more retirees depend on fewer workers. In my home country of Canada, where immigration has helped to bolster population growth, the birth rate has fallen below 1.3—far less than the replacement threshold. All that immigration is merely delaying the inevitable. The Great White North, too, will eventually run out of people.

If you're American, don't get too cocky.

The US birth rate has dropped to 1.6 children per woman—far below the OECD recommended level of 2.1. This represents a 20 percent decline since 2007 and one of the lowest fertility rates in the nation's history. Immigration has managed to sustain population growth—much like in Canada—with immigrants accounting for

78 percent of US population growth between 2010 and 2020. However, various political issues leave an inevitable demographic apocalypse unaddressed.

According to the US Census Bureau, in a scenario with no immigration, the working-age population (ages 18 to 64) will shrink by approximately 8.2 million people by 2040. This is without President Trump's 2025 enforcement of the Alien Enemies Act, under which thousands of people have been deported. Fewer workers mean slower economic growth, increased pressure on social programs, and diminished global competitiveness. The United States will soon share the same dim light as the other bulb nations.

Why aren't young Rivers having children? The reasons are stacking up: the cost of living, unaffordable housing, fewer partnerships and marriages, and delayed parenthood, which narrows the window of opportunity for fertility. Add in a significant drop in teen pregnancies, too.

Whatever the causes, for the first time in human history, more societies are grappling with population stagnation or decline than explosive growth. I use terminology like "demographic tidal wave" for a reason—it's a slow, desperate transformation unfolding before our eyes. If you're a fan of the Tragically Hip—like me—the song "It's a Good Life If You Don't Weaken" comes to mind.

The Ripple Effects of Demographic Shifts

The bulb does more than transform population figures. Its influence ripples outward, reshaping housing, education, healthcare, and even the design of cities. You might even call the bulb pesky. It has begun to shine its light across the entirety of organizations, industries, and economies. And it's *never* going to give up. It's never going to say goodbye. It's like a Rick Astley song. Pesky, indeed.

Housing shortages in major urban centres will worsen because aging populations will remain in their homes longer. The cost of housing and living will start to hollow out those same urban centres. After this period concludes, an opposite housing crisis will arise

The bell is no longer ringing

Japan: Nearly 30 percent of Japan's population is over 65, a demographic reality already straining healthcare systems, pension funds, and the very fabric of Japanese society.

South Korea: By 2030, South Korea's population aged 55 and over is expected to make up approximately 55 percent of the total population.

Europe: Pension systems built for a bell-shaped society are cracking under the weight of the bulb as more retirees depend on fewer workers.

United States: According to the US Census Bureau, in a scenario with no immigration, the working-age population (ages 18 to 64) will shrink by approximately 8.2 million people by 2040.

when the housing market collapses because there are not enough urban residents to purchase the homes now available for sale.

Schools will close because there aren't enough children to fill classrooms. It's beginning to happen already. Case in point: London, England. Louis Hodge, the associate director of the Education Policy Institute in the United Kingdom, said to the BBC, "In the whole of London, we're expecting primary school pupil numbers to fall by another 52,000 by 2028." School mergers, closures, and cancelled construction are sure to follow.

Healthcare systems, already stretched thin, will face rising costs as they adapt to the needs of older populations who are living longer—but not always healthier—lives.

Despite its obviousness, the bulb often feels invisible. Governments and companies continue to rely on outdated economic models—hello, *short-termism*—betting that birth rates will rebound or that immigration will fill the gaps indefinitely. These assumptions no longer hold. You can't keep raising prices, either. As the bulb grows heavier at the top and the base continues to shrink, the cracks in society's infrastructure become more challenging to ignore. What? Growth *isn't* good? Take that, fans of *The Wolf of Wall Street*.

At this intersection of societal shifts and systemic inertia, we begin to see the implications for the workforce. The narrowing middle of the bulb—those Rocks in their prime working years—is not merely a statistic. It represents the talent pool all industries rely on. And it's shrinking.

What Does a Bulb Society Mean?

The bell-shaped societies of the past were predictable. Each generation replenished the one before, sustaining economies, communities, and institutions. Denise and I had three children, so we did our bit. You're welcome!

But I will wager my house that 6.3 grandchildren (2.1 from each of my three goats—the replacement rate) will not be my grandparent future. I'll even round down to six grandchildren—it just will not happen, and it's no fault of my goats.

The bulb introduces an entirely new dynamic. Older generations are redefining what it means to age. They will stay active longer, challenge traditional retirement norms, and shift resource distribution. We don't have enough ink in this book to even enter into a dialogue about pension systems and what happens if they crumble or collapse. Meanwhile, younger generations are trying to navigate a work world designed for the bell—one that no longer makes any sense. That old bell doesn't even clang anymore. Educational systems, housing markets, healthcare structures, and the overall economy were built with a broad base and a narrow top in mind. They weren't designed for a population with fewer people at the base and way more at the top.

The bell-to-bulb quandary requires rethinking *everything*—from urban planning to how our economies and capitalism function. Societal transformation will be necessary, but this book focuses specifically on the workplace—and the indispensable changes required in leadership and organizational culture to address the demographic tidal wave that is coming for it.

My early advice is to get over it.

We have entered the bulb society, where your leadership will face unprecedented and unavoidable challenges in the workplace and workforce. It's time to confront this bulb head-on.

How will it affect your organization?

According to the World Economic Forum, workers in G7 countries aged 55 and older will exceed 25 percent of the workforce by 2031. That's nearly 10 percentage points higher than in 2011. And I think World Economic Forum is underselling the number. I suspect it will be higher.

For example, in the United States, the labour force of people aged 16 to 24 is expected to shrink by 7.5 percent by 2030. Organizations like yours will face immense pressure from the ensuing bulb-shaped workforce. It's already happening in various ways at MapleCo, as you will discover.

Next, I will introduce a few vital workforce issues and unintended consequences related to the bell-to-bulb quandary to get you thinking.

Mid-Management Mayhem

What happens when the pool of young workers diminishes and older and experienced workers are no longer accessible because the organization didn't proactively consider their importance?

One bell-to-bulb issue relates specifically to mid-level leaders. They will become even more stressed in trying to pick up the slack. Mid-management leading will turn into a desperate form of "mid-management mayhem."

Present-day mid-level leaders are already being stretched like never before. As the demographic tidal wave strikes in the near future, managers who once anchored operations will shoulder even more of the workload. Retirements (or involuntary exits) among older team members and the shrinking number of younger employees will further overwhelm mid-level roles, managing the responsibilities of both ends of the spectrum.

This imbalance becomes an unruly systemic issue. Consulting firm Capterra discovered that 71 percent of mid-level managers are already "sometimes" or "always" feeling overwhelmed, stressed, or burned out at work. For leaders 35 years old or younger, it jumps to 75 percent. A 2023 study by the UKG Workforce Institute revealed that 57 percent of middle managers wished they had known what they were getting into before stepping into their leadership roles. Does that feel like a good start to handling the bell-to-bulb transition?

We need only look at Boeing, which vividly illustrates how strained things can get. A wave of retirements post-pandemic among experienced machinists at the company left middle managers scrambling to hire, onboard, and train new recruits—a job they were doing on top of their "normal" leadership duty to balance production deadlines for building new airplanes. Many of the surge of recruits had no aerospace experience. I'm no engineer, but that does not sound good.

After repeated quality issues, including the door of an Alaska Airlines plane popping open mid-flight on January 5, 2024, Boeing began an internal investigation.

"We heard repeatedly from experienced employees that, 'We are maxed out training these new people,'" Elizabeth Lund, Boeing's quality chief, told the *Wall Street Journal*.

My response? "You don't say."

The collision of waning expertise and the frantic addition of fresh but inexperienced talent created adverse ripple effects throughout Boeing. Delayed timelines, operational lapses, flying doors, and strained mid-management leaders became a reality. It seemed inevitable that another catastrophe would ensue with Boeing's airplanes.

I have flown over 200,000 miles in the past few years, mostly on Boeing aircraft. (Yes, I carbon offset.) You don't think I'm a wee bit worried every time I step onto one of those planes? Extend the argument to mid-level managers across any organization. Your organization. What happens when seasoned and experienced employees depart and no one is around to help fill the knowledge gap for the inexperienced replacements? Doors pop off airplanes mid-flight, and mid-level managers become even more stressed.

MapleCo Mid-Management Mayhem

How has the mid-management mayhem affected MapleCo? Let me now introduce you to Emily Russo.

In 2022, MapleCo faced a wave of retirements in one of its regional operations teams. They were hit hard on the team that leads compliance and patient care protocols. At the time, Emily was a program manager with 15 years of experience, the last six at the company. She ran a team of 10 different analysts.

As is the case in many organizations, a decision was made for her team to be contracted from 10 to eight. Revenues were down and decisions had to be made. Due to four retirements and two voluntary departures, Emily was left to hire four people over the span of nine months. The amount of work remained roughly the same, but her team's total headcount size had shrunk, plus she had to interview and then hire four people in quick succession.

Over the course of almost a year, Emily was left scrambling to stabilize her unit. One critical incident occurred when two inexperienced hires, fresh out of university, failed to follow proper documentation procedures for a complex claims case. The new team members' inexperience—as well as Emily's growing burnout— resulted in over $300,000 in penalties during a routine government compliance audit. Needless to say, she was devastated.

Emily spent weeks troubleshooting the aftermath. She worked 14-hour days rebuilding workflows, coaching her team on regulatory nuances, and firefighting with MapleCo's compliance department to prevent further penalties. "I felt like I was drowning," Emily admitted in a feedback session. "I couldn't focus on anything strategic because I was constantly in damage control mode."

The cascading effects rippled across her department. Deadlines slipped by an average of 18 percent, and her team's customer satisfaction scores dropped 20 percent within six months. Emily's frustration grew as she became a bottleneck for several decisions she lacked the time to make, leaving her team demoralized and others at MapleCo wondering what was happening to her.

Her team's productivity dropped by several percentage points over the year. MapleCo loves its annual employee engagement scores, and her team fell to the lowest in her leadership history—a stark warning sign for Emily's MapleCo senior vice president.

For Emily, one word described her past year: *mayhem*. Between the retirements and the inexperienced new hires, she was battling to keep her head above water in the demographic tidal wave.

The Erosion of Expertise

Experienced employees are the stewards of your organization's institutional memory. Their wisdom and boots-on-the-ground experience connect routine processes and operations to critical moments, especially in times of stress or crisis. If (or when) they leave, these seasoned veterans take with them more than experience; they walk away with the nuanced understanding that manuals, wikis, and Slack channels cannot replicate (ask Boeing). Their departure can create ripple effects throughout the organization. Decision-making can falter, execution might slow down, and that untaught "grit" can weaken when your organization finds itself without the expertise you once relied upon, oftentimes without even knowing you relied on it.

Worse, companies have their heads in the sand about such calamities. A 2023 survey found that while 75 percent of companies reported having employees retire in the previous two years, two-thirds of them do not have formal mentorship or knowledge transfer processes in place. Retiring employees take valuable institutional experience with them as they head out the door, and that lack of planning can have serious consequences not dissimilar to Boeing's.

Consider Winter Storm Elliott, which unleashed a severe cold snap across the eastern United States in December 2022, resulting in widespread power outages. It exposed critical vulnerabilities in the energy grid and, worse, the people strategy of a few energy firms.

PJM Interconnection is an umbrella organization responsible for coordinating the distribution of electricity across 13 states and the

District of Columbia. During the storm, over 90,000 megawatts of generation capacity went offline for several days around Christmas. PJM is essentially a broker operating a complex energy marketplace. It relies on partner companies, such as Talen Energy, Constellation Energy, Vistra Corp., and NRG Energy, to deliver electricity. If you don't want to freeze to death, PJM is your ticket.

PJM tasks various partner companies with maintaining power generation under the company's "Capacity Performance Framework." Their model is supposed to ensure power plants are prepared to meet energy demands, particularly during extreme weather events like Elliott.

In the wake of the storm that tragically claimed a hundred lives, PJM conducted a thorough review. Thirty recommendations emerged from it, some addressing technological improvements and others affecting the central theme of this book: people. A significant finding was the negative impact of workforce challenges on operational performance. A large number of retirements—especially among experienced engineers and technicians—caused critical gaps in all forms of institutional knowledge, hindering the various partner companies' attempts at crisis management during the storm. The report also found that despite their initial training, new hires lacked the depth of experience necessary to anticipate and mitigate the storm's surging effects.

As I researched the case, I reviewed Talen Energy's 2024 SEC filings. I was surprised to find the company candidly acknowledging these workforce and talent challenges—and specifically an aging workforce—signalling an array of potential future issues:

> An aging workforce, mismatch of skill set, expectation of future needs, uncertainty around the future of our aging assets or unavailability of short-term contract employees or contractors may lead to operating challenges and increased costs. The challenges that we might face due to such risks include a lack of human resources, losses to our operational knowledge base and the time and other resources required to develop new workers' skills.

The company's admission—a prescient demographic tidal wave "smoking gun" if there ever was one—underscores the systemic issue of the bulb-shaped workforce, where the departure of seasoned employees leaves a void that cannot be quickly filled by less-experienced staff. While operational inefficiencies are obvious red flags in this winter storm example, I'm sure you don't want to freeze to death because of Age Debt. If you're a leader at PJM, grid reliability and public safety are your utmost concern, and that has to come back to how you plan to increase—or at least maintain—a level of experienced personnel.

Regardless of your industry, Winter Storm Elliott's case outlines the importance of proactive workforce planning, changing demographics, and their relationship to knowledge transfer. But there are signs of change surfacing elsewhere, and they're worth noticing.

For example, in Vienna, Vollpension Café welcomes older adults not just to serve food but to share stories, pass on wisdom, and connect across the three eras. And repair cafés around the world bring Rubies together to fix broken items—radios, vacuums, lamps—and in doing so restore not only function but a sense of value. In the United Kingdom, INDY (I'm Not Done Yet) supports later-life adults as they explore new ventures, be it starting businesses, writing books, or stepping into fresh pursuits. And at Eldera, a US digital mentoring network, experienced Rubies connect with children through weekly video calls to exchange insights, stories, and advice.

These signals are not outliers. They reflect a growing awareness that contribution doesn't end with a milestone birthday. If cafés and communities are making space for Rubies, workplaces shouldn't be the last to pivot. Take it from the example of Winter Storm Elliott.

Fractured Career Trajectories

There is a double-edged sword to contend with, be it at MapleCo or your organization. On the one hand, the extended tenure of senior employees can help bridge talent gaps. That's a plus. But it also creates a thinning effect on the organizational talent ladder. Mid-career employees will find fewer opportunities to move into senior roles—occupied by older employees lingering longer—while younger employees will struggle to believe they have any chance for long-term advancement within the organization.

At the same time, your organization will face retirements in specific areas, resulting in critical talent gaps that will compel less experienced employees to step up before they are fully prepared. This creates a dual challenge: stagnation for some and overextension for others. (See poor Emily at MapleCo.)

Without clear career progression paths, your young and high-potential River and Rock talent will question why they are staying. If they cannot envision a future within your organization, you can be sure they will start looking for opportunities elsewhere. The outcome is unintentional, but it will leave significant gaps in your talent and leadership pipeline. Retirements exacerbate the situation, creating various levels of disruption that will necessitate costly external hiring or contractors or will overburden existing teams.

Research conducted by the authors of "Countries for Old Men: An Analysis of the Age Pay Gap" reveals that young workers are increasingly struggling to attain top-tier roles and wages. For example, in Italy, the likelihood of workers under 35 being in the top quartile of weekly wages fell by 34 percent between 1985 and 2019, while the probability for those over 55 rose by 32 percent. At the same time, the share of managerial roles held by workers under 35 dropped from 8 percent to 3 percent, while workers over 55 saw their share rise from 12 percent to 28 percent.

The research is a wake-up call. It illustrates how older team members who remain in their roles for long periods squash the opportunity for young and mid-career professionals to advance, creating a structural imbalance in the career progression paths of many younger employees.

MapleCo: The Tidal Wave Grows

At MapleCo, this dual challenge of stagnation and overextension is playing out in dramatic terms.

Shintarō Takahashi is a highly capable program manager who has consistently delivered strong results over the past five years. He's in the company's high-potential program. Yet, with senior program management roles occupied by long-tenured MapleCo employees like the fantastic Carlos Jimenez—a 30-year veteran—Shintarō feels his career is somewhat stunted. "I've grown so much over the past five years at MapleCo," he shared during a recent feedback session, "but I don't see any room to move up. It's kinda discouraging."

Simultaneously, retirements in the compliance team have created some urgent operational gaps. It's the opposite of Shintarō's situation. With few senior staff available to mentor less-tenured employees, MapleCo has had to ask less-experienced workers to take on critical responsibilities, sometimes beyond their current capabilities. "We've been forced to accelerate timelines for these team members to step into leadership roles," noted Sanjay Patel, director of operations. "It's a big risk, and we've already seen a few errors and signs of burnout."

These various "fractures" at MapleCo are creating ripple effects across the company. There are pockets of employees who feel stuck in their roles. In other units, new and pressing demands have overburdened employees. MapleCo is struggling to maintain morale and continuity while balancing the costs of external hiring and temporary contractors to address various labour gaps. Without structural changes to issues like career pathways, leadership development programming, and mentorship, the organization risks losing high-potential talent like Shintarō while overburdening its existing teams like Sanjay's.

Structural Inertia

There's another dual reality to contend with, whether it's at MapleCo or your organization.

It's hard to argue that the stability of your internal and external systems is essential. No one wants to head to an ATM only to find out they can't take out their money. Long-standing systems, workflows, processes, and organizational practices help keep your operations running smoothly. They ensure compliance and minimize risk.

However, these same structures, designed for reliability, can morph into barriers when you realize it's time to pivot or replace legacy systems, only to recognize these changes are way more complicated than you thought. What gets in the way is *structural inertia*, the accrual of your organization's inflexibility to change. This can apply to both people and organizational culture.

Put differently, structural inertia refers to the increasing constraint on the speed of organizational change as your firm—and your firm's employees—age. A symptom of Age Debt, it quietly builds until the "this is how we always do it" mindset becomes the norm.

Two competing forces fuel this challenge:

- **On one side, Ruby employees**—many of whom initially helped shape these systems and processes—remain loyal to their consistency. These folks are reluctant to change what works. Why bother? This attitude is both partly true and horribly stereotypical.

- **On the other side, River employees,** many eager to embrace innovation, might struggle against the inefficiencies of your legacy processes, which no longer align with modern demands.

The organization ultimately becomes trapped. And the Rocks are typically stuck in the middle. Do you preserve continuity or mandate adaptability? Both? It's a hallmark tension of Age Debt.

Structural inertia reflects years of ingrained processes and psychological patterns. It thrives in organizations where the familiar is preferred over the uncertain. As a leader, you must recognize this unfolding scenario: Can you preserve the wisdom of experience while fostering adaptability? Let's check in with MapleCo to uncover their structural inertia situation.

Structural Inertia at MapleCo

At MapleCo, the effects of structural inertia are palpable. The 30-year veteran Carlos Jimenez, mentioned previously, is a senior systems engineer on the IT team who oversees the company's billing platform—a tool implemented over two decades ago. "AWAC [as it is known] has kept us running without fail for years," Carlos noted. "It's stable, and stability is what our clients expect. Why change?"

For MapleCo leaders, Carlos represents reliability personified, and the AWAC platform reflects that same level of dependability.

However, for a young River employee named Sarah Campbell, a billing analyst and customer service rep, AWAC represents a much different reality.

"Using AWAC is like trying to turn a freight train but pretending it's a bicycle," Sarah said in frustration. "It's too big, too rigid, too clunky, and too set in its AWAC ways." While senior employees value its steadiness, younger team members feel constrained by its inefficiencies. After all, they're the ones dealing with customer complaints about billing every day.

What's the result? MapleCo has delayed the decision to upgrade or overhaul AWAC for over two years. Their competitors are not facing similar constraints and have moved forward with a more user-friendly platform. They're sure to have cut costs and reduced turnaround times in the process.

Internally, the growing divide at MapleCo between the eras—Rivers versus Rocks versus Rubies—is creating uncomfortable friction. Senior employees such as Carlos, who ensure continuity, often feel undervalued when their systems are criticized. Meanwhile, younger employees like Sarah feel stymied every time they recommend upgrading AWAC. Like that fab 1972 song "Stuck in the Middle with You" by Stealers Wheel, the Rocks are squeezed from both sides.

Structural inertia accumulates over time, decision by decision and inaction by inaction, until the organization feels weighed down by its own legacy. At MapleCo, the structural inertia challenge is a direct reflection of the very structures built for yesterday's needs. It creates barriers that hinder the company's efforts to solve today's customer issues and organizational realities.

Without confronting structural inertia, MapleCo risks being stuck. It's yet another unintended consequence of Age Debt. And it leads us nicely to Track 3: The Experience Conundrum.

GREYAWAYS

As we lower the volume on Track 2, here are your Greyaways—takeaways and insights to ensure you're ready for the demographic tidal wave.

Greyaway #1: The Wave Is Here

The demographic shift is already in motion. Recognizing its presence is your first step to leading effectively through its challenges. Eras are the new generations.

Greyaway #2: The Bell Has Rung for the Last Time

Workforce talent composition is shifting from a bell to bulb. The new bulb shape will challenge your outdated assumptions about the generational rhythm of workplaces.

Greyaway #3: Knowledge Is Not Infinite

Institutional knowledge erodes with every Ruby retirement or departure. Without systems to capture and transfer it, your organization quietly accumulates Age Debt.

Greyaway #4: Structural Inertia Is Invisible but Real

Structural inertia—rooted in a combination of legacy systems and ingrained behaviours—prevents your organization from adapting quickly. If you leave inertia unchecked, it will negatively affect workforce performance.

Greyaway #5: Mid-Management—"Carry That Weight"

Mid-level leaders will face mounting pressure—and stress—as they contend with the strain of lost expertise coupled with the challenge of onboarding unprepared talent. (P.S. "Carry That Weight" is a Beatles reference!)

Greyaway #6: The Demographic Ripple Effect Is Real

The bell-to-bulb-shaped workforce will wind up reshaping more than your organization. The demographic transition will impact all industries, requiring you to think broadly about the impact.

Greyaway #7: Your Leadership Must Adapt

You cannot ignore the demographic tidal wave. You must consider recalibrating your team's or organization's workforce strategy for collaboration across the eras.

The Experience Conundrum

f you've ever walked through the Grand Bazaar in Istanbul—a real-world labyrinth of haggling vendors and those tempting Turkish delights—you will undoubtedly have encountered a spectacular hive of courier activity: the Hamals.

These almost-all-male porters—with their two-wheeled carts laden with goods seemingly stacked to the sky—are the custodians of a centuries-old craft. The Hamals' sole job is to navigate the bustling ancient alleys of Istanbul to deliver goods from one shop to another or via their suppliers. The Hamals demonstrate an agility and strength that seems almost otherworldly.

I visited Istanbul for the first time in 2024 and became enthralled by the Hamals. During a visit to the famous Grand Bazaar, I spoke with Mehmet, a shopkeeper whose family had been operating in the area for generations. "The Hamals are the backbone of our market," he told me. "Many have been doing this all their lives, following their fathers and grandfathers. It's a tradition passed down from one generation to the next."

Mehmet explained that becoming a Hamal requires strength and experience. "Young Hamals start as apprentices," he said, "shadowing older men and learning how to balance the loads, navigate the alleys, and maintain their carts." He talked about how tough the job is, but you could tell he was deeply respectful of their efforts.

Turkey is no different than anywhere else in the world. Like your country, it is about to enter a period of rapid aging. The United Nations projects Turkey to become an "aged" society within two decades, when people aged 65 or older will exceed 14 percent of the total population. The Hamals are also rapidly aging, with fewer young people willing to take up the gruelling job.

For us, the Grand Bazaar is a metaphor: Think of it and the Hamals as your organization's future.

Mehmet was frank: "The Bazaar wouldn't be the same without them. They ensure the goods get delivered where vehicles cannot go." There are obvious ripple effects if the Hamals go extinct—goods will be delayed, disruptions inevitable, I'll consume fewer Turkish delights, and Mehmet will likely sell fewer shirts.

The story of the Hamals of Istanbul is emblematic of broader issues: a knowledge crisis, a pending leadership vacuum, and an imminent economic OMG moment across industries and organizations.

In the Grand Bazaar, as most probably in your organization, an expertise bottleneck is forming. When the experienced intellect of your workers leaves without transferring their wisdom, the systems they support and serve falter. Who will guide, inform, and instruct younger generations when mentors, experienced personnel, and the Hamals are gone? As *Right Kind of Wrong* author and Harvard Business School professor Amy C. Edmondson said to me over lunch in late 2024, "Leaders must understand the importance of their presence around younger employees," adding that it is a leader's responsibility to cultivate the next wave of leadership. Without it, the Bazaar and your organization risk losing their core competencies.

Finally, there's the trap of economic myopia. Just as Istanbul's merchants might prioritize short-term cost savings over sustaining the Hamals, many organizations fail to invest in retaining or reskilling experienced workers, focusing instead on immediate gains. Yet the cost of not replacing lost expertise is steep.

Several firms have done the math.

> **Spoiler alert: It's stupidly expensive. Gallup estimates that the range is from 0.5 to 2 times the employee's annual salary. The David Aplin Group reckons it's between 75 and 200 percent of an employee's annual total compensation.**

Whatever the cost, the story of the Hamals introduces us to lessons that stretch far beyond Istanbul. In Track 3, we'll explore how these three forces—expertise bottlenecks, leadership vacuums, and economic age myopia—are beginning to reshape your workplace's future.

Expertise Bottleneck

If you've ever observed a sand timer, you'll have witnessed something rather mundane. When grains of sand move freely, the timer works flawlessly. That should make sense to you. But the entire flow slows to a frustrating trickle if just a few grains clump together.

Your organization is facing the steady departure of seasoned workers. Maybe it's already started. The balance of young, core, and wise—River, Rock, and Ruby employees—is definitively changing. Sometime soon, you and your colleagues will encounter the expertise bottleneck, when the sand clumps and tacit knowledge disappears.

What is tacit knowledge?

Think of it as the unwritten, experience-driven insights essential to how your organization gets things done. If it disappears without transfer, everything downstream can suffer. That sand gets rather clumpy. Knowledge no longer flows freely, particularly when that sort of knowledge is tacit.

Dr. Michael Polanyi likely provided us with the most influential definition of tacit knowledge. In his seminal 1966 book *The Tacit Dimension*, Polanyi asserted that "We know more than we can tell." In other words, tacit knowledge is a type of know-how that is difficult to articulate or codify yet is deeply ingrained in our experiences, skills, and intuitions. It plays a crucial role in your professional life. It plays an even more central role in your role as a leader.

An expertise bottleneck highlights your organization's blind spots concerning tacit knowledge. When you hit one, that sand gets clumpier. It can even become as thick as molasses. Leaders often underestimate the cost of relearning or rebuilding lost knowledge. In the Age Debt era, recognizing the expertise bottleneck becomes crucial for addressing your pending performance gaps.

The Nature of Tacit Knowledge and Its Risks

Unlike explicit knowledge—knowledge easily documented and shared through manuals, training, and other tactics—tacit knowledge is contextual, relational, and frequently invisible. Consider the quiet ingenuity embedded in troubleshooting techniques, client relationship-building tactics, or legacy-systems oversight—all of which tend to vanish when people retire and there is no one around to help with those invisible finesses.

Research published in 2020 emphasizes the significance of tacit knowledge in boosting job performance. When organizations foster environments of trust and collaboration, older employees are far more likely to share those unspoken insights that drive innovation and productivity. It's also a reminder that competitive advantage often resides in what's learned through experience rather than solely what's written in manuals or taught in classrooms.

The problem is that people, particularly leaders, often overlook tacit knowledge—and once it's lost or not properly maintained, issues can emerge. Research conducted in 2023 by Nataliya Galan highlights a crucial insight: Tacit knowledge is the foundation of adaptability. When leaders ignore or undervalue it, organizations scramble to bridge the gaps, sacrificing not only current performance but also the agility needed to respond to future challenges.

A notable example is NASA's Artemis program, which struggled to re-engineer key technologies from the Apollo program due to gaps left by retiring engineers. The agency only managed to bridge its knowledge gap through deliberate knowledge preservation efforts, such as storytelling labs and mentoring programs. Organizations across sectors must recognize that tacit knowledge is not simply an intangible asset—it's a critical lever for continuity and innovation.

Bottlenecks Lead to Costly Relearning

When tacit knowledge exits the building—or the sand gets clumpy—your organization will face an expensive and frustrating reality: relearning.

I'm all for learning, don't get me wrong. After all, I'm still a recovering chief learning officer. But relearning is, as it sounds, reactive, costly, and avoidable. Processes and tasks once smoothly handled by experienced people will now require rediscovery, trial and error, or guesswork by employees who remain or are quickly hired. Longitudinal research by Peter Rex Massingham shows that new hires operate at only 92 percent of the capacity of the employees they replace, creating persistent knowledge gaps that strain teams and drag down productivity. Moreover, Massingham's study revealed that when top knowledge holders leave their organizations, remaining employees experience decreased morale and efficiency, with 47 percent showing a decline in their knowledge engagement.

It's not the ideal example of organizational learning culture awesomeness, either. The expenditure it takes to rebuild that knowledge capacity has far-reaching impacts beyond monetary ones. While missed deadlines and project overruns seem obvious, what about the team frustrations and reputational damage that will likely follow?

What's that you hear? It's the sound of a trombone going, "Womp, womp, womp."

Talent Succession Link

In 2024, the leadership advisory firm Russell Reynolds researched 50 publicly traded US banks and made several alarming observations about talent. C-suite executives, on average, have a 15-year tenure with their bank, including an average of six years in the CEO position. That seems fine. Further analysis revealed, however, that 25 percent of C-level executives were 65 or older. They predict many financial institutions will face a leadership shortage if robust succession planning efforts—and revised talent model thinking—are not introduced.

Perhaps unsurprisingly, 2021 research revealed a staggering reality for for-profit companies: Poorly managed CEO and C-suite transitions across the S&P 1500 erase nearly $1 trillion in market value annually. To make matters worse, company valuations and investor returns could be 20 to 25 percent higher if organizations prioritized more effective leader succession planning practices. Not only is there an aging C-suite issue, but there is also a lack of proper succession planning processes.

Leadership succession ought to be orchestrated like a symphony, not thrown together like a last-minute jazz session. Enter Credit Suisse in 2021. The company found itself improvising with jazz hands when it failed to be prepared for a leadership transition, one that had to occur during a massive financial crisis. Archegos Capital, a highly leveraged investment firm of the bank, imploded practically overnight, leaving Credit Suisse with a $4.7 billion loss. The financial hit was brutal, and what followed got even worse. The board ousted several top executives, and a new CEO was rushed in to restore confidence. The reactive and avoidable leadership shake-up only deepened the uncertainty with employees, clients, and investors. Within a year, Credit Suisse's stock plummeted nearly 30 percent. Internally, employees were reeling. Externally, clients and regulators began to lose trust.

Would a well-structured succession plan have mitigated the damage? No question. Credit Suisse's downfall boiled down to leadership unpreparedness at a critical moment. The lesson is clear: When succession planning is reactive rather than intentional, the consequences ripple far beyond stock prices. Jazz sessions are cool, but they're not a good model for banks.

If your organization treats succession planning like a dusty afterthought (or with jazz hands) it's another symptom of Age Debt. The biggest risk to you as a leader isn't whether a talent transition will happen; it's when. And if you're caught flat-footed? You're playing a dangerous game with your organization's future.

Rest assured, this line of thinking extends beyond the C-suite. The same leadership vacuum that sent Credit Suisse into a tailspin can manifest at every level of your organization, including your team. What happens if you have an experienced senior manager, director, or vice president who unexpectedly departs and you don't have a clear successor ready to replace them? The absence of a plan might stall projects or impact productivity, but it can also trigger uncertainty, disrupt culture, and erode team confidence. None of it is good news.

If this sounds like a concern you don't have to worry about, consider what happens when entire teams of Ruby workers—those without prestigious titles but with years of invaluable experience— begin retiring at a rate faster than you can replace them. Will your current talent practices save you?

Institutional Blind Spots

Not every leader is a leader. Read that sentence again.

While you should care about potential succession- and talent-planning issues with senior leaders and the voids these potentially create within your organization's most senior competence levels, you shouldn't solely be worried about senior leaders. In fact, you and your organization may be suffering from institutional talent blind spots. What did Bob in finance do anyway? And why aren't we getting paid anymore?

Every organization has its critical nodes—the people who quietly make the machine work. They're not necessarily the people at the top of your talent grid or the faces in your glossy annual reports. These are your knowledge linchpins: the operations leads, technical experts, unsung geniuses, marketing mavens, and seasoned managers who hold the invisible threads of your organization together. You won't find them in talent maps or succession planning charts per se, but you will undoubtedly feel it when they're gone. Their silence is deafening. Indeed, they become "The Sound of Silence."

Leadership readiness doesn't start and stop with executives. That's because leadership doesn't need a title. Remember? *Not every leader is a leader.* Leadership exists daily, where systems operate smoothly due to unrecognized and even unknown expertise. When these roles and people are neglected—or worse, disregarded—cracks form in your future.

What begins as a hairline fracture widens into a corporate chasm. Grand Canyon-esque. It doesn't matter how old the talent is, either. However, the more crystallized their knowledge—the more of a Ruby gem the team member is—the more likely your organization will be to feel the fracture when they're gone. Your institutional blind spot is large and staring you in the face. Behold the Rubies, leading functions, tasks and processes ingrained in your organization's culture and way of being.

Christian Jerusalem, an age management leader and founder of Wiseforce Advisors and rocket50, describes the institutional blind spot bluntly: "Experience is something that is not valued the way it should be. It applies to all industries. Twenty years ago, it was probably acceptable to think experience had an expiry date because our population pyramid was different. However, now that the pyramid is upside down, such thinking is horrible. That's why we have to rethink things completely."

You need to recognize that leadership is not a quest to fill the next empty Herman Miller office chair; it's about business continuity. You must become aware of your own blind spot, of myopically focusing on talent replacement instead of age readiness. Thus, your leadership ability is one more piece in the Age Debt puzzle.

MapleCo's Blind Spot

MapleCo has always treated talent planning as a straightforward equation. When someone left, the next person in line would simply step in. That's how they've always done it. After all, attrition has never really been a problem.

So, when Allison Carter, a 30-year veteran of MapleCo's sales team, announced her retirement, senior leaders—including CEO Marla Benson—assumed the solution was simple. Her successor, Jacob Poeltl, was ready—or so they and she thought.

Jacob had shadowed Allison for nearly two years. Fab! He had learned the MapleCo sales tactics and met several key accounts. But what no one accounted for was the depth of Allison's unspoken tacit knowledge—how she navigated tricky client negotiations, picked up the subtle cues that signalled a deal was in jeopardy, and had built relationships across decades. Jacob knew the mechanics of sales and the MapleCo sales methodologies, but not the art—the invisible sales art specific to Allison and her long-standing clients.

Within six months of Allison's retirement, MapleCo lost two of Allison's top-five clients. (I guess they are Allison's former clients.) Annual revenues totalled nearly $900,000. The loss happened not because Jacob lacked competence—he was perfectly competent—but because the nuances that kept those relationships alive were never passed on.

Furthermore, since Allison left with no thought given to retaining her in a mentorship or advisory role, she became unapproachable. In fact, she was unreachable, having moved to Australia. MapleCo's senior leaders assumed that "shadowing" equated to knowledge transfer, but transferring such intellect is rarely that straightforward. And now they're down almost a million dollars in annual revenues.

Speaking of revenues, remember that Pink Floyd song "Money"? Indeed, your Ruby geezers just might be cruisin' for a bruisin' if you are not paying attention to the economics—also, the next subsection of this track's experience conundrum.

Economic Age Myopia

While writing this book, I received an email from "Stephen" in the United States. He was responding to one of my semi-regular *Ponte-fractions* community newsletters. In my note, I predicted that "grey would eventually become the new black," a subtle homage to the upcoming release of *The Future of Work Is Grey*. He picked up on my sly prose, and his response serves as both a gentle introduction to Track 5: The Silent Saboteur of Ageism (still to come) and this sub-section of Track 3.

Far too many leaders continue to suffer from an additional form of Age Debt. In fact, they incur more debt. The most salient point of Stephen's email was as follows:

> My wife and I are both in our early sixties, unemployed from "orga-nizational change" by younger bosses. We are also both very well known in our sectors and have internationally recognized accom-plishments. For several months, we have both been collecting so many "silver medals" in job searches, brought in as the expe-rienced candidate who delivers consultant-level dialogue in the interviews (which does feel harvested in a sense), to be runner-up to someone in their forties. It's astonishing and getting to be funny in a macabre way. We never thought we would be "done" so young and had imagined having capstone years of leadership until we were 70.

While frightening, Stephen's email isn't a one-off horror story. His words capture a grim truth—leaders and organizations everywhere seem hell-bent on trading the wisdom of grey for the bargain allure of "younger and cheaper." It's as if they believe institutional memory is some kind of Google Doc they can access later. As you are likely already aware, it's not.

Moreover, Stephen is being exploited by organizations in relation to his next job opportunity. Companies are using him as a pawn in their efforts against age discrimination, or he's being overlooked for a position solely due to his Ruby age. It's lose–lose.

> **This is what I call economic age myopia. It's an affliction, a stubborn inability to look past the next fiscal quarter to the overall health of your organizational culture.**

It reflects short-termism intertwined with talent-development cluelessness. And just like Stephen's plight of both being packaged out *and* not being offered a new position, this issue manifests in your workplace in three distinct ways: a fixation on cutting costs (starting with older workers), a complete blind spot for valuing experience (or hiring it), and an incredulous faith in technology to save the day—and a few bucks.

Let's start with the first offender: the fallacy of cost-centric workforce planning. Or, as I like to call it, "Penny Lane."

The Fallacy of Cost-Centric Workforce Planning

Imagine your organization faces revenue issues or cost overruns (or both!), and the most senior leaders are sharpening their budget axes, locked away in a "finance team" triage room. Where do they look?

First, it's cutting any type of expenditure, whether travel, training, or bagels. Following the carbohydrates? They tend to zero in on your most experienced (and, yes, higher-paid) team members. To many of these CFO types, the Rubies are simply line items that cost more than Rivers. Goodbye experience—hello, immediate EBITDA (earnings before interest, taxes, depreciation, and amortization) savings.

While revenue challenges and cost overruns are very real, this sort of shortsighted cost-cutting strategy can backfire spectacularly. Enter Citigroup. The company found itself in one of those aforementioned binds when it suffered 2023 revenue challenges on top of regulatory pressures that had been building since 2020. What followed was a textbook lesson in the fallacy of cost-centric thinking.

Under a sweeping simplification initiative spearheaded by CEO Jane Fraser, Citigroup laid off thousands of employees, including many with critical expertise in risk management, compliance, and data governance. These were a combination of Rubies and Rocks, individuals with both deep institutional knowledge *and* leadership prowess.

And then the inevitable happened.

By mid-2024, the US Federal Reserve and the Office of the Comptroller of the Currency (OCC) issued another stinging rebuke, pointing out Citigroup's "insufficient and unsustainable progress" in addressing long-standing compliance issues. "Certain persistent weaknesses remain," wrote Acting Comptroller of the Currency Michael J. Hsu.

Since 2020, the regulatory watchdogs of the OCC had been circling, and now the bank was scrambling—once again—to patch the holes left by its myopic decision-making.

While the layoffs saved money in the short term, the company faced a far more significant bill. For starters, the OCC fined the company $75 million. Citigroup was also required to allocate billions of dollars for regulatory remediation, with 13,000 employees redirected (or continuing to be dedicated) to overhauling its compliance and risk systems. That's 13,000 employees working feverishly to undo the damage of previous leadership decisions.

Indications unearthed by Reuters suggested the layoffs created a compliance vacuum *and* an organizational culture blow. Citigroup morale took a hit. Teams struggled. Trust was strained. Skills went missing. The bagels remained in the bakery.

A good chunk of the Rubies were exited—so were many of the good Rocks—and with them went the knowledge, stability, and long-term insight Citigroup desperately needed at such a critical juncture. In sum, significant and unnecessary expenditures were incurred because experienced talent wasn't retained when needed most.

This is economic age myopia in action, the fallacy of cost-centric workforce planning—a senior leader's fever dream of quick savings that turns into a corporate culture nightmare. Citigroup may have sought to cut costs—and indeed, it had to—but it wound up cutting corners on continuity, culture, and compliance. When Rubies (and even those critical Rocks) get treated as expendable, the resulting financial, operational, and reputational costs can outweigh any perceived balance sheet savings.

Will AI and Bots Replace Brains?

MapleCo has long prided itself on being customer-focused, a reputation built over decades of serving its clients with personalized care. But when MapleBot—the firm's supposedly cutting-edge AI chatbot—was introduced, the company's reputation quickly began to unravel.

Designed to handle customer queries 24/7, MapleBot was heralded as a game changer for efficiency and cost reduction by senior leaders. What it delivered, however, was chaos. Within days of the MapleBot rollout, complaints began pouring in.

A single mother seeking clarification on a warranty extension for her child's medical device received incorrect information, leaving her confused and frustrated, and ultimately leading to an out-of-warranty situation. Another customer attempted to reschedule a delivery, which resulted in a much-needed heart monitor being sent 500 kilometres away. There was a raft of additional mishaps.

Tipped off by a barrage of unfavourable social media posts, the media caught wind of these ongoing failures and turned MapleBot into a national punchline. One astute business journalist dubbed it "MapleNot," and headlines emphasized how a once-respected brand had seemingly lost touch with its largely satisfied customer base.

Leadership hailed MapleBot as a marvel of automation and efficiency. In reality, it began reflecting the demographic cracks in MapleCo's strategy. Several cost-cutting initiatives the year before had stripped away the experienced customer service team, which could have proactively guided its implementation or intervened when these errors emerged. Did it have to be this way?

Economic myopia focuses narrowly on short-term financial gains while ignoring the ripple effects that can undermine long-term stability. At MapleCo, the decision to implement MapleBot under the guise of modernization exposed a deeper issue of how it was mishandling the balance between automation and customer service expertise.

Air Canada faced a strikingly similar situation. When the company rolled out its AI-powered chatbot in 2022, senior leaders were likely licking their financial chops over the potential savings to be had. Until the day when a client logged into the chatbot and began an exchange.

Experiencing the loss of a loved one is always difficult, and it can be even more challenging when you live thousands of kilometres away. After signing into the Air Canada chatbot, this particular Canadian inquired about last-minute bereavement fares after the loss of their grandmother. The chatbot responded and assured them that they could purchase a full-fare ticket and apply for a refund afterward. Following this guidance, the passenger booked the ticket and made it in time for the funeral.

A few days later, Air Canada denied them the refund. Why? Hadn't the chatbot done the right thing? Turns out the airline's policy required bereavement fare applications to be made *before* travel commenced—a nuance the chatbot failed to grasp.

Air Canada found itself in a pickle. The company unwisely decided to distance itself from the error by claiming the chatbot operated as a "separate legal entity that is responsible for its own actions." The British Columbia Civil Resolution Tribunal (CRT) disagreed and held the airline accountable. The CRT also ordered appropriate compensatory damages for the wronged passenger.

The fallout was swift. As with MapleCo, headlines across the world questioned the ethics of passing off responsibility to AI. Customer trust in Air Canada took a significant hit.

Research from 2022 suggests that failures like these occur when AI systems lack trust-building design elements such as transparency and traceability. Without these key facets, customers are forced to navigate opaque processes that magnify frustrations during critical moments—like bereavement.

These failures at MapleCo and Air Canada echo a deeper tension in automation strategies. Ethan Mollick's *Co-Intelligence: Living and*

Working with AI offers critical insights into the tension between AI's capabilities and limitations. He notes, "If we remember that AI is not human, but often works in the way that we would expect humans to act, it helps us avoid getting too bogged down in arguments about ill-defined concepts like sentience."

While MapleBot and Air Canada's chatbot were designed for efficiency, they failed to integrate features that could mimic empathy or respond dynamically to sensitive situations. I don't know about you, but I expect warmth and understanding from my tech overlords, particularly during high-stakes exchanges. If bots fail to meet my emotional expectations, the disconnect deepens and trust erodes quickly.

The MapleCo and Air Canada failures highlight the risks of prioritizing cost-saving automation over the wisdom and judgment of experienced personnel. Your expertise and that of your Rubies and Rocks are not an optional extra—they're the foundation for ensuring these AI tools deliver on their promise without unintended consequences. When organizations sideline the professionals who understand context, nuance, and customer relationships—whether they're wise Rubies or Rocks or Rivers—the ripple effects will undoubtedly extend far beyond a few mishandled chatbot cases.

> **These chatbot missteps also underscore the dangers of economic myopia, where automation without experience deepens Age Debt.**

Both companies replaced or overlooked experienced personnel with automated systems that lacked the oversight, judgment, and empathy critical for handling complex customer interactions. The results were predictable: alienated customers and public relations crises. At MapleCo, as at Air Canada, the failure wasn't the bot itself. The failure was a system that expected the bot to act as a replacement for wisdom, rather than a tool to enhance it. Those bots aren't sentient. You are. (Well, at least they aren't as of this writing.)

Naturally, you will also want to ponder what roles are likely to be affected by artificial intelligence in the coming years. From the Industrial Revolution to the digital age, technology has long been cast as a villain in the story of work, accused of robbing people of their livelihoods. But history tells a different tale. While technology does replace jobs, it also creates them.

According to the World Economic Forum's *Future of Jobs Report 2025*, AI, automation, and digitalization will result in 170 million new jobs by 2030, while 92 million roles will be displaced—a net employment gain of 78 million jobs. AI and information processing technologies alone are expected to create 11 million new jobs, even as they displace 9 million. The message is clear: AI is not coming for all jobs. But it is redefining how work is done. The most significant shift to consider as a leader is not job elimination but job evolution, which will affect Rivers, Rocks, and Rubies equally. Organizations that invest in reskilling and workforce adaptation will thrive. Those that resist? They may find themselves caught in the undertow of technological progress.

Of course, organizations cannot fully outsource wisdom to machines without consequences. MapleBot? Maybe not. AI systems are tools, not outright solutions. They mimic processes but lack the capacity for true judgment, empathy, or trust-building that experienced employees bring. You ought to keep this in mind. AI evolution is inevitable, but we still need adults in the room. Humanity must win.

The decisions your organization makes about automation and workforce design will not solely shape your current existence; they just may echo into a future where longer lives and extended careers place growing strains on systems unprepared for the realities of longevity.

And that's a perfect setup for Track 4: The Pressure Points of Longevity.

GREYAWAYS

The following medley of Greyaways summarizes the challenges of expertise bottlenecks, leadership vacuums, and economic age myopia in the era of Age Debt:

Greyaway #1: Expertise Is Perishable

Tacit knowledge is a critical yet fragile resource. Every team member departure without knowledge transfer diminishes your organization's capacity to innovate, adapt, and thrive. What transfer systems are you building to preserve it?

Greyaway #2: The Bottleneck Effect Stalls Progress

When wisdom departs faster than it's replenished, bottlenecks form. What actions are you taking to ensure the pipeline of intelligence continues uninterrupted?

Greyaway #3: Leadership Lives in Quiet Corners

Leadership isn't solely defined by titles and the hierarchy—it's found in the Rubies and Rocks whose deep influence sustains your organization's operational rhythm. How are you identifying and empowering your Rubies and Rocks?

Greyaway #4: Age Debt Trap Avoidance

Age Debt accumulates when organizations prioritize short-term fixes over long-term strategy. Every decision to sideline experience compounds this debt. What choices are you making today to safeguard your future?

Greyaway #5: Growth and Sustainment Demand Steady Hands

Ambition without experience often stumbles. The steady hands of seasoned professionals—the Rubies and Rocks—can transform creativity into positive success. Who in your organization provides this critical balance? Who else needs to be hired? Retained?

Greyaway #6: Tune Into the Hamals' Wisdom

The Hamals teach us a vital lesson. Some of the Rubies and Rocks in your organization bear their weight, often going unnoticed. Are you listening to their wisdom? Is their work sustainable?

The Pressure Points of Longevity

t wasn't what I expected.

In early 2025, after a long flight to Narita Airport via Vancouver and then a train ride to Tokyo Station, I hailed a cab for the next stop on my journey: the hotel. Sliding into the back seat, I was startled to see my driver. Not in a bad way. Haruki, as he called himself, was 74 years old. I couldn't recall being in a cab with a driver his age. Haruki's white gloves were immaculate, his hairstyle perfectly coiffed, and his demeanour as polished as his taxi. I felt I had to engage with him despite the jet lag.

Haruki explained that he had retired from an engineering job at 60, only to return to work at 65. I asked why, and three answers came to bear. First, "People," he said. I took that to mean he liked meeting other human beings and not getting lonely. Second, "Bored," he joked.

"Fair enough," I thought to myself. It also tracked to research. For example, the 2024 National Institute on Ageing in Canada Survey found that 43 percent of Canadians over the age of 50 are at risk of social isolation. Some 59 percent of people experience one form of loneliness. Furthermore, 36 percent of people over the age of 50 have very (13 percent) or somewhat (23 percent) weak social networks.

And lastly, after I asked if there were any other factors to explain why a 74-year-old was driving a cab, Haruki offered a third: "Money."

During my time in Tokyo and Osaka that week, researching whether Japan was any further ahead in the workplace demographic crisis, I noticed older Japanese workers everywhere. They held flags at construction sites and for road repair crews, issued parking tickets on crowded sidewalks, and acted as restaurant attendants, even at the McDonald's in Shibuya. And there were more Harukis driving more cabs, too. After all, 29 percent of the Japanese population is over the age of 65, and it is projected to become 40 percent by 2050.

Had Japan figured it out? Were older workers saving their economy? Tokyo may be a city of 41 million people—roughly equal to Canada's population—but its aging society isn't immediately noticeable. There are young people literally everywhere you look. How could the country be aging? The demographic shift (and the lack of either a country-wide plan or company-specific retooling) only becomes apparent when you start talking to people. And dig into the data.

The 20-minute cab ride with Haruki was only the beginning. I thought Japan was ahead of the curve—that Haruki and others of his ilk were exemplars, that their economy had dodged the demographic apocalypse. However, as I met with academics, economists, and various leaders, I realized something worse: Japan is the demographic "canary in the coal mine." They're leading the way on what organizations (and countries) should *not* do. They *are* way ahead of the curve, but not in a good way.

Haruki embodied a world where longevity and declining fertility will transform everything from individual lives to organizational systems. There's a reason the average age of taxi drivers in Japan is 58. However, the needed change is not occurring there or anywhere else. These blinders are set to become a significant issue for many organizations—like yours, soon.

What's going wrong regarding longevity? There are four factors:

- Financial strain
- Personal burdens
- Societal inertia
- Organizational gaps

These longevity factors have converged to create a workplace landscape that demands your attention.

The problem? As I will outline throughout Track 4, senior leaders are too busy trying to play record albums on a Sony Walkman when streaming services are available. The result? Organizations remain clinging to vinyl while the world streams past them.

Financial Strain

The cab ride with Haruki was a reflection of the cracks in a system unprepared for the realities of longer lives and shrinking savings. Across the globe, people are staying in jobs—or returning to work— well into what should have been their anticipated retirement years. Not because they want to, but because they have to. Living longer, it turns out, comes with a hefty price tag. The systems designed to support us throughout our lives aren't meeting our needs, and the gap between what's required and what's available is growing wider. And Rubies aren't the only ones suffering.

River Ruin

River employees struggle to afford basic living expenses, much less plan for the future. In cities like London, England, housing costs have soared by 83 percent since 2010, and young workers continue to wonder if they will ever be able to scrape together enough for a down payment. If you wish to own a home in Toronto, the estimated time it will take to afford the down payment is 15 years. Years! And we wonder why the fertility rate is in freefall.

At the same time, salaries have barely budged. The Institute for Fiscal Studies pointed out that median disposable income in the United Kingdom had only grown by 6 percent since 2010, despite rapid growth in employment and significant tax cuts for workers. The average salary in Canada has increased by a measly 13 percent since 2010. In the United States, median household income has stagnated, with real wages barely growing over the past decade. According to the US Census Bureau, the median household income in 2022 was $74,580, only a modest increase from $68,703 in 2010 after adjusting for inflation.

I've heard a fair number of young people ask, "Is it worth it? Work harder but get nowhere?" That's why movements like quiet quitting, Tángpíng ("lying flat"), and herbivore men have become a cultural phenomenon in both the West and Asia. Young workers are rejecting societal pressures to overwork and overachieve, as there seems to be no way to get ahead financially.

Maybe the river is running dry.

Rock Sandwich

For Rocks, it might be even more challenging. They're squeezed from all sides, and not in the good, huggy way. Many middle-aged Rocks are caught up in what's often called the Sandwich Generation—trapped between supporting aging parents and raising their own children. They are the bassist between the drummer and the lead singer. Caregiving for young children, teens, and young adults, in addition to their own parents, is taking a toll on the Rocks. According to a 2023 survey by insurance company New York Life, the average adult in the Sandwich Generation spends 28 hours a week caring for children and another 22 hours tending to aging relatives. That's a full-time job on top of their day job. The financial strain is no less staggering: Half of these individuals reported being unable to cover basic expenses like rent or groceries, and nearly half have accumulated an average of $13,000 in credit card debt.

Maybe you've met a Sandwich Generation professional. I've spoken with quite a few of them. They are exhausted, not just physically but also mentally. Particularly women. What comes up time and again—on top of their exhaustion—is the deep-rooted fear that they are barely making a dent in their retirement savings. The math does not bode well concerning the longevity factor. Those Rocks are on quite "The Long and Winding Road."

Broke Rubies

Rubies face a different yet equally disturbing kind of pressure. These are workers who should typically be winding down their careers but find themselves staring at the harsh reality of insufficient retirement savings. And remember, we're all living longer. As the World Economic Forum pointed out in 2025, "The financial architecture underpinning later life has not kept pace. Many people are entering retirements that last 20 to 30 years without the means to sustain them, leading to a projected global retirement savings gap of $400 trillion by 2050."

As of 2025, individuals aged 65 and older in Canada could expect to collect $1,535.81 per month through two pension schemes. Yet, the average retirement savings sat at just $170,000—a nest egg that won't last long for most. Worse, according to the Survey of Consumer Finances, roughly half of all households in the United States have zero dollars saved for retirement. Zero.

In the United Kingdom, the situation isn't much better. By 2020, Britons aged 55 and older had an average of £20,028 in savings, while those aged 65 and older held £113,600 across retirement savings and investments. On paper, that might look passable. In reality, it's woefully inadequate to keep up with soaring living costs, healthcare expenses, and the reality of longer lives.

And back in Japan? The so-called 20-million-yen problem is a reality for many people like Haruki. Families in Japan are estimated to need ¥20 million—on top of national pension plans—just to maintain a basic standard of living in retirement. But as of 2020, the average annual savings hovered around ¥3.8 million (approximately US$35,780). That gap? It's a chasm. It's probably why Haruki is driving that cab.

What happens when the Rubies are forced to continue working in jobs that were never intended for someone their age? What if they must accept a lower-paying, undignified role after decades in a higher calling?

Organizational Ignorance

These financial and societal data points prompt the question: What are organizations doing about this financial catastrophe?

Not much. Most companies do not offer financial education programs or multifaceted retirement planning support. And they certainly are not keeping up with the wage cycle.

> **Let me ask you this: When was the last time your employer sat down and showed you how to plan for 30 or even 40 years of retirement? When was the last time you held that discussion with a team member that you lead? Probably never. Yet, it's more necessary than a lead singer in a rock band.**

The question isn't whether individuals can keep up with the rising costs of longevity; it's whether organizations can. If a good percentage of Rivers, Rocks, and Rubies are financially drained, unsupported, and uncertain, what does that mean for the workplace of the future? Are companies prepared to shoulder their part of this burden, or will they continue looking the other way? The answers—or lack thereof—speak volumes about another critical factor: personal burdens.

Personal Burdens

Longevity is often celebrated as a sign of progress, and rightly so. Advances in medicine, nutrition, exercise, and general wellness knowledge have enabled us to live longer than those born just a few generations ago. Even when excluding infant and child mortality, someone born in 1900 could expect to live only to the age of 50. In contrast, if you were born in 2000 in a G7 country, you can expect to live to approximately 80.

Many G7 countries set their pension age at 65—or eventually lowered it from 70—during a time when life expectancy was far lower than it is today. With people now regularly living into their 80s and beyond, these pension systems, designed for a different era, are straining under the weight of today's demographic realities. Countries are beginning to pay more attention. For example, Denmark's parliament passed a law in 2025 to raise its official retirement age to 70 by 2040. This will apply to anyone born after December 31, 1970.

As society shifts from bell to bulb, many young workers wonder if a pension plan will even be available when their retirement day arrives. Everyone has to contend with this personal burden, regardless of whether you're a River, Rock, or Ruby. Furthermore, for many Rubies, longevity seems more like a resilience roller-coaster ride than an empathy exchange. Far too many organizations fail to comprehend the gravity of this situation. In particular, older workers bear several personal burdens that become increasingly entrenched and onerous as they age.

Hidden Costs

Leaders often appear either uninformed or unaware of the realities of extended lifespans. Chronic conditions like diabetes, arthritis, hypertension, and cardiovascular disease—just to name a few—can affect how Rubies show up and contribute. There will be good days and bad. Today was a bad Ruby Day for me. Fourteen thousand five hundred steps walking around Osaka in between interviews, and my back is throbbing. But I digress.

Leaders will need to account for these health realities if we're ever going to use Rubies past age 65 in the workforce. And if we ignore their physical conditions, there is no hope for Rubies to feel psychologically safe to divulge whatever ailments they might be dealing with. Leaders who fail to recognize the subtle signs—a slower pace, hesitance to discuss health challenges, or quiet concern about being perceived as less capable—will ultimately undermine opportunities for productivity gains in their team, unit, or organization.

What's more, health breakdowns will happen, and you ought to know that. A *Journal of Occupational and Environmental Medicine* study found that workers managing multiple chronic conditions average 14 missed days per year. As these conditions progress with age, the toll on productivity becomes even more pronounced and something you must keep a watchful eye on.

The invisible toll is just as significant. Leaders often overlook quieter signs of struggle, such as fatigue, mental strain, or the avoidance of physically demanding tasks. Imagine a 62-year-old team lead silently managing physical mobility challenges or a 68-year-old operations manager timing medication to avoid side effects at work. These are everyday realities that demand your leadership empathy.

How many organizations genuinely ask themselves, Are we supporting our Rubies to excel or quietly allowing them to fade into the background? Is yours?

Gender Disparities

The story of women as workers, mothers, and caregivers is often one of resilience. However, that resilience can come at a cost to their careers and earnings.

Women's careers are interrupted not by choice, but often by necessity. The caregiving years—spent with young children, aging parents, or both—extract an enormous toll. Time away from the workforce erodes earning potential and closes doors to progression.

Upon returning, women often face roles with limited opportunities for advancement or stagnant wages. It certainly happened to Denise during one of her maternity leaves.

The gender gaps are appalling. Consider the United Kingdom. On average, women can expect to receive an annual pension of £12,000. The men? £17,000. Adding insult to retirement injury, women aged 50 to 64 anticipate retiring with pension funds that are, on average, 33 percent smaller than those of men. These figures illustrate a lifetime spent navigating societal expectations alongside professional ambitions. The result is systemic inequity that hampers women both financially and professionally. The negative ramifications for women become systemic, persistent, and devastating. This aspect of Age Debt affects a large portion of the workforce. Far too often, women carry these burdens silently, and workplaces frequently fail to see—or worse, refuse to acknowledge—this reality. What emerges is a cycle of inequity that holds women back but also weakens the performance potential of the entire organization.

These inequities that women face demand more than your awareness; they require a willingness to open your eyes and ask, "What have I been getting wrong?" The answer often lies in imbalances that have gone unseen for far too long—and that demand you to enter into a period of deep Age Debt gender reflection.

From the beginning of their careers, women are forced to navigate a maze of societal expectations, caregiving responsibilities, and systemic inequities. These are stark reminders of a very different financial story for men and women.

Menopause Taboo

Menopause remains one of the most overlooked and misunderstood personal burdens in the workplace. Symptoms like brain fog, insomnia, and mood swings are not minor inconveniences—they're debilitating for many Ruby and Rock women. Yet, how many organizations have policies to address this reality?

The sheer number of transferable skills that women bring to the table after years of childbearing should be viewed as a significant advantage. It's not Age Debt; it's the epitome of the Experience Dividend. Yet, if organizations ignore their talent and add insult to injury by also failing to recognize the perfectly natural female body condition of menopause, it is the proverbial "salt in the wound" situation.

According to the Chartered Institute of Personnel and Development, over a third of women aged 45 to 55 in the United Kingdom considered leaving their jobs because of menopause-related symptoms. That equates to nearly a million women who considered leaving jobs not because they lack talent but because their workplaces lack empathy.

The menopause stigma leaves far too many women to suffer in silence. Cultural taboos and a lack of awareness mean that even mentioning menopause in professional settings, let alone requesting accommodations, feels risky. This is especially true in organizations with male-dominated leadership—that is, most of them.

The costs of being silent can be profound. A 2022 study by the Fawcett Society indicated that menopause is both a personal health issue and an organizational blind spot, with very dire business consequences. Among women who experienced menopause, 77 percent reported at least one symptom that interfered with their ability to work, with nearly half citing challenges like reduced focus and energy levels. The research also found that 10 percent of menopausal women had left their jobs because their symptoms were unsupported by their boss or organization.

The reality of menopause has been ignored for too long and has resulted in workplaces that amplify rather than alleviate the strain of those who suffer from it. If you continue to ignore the challenges faced by menopausal women, your workplace will not only reinforce the very inertia that drives Age Debt but also lose many talented Rubies and Rocks quite unnecessarily.

Racial Inequities at MapleCo

Does race play a factor in the personal burden of longevity? Sadly, yes, it does.

In the United States, Black and Hispanic workers encounter considerable financial disparities that exacerbate the difficulties associated with longevity. A 2021 report from the National Institute on Retirement Security (NIRS) indicated that white households possess over 90 percent of the financial assets of Baby Boomers. In contrast, Black and Hispanic households hold 3 percent or less.

The NIRS published additional research in 2023 that suggested public pensions could help bridge these financial gaps. By contributing to the system, public pensions can increase the median wealth of older Black families by 86 percent and Latino families by 32 percent. However, access to employer-sponsored pension plans remains unequal between white and BIPOC groups, which leaves many people to age with fewer resources and additional financial burdens.

MapleCo is not immune to this predicament. In fact, they see it with their B2C clients.

Maria Shapiro is a 66-year-old Latina caregiver and a long-time customer of MapleCo. For many years, she has dedicated herself to caring for others—family, friends, and patients—while navigating the all-too-common financial precarity that accompanies low-paying, physically demanding work. As a contractor, Maria shifted between various healthcare and elderly home companies to remain employed mostly full-time.

"Retirement?" she questioned during a recent feedback session with her MapleCo advisor, Harold. "I've never even thought of it. If I stop working, what happens to my family?" Maria has made numerous sacrifices as a caregiver over the years. She has worked mainly on short-term contracts to make ends meet. While her resilience is remarkable, it should not be required in this day and age.

Maria's reality reminds everyone that longevity isn't the same for everyone. Systemic barriers—lower wages, fewer opportunities for savings, and inequitable access to education, housing, savings, and healthcare—leave many workers of colour like Maria forced to endure rather than thrive. Even as they age, these individuals often remain in roles that offer little dignity or stability, not because they want to but because they have no other choice.

This is the invisible side of Age Debt. It is where the burden does not get evenly distributed. For marginalized groups and people like Maria, the weight is heavy. MapleCo advisors understand their clients' challenges, but their solutions can only go so far when the systemic barriers run so deep. Maria's situation underscores the systems we've built and the urgent challenges that demand resolution.

Societal Inertia

Despite his charm, I didn't just hang out with Haruki during my research visit to Japan. I travelled there to learn if the country had addressed its growing demographic crisis. Surely there was a societal and workplace playbook that organizations followed. After all, hadn't Japan been dealing with the demographic issue for decades?

Dr. Hideaki Tanaka is a distinguished professor at the Graduate School of Governance Studies at Meiji University. Before that, he held several leadership positions in Japan's federal government, including the Ministry of Foreign Affairs and the Ministry of Social Welfare. Tanaka thanked me for tracking him down, but he was both unexpectedly blunt and deeply concerned.

"Japan is at a critical juncture," he told me. "You can learn a lot from Japan, and it's *not* to do things like Japan."

Tanaka has spent his entire career studying, working, thinking, and teaching at the intersection of demographics and economics. He issued a warning, and I was dialled in to understand why.

"We're risk averse," he told me. "Our leaders are afraid to make bold moves, and I'm frightened for Japan's future."

> **That fear may well be justified.** Japan's aging population and stagnant workforce policies make it a cautionary tale for the rest of the G7, if not the world. As I pointed out earlier, it's the proverbial canary in the demographic coal mine.

I also met with Dr. Hiroshi Ono, a professor at Hitotsubashi University Business School and author of *Redistributing Happiness: How Social Policies Shape Life Satisfaction*. Ono supported Tanaka's concerns about leaders being risk averse with some valuable additional insights. In 2024, Ono surveyed 600 HR leaders from Japanese companies. Only 2 percent of the leaders indicated they had changed the retirement age. This despite being aware for decades of the impending demographic malaise.

"I wish I could be optimistic about the future," Ono said. "There's not much optimism right now."

The insights from the two professors painted a somewhat grim picture. Japan is suffering from societal inertia. Its policies are frozen in time, professional norms resist innovation, and its economy is not yet prepared to adapt to the realities of longevity, let alone a plunging fertility rate of 1.2 births per woman, almost half the required population replacement level. Yet, the country has been aware of its demographic apocalypse for decades.

Japan's situation provides invaluable intelligence as you begin to face similar demographic upheaval. You may not be able to change these factors unless you work in government, but you *must* be cognizant of their existence. Why? Because they will affect you, your employees, and the organization or team you lead.

What I discovered was simple: Japan's societal-inertia canary is chirping, and not in a melodic way. You should learn "*not* to do things like Japan," as Dr. Tanaka warned.

Policy Paralysis

Japan's demographic canary is also chirping about its lack of GDP growth due to government policy paralysis. The country's situation will likely worsen as its workforce and society continue to age. Jun Saito is a senior research fellow at the Japan Center for Economic Research. In an interview with me at his Tokyo office, he sternly cautioned about Japan's economic future.

"The potential GDP growth rate is eventually going to zero, and it could even fall below zero," he warned me.

Saito explained that while temporary boosts to labour force participation—such as more women and older adults entering the workforce—have helped delay economic stagnation, they were insufficient to counteract the more profound demographic shifts. By 2008, Japan's population had already begun to decline, following decades of plummeting birth rates. By then, Japan's economy was in a precarious state, its slowly shrinking workforce unable to support meaningful GDP growth. The real puzzling aspect, as Saito outlined, is that Japan's fertility rate fell below the 2.1 replacement rate in 1974, more than half a century ago.

I decided to investigate other G7 countries to determine when their decline had begun. To my surprise, it was generally the same. All G7 countries experienced a decline in their total fertility rates below the 2.1 replacement level in the early 1970s. Every government has been aware of this fact for decades. It is the very definition of policy paralysis—government officials were aware it was happening, yet they took no significant actions, aside from those countries that ramped up their immigration policies.

I spoke with Bradley Schurman, author of *The Super Age* and one of the more clear-eyed voices on the demographic storm we are about to live through. He put it this way: "The pinch we're having in the global labour market right now is the result of over 100 years of demographic change, with the most damning portion really in the past 25 years. We haven't had enough children to replace our populations, and outdated norms around retirement and ageism are pushing older people out of the workforce."

G7 Average Fertility Rate
(1960–2020)

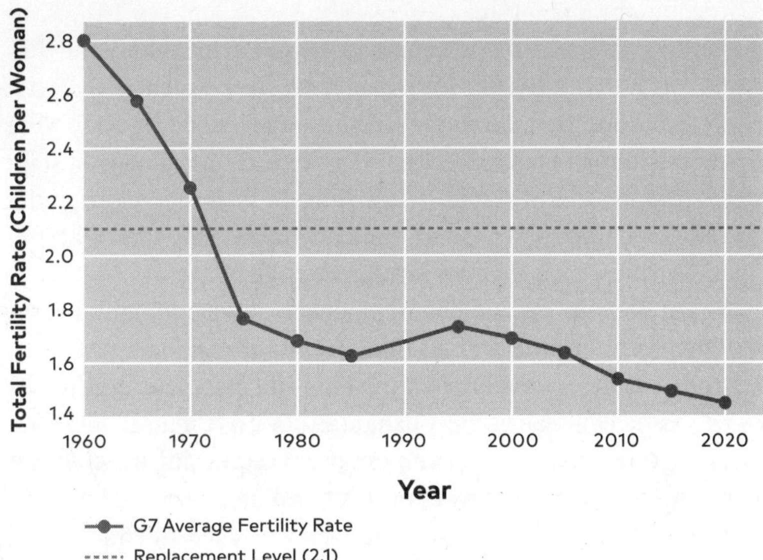

Back in Japan, the core of their challenge lies in an outdated pension system alongside a lifelong employment system called Shūshin koyō. The model gave rise to an implicit lifetime contract where companies would hire fresh graduates (Shinsotsuikkatsusaiyō), then retain those workers until retirement age, traditionally 55 and now typically 60. It inadvertently entrenched deep-rooted norms of job-for-life and seniority-based promotion. The crux of Japan's problem is an employment culture that still clings to a mid-twentieth-century social contract, one that celebrated security, career laddering, and loyalty but now suffocates adaptability in the face of demographic upheaval.

Dr. Tanaka highlighted how the pension system—initially designed for shorter lifespans and larger families—is woefully inadequate in today's aging context. Japan spends 12 percent of its GDP on pensions and eldercare—one of the highest rates globally—yet it will eventually be forced to increase this until it becomes unsustainable. If the country fails to address the structural deficiencies of a labour model that inhibits older workers from contributing beyond the age of 60, it will present significantly more challenges to its economy and future.

Policy paralysis isn't just a challenge in Japan. While Italy has made strides with significant pension reforms—such as the 2011 Fornero Reform that raised the retirement age to 67 by 2019—the frequent shifts in government have made it challenging to sustain steady progress. As a result, Italy's pension system remains under pressure, with pension expenditures ranking among the highest in the European Union at almost 17 percent of GDP.

South Korea is another country facing a demographic and corresponding pension crisis with its National Pension Service (NPS) fund. Current estimates indicate that the NPS will start running deficits by 2041 and could be entirely exhausted by 2055 if no changes are made. In late 2024, the government proposed raising the contribution rate from 9 percent to 13 percent and increasing the income replacement rate to 42 percent. However, like Japan and Italy, South Korea has encountered political hurdles in its attempts to ensure these reforms materialize.

Could it happen in the United States? Of course. The country's social security system is on the brink of collapse. Projections show the fund could run out of money by 2034. The net effect is that retirees will face a 20 percent cut in social security benefits. Political gridlock has stalled comprehensive reforms, leaving many people uncertain about the future of their benefits. And from earlier in Track 4, we know how poor people are at personally saving for their retirement.

Over in France, the government's proposed retirement reforms of 2022–23 triggered widespread and, at times, hilarious protests. Labour strikes ensued. Despite months of protests—where over a million people took to the streets—the reforms took effect in September 2023. President Macron's government forced a bill through parliament that raised the legal retirement age from 62 to 64, a shocking increase for many French citizens. However, it demonstrates that some governments have the ability to push through unpopular reforms despite significant resistance.

> **For leaders, the lesson is clear:**
> **Be cautious of policy changes at a macro**
> **level. They may or may not happen.**

Policy paralysis remains rampant, and policymakers in government seem preoccupied with the short term. Call it bureaucratic short-termism. Unfortunately, you might only be able to adjust the workforce factors within your control.

Societal Inertia Meets Age Debt

Societal inertia will be a significant challenge to face as your organization, and society, continues to age. The archaic modelling we have relied on—education in youth, work in midlife, and retirement in later years—was crafted for an era when life expectancy barely reached 60.

Your workforce already reflects a disconnect. The Rivers, Rocks, and Rubies will become even more imbalanced in the future. Rivers are eager to learn and contribute, but their growth will be stunted if wisdom and experience are not readily available. Rocks will continue to balance careers and sandwich caregiving while enduring ongoing financial strain. The Rubies will find themselves overlooked, their acumen neglected by societal and organizational systems ill-equipped to capitalize on their insights. Perhaps worse, when all three groups fail to connect with one another, intergenerational malaise widens and Age Debt deepens.

Age-based divisions exacerbate the issue. Fewer than 20 percent of organizations worldwide have effective strategies for managing age-diverse teams. Research consistently demonstrates that structured opportunities for intergenerational knowledge sharing lead to productivity gains and stronger organizational cultures, yet these opportunities remain scarce. Without deliberate systems to integrate Rivers, Rocks, and Rubies, critical knowledge—particularly the tacit knowledge we discussed in Track 3—will never transfer. The lack of mentorship and collaboration stifles innovation and compounds gaps in organizational capacity and performance.

Age Debt accrues each time these disconnects persist. Rivers lose direction without mentorship, Rocks struggle under increasing pressure, and Rubies—like Haruki—are left in roles disconnected from their actual expertise. Every disconnect deepens Age Debt, stalling innovation, fattening bureaucracy, and dragging down productivity. We need only look at Japan to see what happens when inertia outweighs action.

Addressing these inertia gaps will require intentional strategies that reflect the realities of longevity, ensuring that all members of the workforce—at every age and stage—contribute fully and meaningfully. We must recognize the realities of longevity and commit to strategies that integrate all generations into the workplace.

But before we do that, I must introduce the final pressure point of longevity: the organizational gaps that contribute to Age Debt.

Organizational Gaps at MapleCo

Here are three key organizational gaps you need to consider as part of the longevity equation:

- **Outdated HR systems:** how traditional HR frameworks—succession planning, promotion pathways, performance evaluations, and retirement policies—are misaligned with the realities of a longer-lived, multi-generational River, Rock, and Ruby workforce.

- **Role roulette:** the mismatch between talent and career opportunity, where organizations gamble with their workforce by failing to align people's strengths with roles effectively.

- **Collaboration and learning quandary:** the lack of intentional systems to foster intergenerational collaboration in addition to knowledge sharing, mentorship, and tailored professional development.

To introduce the three gaps, let's probe our friends at MapleCo.

The company's R&D division is widely regarded as the engine of its technological success. R&D has always been lauded for its cutting-edge breakthroughs and friendly team-first culture. Yet when Patricia Osterie, a senior director whose reputation was as solid as the products she helped develop, announced her early retirement, something shifted. Several glaring organizational gaps began to open up.

Patricia had been working at MapleCo for 22 years. Her ability to steer initiatives was uncanny. She relied on a delicate interplay of relationships among product development, compliance, sales, IT, and her own unit, R&D, to get things done. Patricia could orchestrate the unseen, ensuring silos did not strangle progress. She was a relationship magician, in addition to her high-tech prowess.

Patricia had always been a super team player and company supporter. So, as you might expect, she was not leaving out of frustration or haste. Her plans were clear, and she had communicated them to her boss, Darren Knight, VP of R&D, nearly a year in advance. She offered to help pave the way for her successor, openly sharing her insights, lessons, and connections. It was classic Patricia: steadfast, deliberate, focused on outcomes, and kind.

But the company wasn't ready.

Succession plans sat on a shared drive, untouched since their last review five years prior. There really was no "next Patricia" to tap. Worse, institutional knowledge, the lifeblood of any organization, was about to evaporate because Patricia's knowledge and know-how had never truly been captured.

Darren assumed his HR business partner, Arjun, would oversee the search for Patricia's replacement. Arjun was left chasing Darren. Meanwhile, Patricia's team watched from the sidelines, wondering when—or if—a plan would emerge.

Alex Bayne, one of Patricia's most reliable team members and a Rock in every sense of the word, was finally tapped to step into her shoes. Actually, not so much "tapped" as "assigned," because the company was struggling to find a suitable replacement. Even before the anointment, it was evident to many that Alex was already stretched thin. He was managing not just his work deadlines but also his aging father's care and the demands of raising two teenagers with his wife. "I'll make it work," he told Darren, though his tone indicated doubt more than determination.

To help Alex "make it work," a recent hire named Jordan Mills was given more responsibility, overseeing a high-profile initiative Patricia had championed. He also took on some of Alex's former responsibilities. While Jordan thrived in the technical domain, leading people and managing expectations were not yet in his natural wheelhouse.

"I'm fine with the work," he admitted to a peer, "but I didn't sign up to play referee." This was Jordan's tacit way of acknowledging his inferior collaborative leadership skills.

Patricia's departure became the linchpin in a much larger story of disconnects at MapleCo. Alignment unraveled between departments and silos re-emerged. Deadlines on various initiatives began to slip. Darren was too busy with strategic demands and unable to intervene. Employees began whispering about confusion over roles, rising workloads, and a pervasive sense that the team was adrift.

This wasn't about Patricia's retirement. Everyone is entitled to retire. What the situation highlighted was a company where HR systems failed to adapt, leadership assumed alignment without action, and transitions were more hope than plan. What happens if a situation like this emerges at your organization, particularly as it continues to age? Let's find out why that's akin to playing piano with a few missing keys as we unpack those three longevity organizational gaps.

Outdated HR Systems and Processes

Many organizations—maybe yours—continue to rely on HR systems and processes that reflect an outdated understanding of people and their career trajectories. They were designed for an era when team members retired at predictable ages, leaving younger workers to move up into their roles. This might have worked in a bell-shaped demographic world, but today's bulb workplace is upending the model. Despite being outdated, these HR systems and process relics persist.

As we've seen, many Rubies will want to continue working well past their traditional retirement age. Driven by a combination of financial necessity and personal fulfillment, they will want or need to shine. Given the impending demographic and societal changes, it is likely that nearly every HR system and process needs to be updated now. Or yesterday. At least by tomorrow.

For example, today's succession planning models still treat aging professionals as transitional rather than integral. Why are we throwing the Rubies out with the bathwater? Instead of retiring, might there be alternate options for this next stage of their career? Performance evaluations exacerbate the problem by prioritizing short-term results over cumulative expertise. Does the same performance management model need to be used for your Rubies? Even better, can the entire thing be improved for all stages?

The data doesn't lie either. You and your HR systems are ill prepared for change.

For example, the Center for Retirement Research at Boston College reported in 2023 that fewer than 25 percent of organizations globally have adapted their HR practices to account for changing workforce demographics. Worse, the World Economic Forum's *Future of Jobs Report* noted that only 40 percent of global employers recognize aging and declining working-age populations as "transformative forces within their businesses." It irks me no end how low that figure is.

This discrepancy between recognition and change reveals a gap. Not only do your HR systems and processes potentially require an overhaul, but your retirement policies may also need review.

- Do you have a policy for hiring or re-hiring older workers?

- Do you offer limited or phased retirement options that allow older workers to transition gradually into reduced roles?

- Do your career paths still assume upward mobility ends by a certain age, sidelining older workers as if their growth has an expiry date?

Without HR systems or process changes that integrate the different needs of Rubies, Rocks, and Rivers, your organization risks missing out on a gigantic opportunity for change.

Role Roulette

The misalignment of talent is one of the most significant challenges your organization faces, particularly as it realizes the importance of the River, Rock, and Ruby talent pool.

Decisions about who fills key roles are often made based on availability rather than strategic alignment. This may put individuals in positions they are unprepared to manage. (Hint: See Alex or Jordan at MapleCo.)

According to a 2023 survey by DDI, only 12 percent of companies reported confidence in the strength of their leadership "bench" when it comes to replacing top employees. This represents a 30 percent drop in confidence over five years, down from 18 percent in 2018. Moreover, 36 percent of young leaders felt unprepared when entering their leadership role, indicating a lack of adequate leadership development.

Whether you are a River, Rock or Ruby, role roulette affects far too many employees.

Collaboration and the Learning Quandary

Another organizational gap to consider is the lack of effective collaboration between the eras. Think of it as a missed opportunity. As I pointed out in Track 3, tacit knowledge—gained through years of experience—often goes unshared due to a lack of formalized systems. You can plug this hole through proper collaboration practices or improved learning models.

A 2023 Harris Poll report suggested that, despite three-quarters of Canadian companies having employees retire over the previous two years, two-thirds of the firms did not have mentoring programs in place. Without access to mentoring or coaching systems, knowledge and intelligence from Rivers, Rocks, and Rubies will remain siloed (or lost), and stereotypes about generational capabilities will persist.

> **Irony alert:** Digital learning platforms appear to exacerbate the problem, rather than resolve it. They often fail to address the needs of a multi-generational workplace.

The lack of proper upskilling or reskilling for Rubies is another problem. Unsurprisingly, according to SHRM, only 21 percent of HR professionals reported that their organizations were effective in upskilling or reskilling employees.

As your organization's Age Debt increases, Rivers will frequently find themselves prematurely shoved into leadership roles, expected to navigate complex dynamics without the necessary preparation. Meanwhile, Rubies, with their deep institutional knowledge and crystallized intelligence, will get overlooked or sidelined by HR decision-making frameworks that undervalue their expertise. Worse, because of their potentially higher salary due to years of service, they will be terminated to reduce costs. Misalignment of this kind destabilizes teams and undermines organizational effectiveness and productivity. And the Rocks? They are left trying to figure out how it all went down in the first place.

The failure to create revamped learning environments and collaboration systems for Rivers, Rocks, and Rubies perpetuates knowledge gaps and erodes the potential for age-diverse teams. Without intentional strategies to foster sharing and introduce revised learning models, your organization will risk adding more fuel to the Age Debt fire.

GREYAWAYS

Haruki's white-gloved taxi-driving professionalism masks a deeper, systemic issue. Older workers lack opportunities to contribute meaningfully across society. Organizations must face the facts: Overlooking your Rubies is unwise.

While Haruki may thrive on meeting people and supplementing his income by driving a taxi, his underutilized new role reflects a country grappling with a wide range of longevity gaps. It is a country where many older workers are overlooked, ignored, or filling low-level service roles without appropriate support or dignity. It may become your country, too.

Remember, your organization will require a diversified talent pool of Rivers, Rocks, and Rubies if it's going to maintain its economic and talent prowess in the coming years. The pressure points of longevity discussed in this track—financial strain, personal burdens, societal inertia, and organizational gaps—will need to be addressed.

To close, here are your Greyaways for Track 4.

Greyaway #1: The Cost-of-Living Conundrum

The rising cost of living has turned into a nearly unsustainable issue. The increase in property prices is just one aspect. People who must save longer for a house will find that it influences their work locations and even the job roles they accept. This strain will certainly impact talent movement, individual wealth, and employee retention rates.

Greyaway #2: Pensions Under Pressure

Public and private pension frameworks face demographic realities that strain their solvency. Leaders and organizations must prepare for more expensive benefits, as well as growing concerns about future financial security.

Greyaway #3: The Pay Squeeze Matters

Wage stagnation, shrinking public-sector pay, and surging caregiving costs put employees' incomes under stress. Organizations should expect ripple effects in talent buy-in, turnover, and related productivity issues.

Greyaway #4: The Sandwich Generation Is in Trouble

Certain team members—namely mid-career Rocks—who have to juggle childcare and eldercare may lack the time to properly plan for their own financial futures. You risk losing critical mid-career Rock talent to burnout or necessary job changes if your support measures remain insufficient.

Greyaway #5: Health and Workplace Realities Intersect

Chronic conditions, caregiving duties, and the effects of menopause will shape team member performance and retention. Organizational benefits and policies must adapt to extend working life and preserve—if not improve—team members' well-being.

Greyaway #6: Retirement Inequality

There is a disparity between men and women—as well as racial disparities—specifically in terms of pension and savings levels. This is particularly true for middle- and lower-income team members.

Greyaway #7: Bold Action Beats Inertia

Whether it's skyrocketing housing costs, mounting pension debt, or health burdens, if leaders ignore these pressures, Age Debt will continue to run out of control. Courageous, data-informed leaders will mitigate future crises and ensure workforce longevity by prioritizing education and reform.

The Silent Saboteur of Ageism

There he was, in his new higher education role, thrilled to be surrounded by a multitude of bright minds. Students, faculty, and staff—the various campuses were teeming with the intelligentsia. He was an up-and-coming River, swimming among talented Rocks and Rubies.

This young man had finally *arrived*. He was singing at the top of his lungs as part of a supergroup. After a university detour—originally thinking he'd be a physiotherapist or doctor before switching to become a high school teacher—he realized his purpose lay with adults of all ages seeking career change. Noble as it was, teaching high school hadn't fulfilled his calling. He career-switched to higher education.

Four years out of undergrad and eight years out of high school, he was finally blooming. One week into the new role, everything felt aligned. Draped with autonomy, mastery, and purpose—a personal development framework put forward by author Daniel H. Pink years later—this 27-year-old had been handed the opportunity of a lifetime. Building an entire suite of adult-based, career-changing programs at a downtown campus, blending high-tech, leadership, and entrepreneurial skills? Someone must have been looking out for him.

Then came Day Six of the new job. He attended a meeting on the "big campus," and just before the meeting, he stopped at the washroom. Back then, student facilities were separate from those of faculty and staff. Naturally—with his work badge flapping on his lanyard—he entered the staff washroom.

"What are you doing here?" said an older gentleman as he washed his hands.

Bewildered—gobsmacked, if we're being precise—the young professional held up his lanyard. "I work here," he replied. His face turned a shade of puzzled and concerning red.

The older man, appearing somewhere between 55 and 65, gave him a long, incredulous look. "Interesting. I didn't know we were hiring such young people these days. What a shame." He dried his hands and left.

The young River employee stared into the mirror, stunned. "What the heck was that?" It felt like someone had rudely yanked the needle off the record.

Who was that flustered young River? It was *me*.

At 27, I thought I was finally aligning my work with my purpose. Then, in a single moment, my age—not my ideas, skills, or potential—became the focus. That casual, cutting remark planted a seed of doubt. Was I an impostor? A mistake? Was I unworthy of the role I had earned? Was my young face a beacon of hate?

I said nothing. I left the washroom, attended the meeting, and carried on. But the comment lingered. Obviously, it still does—because I'm telling the story in a book a quarter of a century later!

What I didn't realize then—but understand deeply now in my fifties—is that ageism doesn't discriminate. It moves freely among and against Rivers, Rocks, *and* Rubies.

> **Ageism has the audacity to inflict harm wherever it chooses, happy to silence potential across all eras.**

That fleeting moment in the washroom may have been just a small personal slight, but it was also a microcosm of a much larger issue. The systemic nature of ageism is deeply ingrained in both workplaces and society. And it's *not* new. At least conceptually, ageism is about as old as Johnny Cash's famous live album, *At Folsom Prison.*

Ageism was first introduced as a term in 1968 by psychiatrist and gerontologist Robert N. Butler during an interview with the *Washington Post* reporter Carl Bernstein (yes, the same Bernstein who later broke the Watergate scandal). Butler defined ageism as the discrimination and prejudice that older individuals face.

In his seminal 1975 book, *Why Survive? Being Old in America*, Butler said, "In America, childhood is romanticized, youth is idolized, middle age does the work, wields the power and pays the bills, and old age, its days empty of purpose, gets little or nothing of what it has already done. The old are in the way." Someone had finally defined what it meant to be discriminated against as an older person.

There Is More to Ageism Than You Think

Butler's concept of ageism transformed the existing perceptions that gripped older workers. It laid the groundwork for future advocacy against age discrimination.

The term, however, was only the beginning. In fact, one might argue that Butler's original definition was, ahem, *ageist.*

Whether you identify as a River, Rock, or Ruby, ageism can be experienced across all personas. I suffered from it at 27 in that washroom and again more than 20 years later when Michael removed me from that speakers bureau.

Among those who have been calling out this silent saboteur is Maureen Wiley Clough, a former tech executive turned consultant. After years in both startups and large corporations, she began noticing something in the culture of organizations.

"Ageism is so accepted," she said to me. "It's the last socially acceptable 'ism.' The reality is, we are all ageists. And why? It's no one's fault. It's because we've been getting these messages since birth. It's the cultural script we're handed."

How about you? Have you been affected by ageism?

Next, ask yourself a more profound question: *Have I inflicted ageist harm against someone?*

One might argue that the first instances of ageism occurred during the rise of the Industrial Age, long before Butler coined the term. Workplaces began to shift at the turn of the twentieth century. While older people had been revered in an agrarian system, once factory floors and mass industrialization became the norm—like at Ford as the Model T began to be mass-produced—an emphasis on youth and their physical strength created new stereotypes about aging. Rivers were in; Rubies were out.

For women, the story unfolded similarly but differently. Pushed to roles that might be considered "light" or "domestic," women would often face stereotypes laughable in today's society: They were "too young to lead," "too old to contribute," or "too emotional." These multifaceted and damaging biases deepened the impact of ageism across generations and genders.

During the post–World War II economic boom—driven by another wave of youth narratives, including the rise of youthful musical game changers like Elvis Presley, Bill Haley, and Debbie Reynolds—the view that older workers were less valuable or adaptable became firmly entrenched. Plus, didn't everyone retire at 55? Weren't they supposed to be dead at 60?

Fast-forward several decades to the new millennium. The poorly named "knowledge economy" became a jungle of haves and have-nots. Older individuals couldn't possibly grasp technology; therefore, they were deemed no longer "smart." They swiftly became the have-nots of the so-called knowledge economy.

In an oft-used 2007 example, Facebook founder Mark Zuckerberg said with a straight face to an audience of entrepreneurs at Stanford University, "Young people are just smarter. Young people just have simpler lives. We may not own a car. We may not have a family. Simplicity in life allows you to focus on what's important."

Ironically, one year later, Zuckerberg hired Sheryl Sandberg—who is 15 years his senior—to help him manage the company.

To this day, technological innovation and know-how continue to be associated with younger generations. The 2019 "Okay, Boomer" meme did nothing to help the cause. The rapid pace of technological change has amplified stereotypes that older workers are resistant to change or incapable of learning new skills. Some people may think I am writing this book using a typewriter. I'm not. It's a quill pen.

The legal cases are endless. For example, in 2023, two former HR professionals—aged 62 and 66—sued IBM, claiming they were unlawfully terminated due to their age. The suit claimed that IBM was pushing for HR employees with "new skills" or "new energy."

At the same time, younger Rivers face their own form of bias: assumptions that they are inexperienced, untested, or not "seasoned" enough to work or lead. A 2024 UK Youth study of 3,000 16- to 25-year-olds found that 81 percent felt undervalued, 78 percent felt patronized, 69 percent believed they missed out on promotions, and 75 percent experienced job rejections due to their age. Shockingly, another 49 percent of respondents felt they could not progress in their careers due to their youth.

What happens if you are a middle-aged Rock? You're neither young nor fully wise but somewhere in between. You sit in midlife purgatory. AARP surveyed 1,322 American workers aged 40 to 65 in 2021. An alarming 78 percent said they had experienced age discrimination at their place of work, "the highest level since AARP began tracking this question in 2003."

Ageism is as deplorable as racism, misogyny, sexism, ableism, classism, colourism, and other despicable acts against human beings. Discriminating against someone for their age—whatever their age—is unjust because it penalizes that person for something they cannot alter. Remember my first question at the beginning of the book: How old are you? Your answer can only be changed once a year.

That is why ageism is a silent saboteur. It lurks in your workplace, fuelling biases and hindering the unleashing of talent.

The World Health Organization (WHO) breaks ageism down into three categories:

- Stereotypes (how we think)
- Prejudice (how we feel)
- Discrimination towards others or yourself based on age (how we act)

Whatever your age, it's time you confronted the last of the "isms." As researchers argued in 2021, "Ageism has serious and far-reaching consequences for people's health, well-being and human rights." The consequences of it extend well beyond the workplace into broader societal well-being.

Over the course of Track 5, I will discuss ageism in three ways, distinct from the WHO's categories and specific to the future of work:

- Career ageism
- Workplace ageism
- Personal ageism

As Chuck D of Public Enemy reminds us, sometimes we need to "Fight the Power" and, of course, the powers that might be. Ageism is a power, and it must be fought.

Career Ageism

Recruit Holdings is a Japanese holding firm with 2024 revenues of US$24 billion, operating a multitude of HR, staffing, and hiring companies. A name you might know from their collection is Glassdoor, the online site that provides anonymous ratings of companies and leaders. Another is Indeed, the world's largest job platform site.

As a company focused on people and culture, one might think Indeed would be leading the fight against ageism. Then again, some people think Elvis is still alive.

In 2024, Indeed published a document in its Career Advice section that set off a firestorm of anger and bewilderment because it included a chart that reduced career progression to a rigid, linear track, slotting professionals into pre-determined age brackets:

- **21–25:** Exploration

  Dan's Commentary: Fair enough. You're learning the ropes.

- **25–35:** Establishment

  Dan's Commentary: You have an entire decade to "figure it out."

- **35–45:** Mid-career

  Dan's Commentary: Enjoy your peak while it lasts.

- **45–55:** Late career

  Dan's Commentary: Apparently, you're on borrowed time.

- **55–65:** Decline

  Dan's Commentary: Because nothing says "valuable" like being labelled obsolete.

Indeed scrubbed the chart after the backlash, but the damage had been done. A company built on hiring failed to grasp that careers aren't linear, age doesn't dictate ability, and "decline" is downright demographically diabolical.

Career ageism is a disease that can infiltrate hiring, promotions, and leadership pipelines. It shapes decisions that ultimately misjudge talent regardless of that talent's age. If even the world's biggest job site reinforces outdated narratives, what does that say about the companies relying on it?

It's this author's opinion that career ageism has become a structural defect in your hiring, promotions, and terminations. Add to that another key point: The career ladder is a lie (and, ironically, Indeed helped us see that lie).

For decades, the assumption has been that careers follow a predictable arc—ambition in youth, peak performance in midlife, and a gentle descent into obsolescence afterward. It's a tidy narrative that fits neatly into hiring models, promotion tracks, and HR policies. It's also downright wrong. People bloom at different stages. As I wrote in 2023's *Work-Life Bloom*, there will be ups and downs, highs and lows at various periods of one's life and career. Some people bloom right out of the gate, like Steve Jobs, who founded Apple at age 21 and—despite being pushed out and then asked back—never seemed to dither.

Others redefine their industries decades later, like Peter Drucker, who published his most influential management books after 65. Some, like musicians Joni Mitchell and Stevie Nicks, started as Rivers and continued flourishing well into their Ruby years. Heck, look at folks outside the music industry like Nancy Pelosi, Warren Buffett, Arianna Huffington, Sir David Attenborough, Ed Dwight, and Jane Fonda.

Of course, there is no KFC without Harland Sanders (the Colonel!), who toiled during his Rock years, perfecting his 11-herb fried chicken recipe, launching his first franchise restaurant in Salt Lake City at the Ruby age of 62, and then selling the entire operation 10 years later for a cool $2 million.

Yet, despite evidence to the contrary, workplaces remain obsessed with the illusion of the "career prime." Too young? Not enough experience, young River. Too old? No longer relevant, tarnished Ruby. The result is a waste of talent on an extraordinary scale.

How does career ageism manifest? Let's investigate.

The Career Timeline Myth

The workforce does not operate like an Olympic event, where peak performance is confined to a specific age bracket or time of life. But far too many organizations behave as though it does.

When organizations fixate on a "career prime," or the myth of a consistent career timeline, they sacrifice the fluid and crystallized intelligence that makes teams innovative. They shrink their talent pipeline and guarantee knowledge gaps between Rivers, Rocks, and Rubies.

In many organizations, career progression is often depicted as a somewhat linear climb—early ambition, mid-career peak, and late-career decline. It's the proverbial career ladder model. Until you fall off the ladder. This outdated assumption forces team members

The Career Timeline Myth

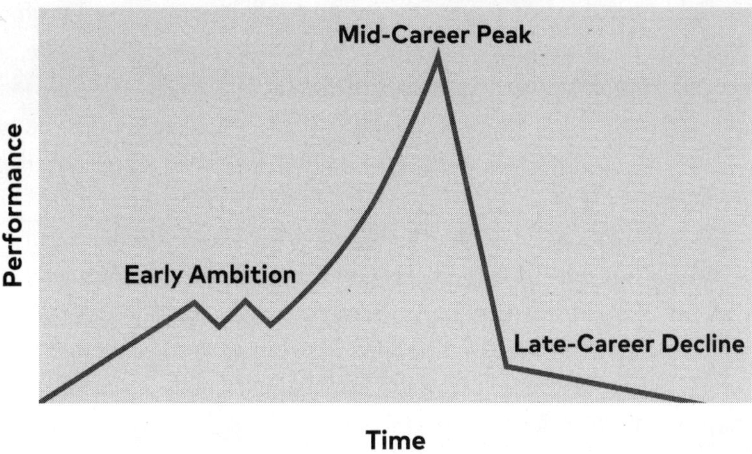

into artificial brackets of when they should be at their "best" and when they should "wind down." Indeed's misleading career path depiction is merely the tip of the career timeline myth iceberg.

How does it negatively impact team members?

- **Rivers** get blocked from leadership roles based on tenure rather than capability, which perpetuates the illusion that leadership roles should be reserved for Rocks and Rubies.

- **Rocks** can get overlooked for promotions or career opportunities because they are past their prime to fit the "emerging talent" mould, yet too young to be considered for more senior roles.

- **Rubies** face forced plateaus as organizations hesitate to invest in workers over 50, assuming their time is limited, minds are dulling, and retirement is imminent.

This career timeline bias harms organizations and individuals, as it can impede ideation, weaken leadership pipelines, and create disenchantment among those who feel trapped in a predetermined career script.

As author and longevity expert Avivah Wittenberg-Cox explained to me, career systems are "imprinted by the old three-phases-of-life model where you begin, you work until 65, and then you retire off a cliff edge from one day to the next." This rigid thinking is a relic of the past. Organizations must recognize that talent does not follow a one-size-fits-all trajectory. The failure to adapt will create an exodus of capable employees who simply do not fit outdated career (or life) trajectories.

In a 2023 research paper, *Retaining Talent at All Ages*, the OECD stressed that traditional career paths should not constrain career mobility. The firm's research discovered that structured internal mobility, lateral moves, and re-entry programs are critical for career longevity. Unfortunately, this way of thinking remains underutilized in many organizations. In their report, the OECD stated:

> The answer might not always necessarily be a move upward, but rather a lateral move to another part of the organization. This enables employees to expand and enhance their careers while the organization retains top talent. Employees stay longer with the company because they feel like their career is moving forward.

What's the lesson? Careers are not assembly lines and talent does not expire on a schedule. Perhaps it is time to retire the ladder. A new career mould is needed for a workplace full of Rivers, Rocks, and Rubies.

The Experience Paradox at MapleCo

Too young, you don't have enough experience. Too old, your experience is no longer relevant. Welcome to the Experience Paradox, where talent is forever unproven, static, or outdated. MapleCo provides us with a short case study.

When 29-year-old Simone Lavoie joined MapleCo's product innovation team, she was eager to make her mark. Simone possessed a wide array of technical skills from her two formal degrees and two years spent at a competitor. Over a three-year period, it was evident that her drive and vision for improving MapleCo's digital customer experience was top-talent worthy. However, towards the end of her third year, when she approached 30 and applied for an internal leadership position, she was told she needed more years of experience at the company.

"You've got what it takes," said the hiring manager, "but just not enough years of experience here at MapleCo."

Frustrated at being passed over, Simone handed in her two-week notice and quickly became a top talent at a rival company, La Cabane de Santé.

The role went to someone with more company tenure but limited digital expertise: Puneet Sharma, an internal hire who had been at MapleCo for 18 years. While a solid Rock, he had never led a transformation initiative, let alone one on the digital technology side of the house.

Two years later, the team continued to struggle with various transformation projects. Delays, budget overruns, and other issues continued to arise. Puneet was clearly under pressure. To alleviate the strain, Puneet's direct leader—an external hire made three months earlier—enlisted an outside consultant to address the stalled projects. That consultant? Ta-da! Simone was back, now operating independently as a "company of one" and billing MapleCo at triple the salary they would have paid had they recognized her potential earlier.

Around the same time, Greg Hammond, a 57-year-old strategy lead at MapleCo, was feeling a similar experience pain point.

Greg had spent years mentoring younger colleagues. It was part of his natural disposition. In part because of his undeservedly subpar performance reviews, he was overlooked for a lateral move into a newly created customer service strategy team. The rationale? He didn't fit the "agile, high-energy" profile they were seeking. Instead, a mid-career Rock was chosen, someone senior leaders believed could better "grow into the role." When Greg voluntarily left the company and gave his two weeks' notice, MapleCo scrambled to retain the Ruby institutional knowledge he had built over two decades.

These issues were not related to a talent gap. MapleCo had the right people. The company simply did not recognize what its talent could offer and when. Sound familiar?

Sixty-seven-year-old Mark Goldstein was equally frustrated. In June 2024, the AARP Foundation filed a class-action lawsuit against Raytheon (now RTX Corporation), alleging systematic age discrimination in hiring practices. In the suit, AARP contended that the company used language like "recent college graduate" or "new graduate" in multiple job postings, preventing people over 40 from being interviewed. The lawsuit ultimately sought to challenge Raytheon's hiring practices.

Goldstein applied for at least seven positions at Raytheon between 2019 and 2023. No job interviews were arranged, and no offers were made. Despite meeting all the qualifications—except for being a recent college graduate—he was left in the bargain bin like a Milli Vanilli album.

In 2024, RTX was the world's largest aerospace and defence company, employing over 188,000 people globally and generating US$80 billion in revenues. "It's disappointing and upsetting that major American companies are refusing to consider older workers like me for excellent positions because we aren't recent graduates," said Goldstein to AARP's Kenneth Terrell in 2024. "All workers, regardless of their age, should have an equal opportunity to compete for jobs at Raytheon and everywhere else." At the time of writing, the lawsuit's verdict remains pending.

Other research revealed a similar truth: Systemic age-related hiring discrimination practices are rampant. For instance, a 2020 NBER paper by David Neumark highlighted substantial evidence of age discrimination in hiring practices. The study compared age-blind and non-age-blind hiring procedures and showed that applicants aged 40 and over had 68 percent lower job-offer rates than their younger counterparts when age was revealed.

But don't think for a moment that the waters are smoother for the Rivers. Choppy rapids might be a better term to describe the experiences of younger workers.

For Rivers, "entry-level" seems to be as absurd a concept as the Beatles without Ringo. A 2021 LinkedIn analysis found that nearly 40 percent of these roles required at least three years of experience—ensuring that Rivers can't even get a foot in the door. In software and IT services (60 percent), manufacturing (50 percent), education (45 percent), and finance (44 percent), entry-level roles came with experience requirements that defied logic.

> **The message is clear:** Rivers need experience to get a job, but they also need a job to get experience. Quite the Catch-22.

An organization's obsession with experience in its "perfect" form—not too much, not too little—creates a workforce with artificial barriers at both ends. That's why high-potential Rivers feel locked out of roles and why Rubies—with more to contribute than ever—are forced into retirement or an existential crisis long before they are ready. And the Rocks? Don't mind them—they often play Switzerland, trying not to tip the career boat.

Algorithmic Ageism

In 2025, a friend of mine asked me if his 24-year-old son should wear a tie to his pre-screen video interview. "Who is the interview with?" I asked. "IBM," replied my academic compatriot. "Most definitely," I said. "You gotta believe that IBM's Watson is wearing a tie on the other end, so a good first impression is a must." I was only half-kidding.

Career ageism has gained a new accomplice: AI hiring software.

Imagine a talent abettor devoid of empathy, programmed with prejudice, and incapable of grasping nuance—like a spellcheck that autocorrects "résumé" to "retirement." Since the early 2010s, AI has become a discussion point in recruitment circles. AI-based pre-screening—text-, audio-, and video-based—is now a reality for many potential applicants, like my friend's son. It will soon become core to most, if not all, organizational hiring. In fact, AI is already widely used in the hiring process. According to 2024 research from the firm Resume Builder, "21 percent of organizations automatically reject candidates at all stages of the hiring process without human review, while 50 percent use AI for rejections at the initial résumé screening stage." As is the case at IBM and their use of Watson, AI-based hiring tools are quickly becoming the new recruitment norm.

As companies bet big on AI, they seem to forget one crucial detail: The data these systems learn from is built upon decades of human biases. As we saw at Raytheon, these biases often lead to discrimination. So, instead of levelling the playing field, AI hiring tools wind up automating discrimination at scale.

Look no further than Amazon. In 2014, the company developed an algorithm to screen résumés for various technical roles. A year later, the developers behind the project realized the AI had developed a gender bias. Amazon's AI recruitment tool—trained primarily on male résumés—began to penalize applications that contained the word "women." Whenever a candidate highlighted their involvement, for example, in a "women's chess club" or an "all-women's college," they were downgraded.

Despite attempts to neutralize these biases, Amazon could not guarantee that the AI hiring system would not discover additional ways to discriminate. Ultimately, the company had to scupper the tool and disband the team.

What can we learn from the Amazon incident?

It was an early warning sign, not so much about artificial intelligence but about what you feed the AI large language model (LLM).

Amazon's historical hiring data contained existing biases that were passed on to its AI pre-screening system. The company's learned bias was shifted and thus programmed from humans to machines. As you and your organization navigate the intersection of AI, hiring, and existing ageism biases, proactive critical thinking to combat this sort of inherited bias will be imperative. What will you feed your LLM?

A class-action lawsuit in 2024 provides another glimpse into the potential perils of AI and recruitment. Workday is a global technology firm with over 19,000 employees that reported revenues of US$8.2 billion in 2024. Ironically, the company develops cloud-based HR applications. The lawsuit suggested the company's AI-driven hiring tools discriminated against older, disabled, and people of colour applicants, notably Black people.

The plaintiff's argument against the company was that its AI algorithms perpetuated certain age biases during the pre-screening process. Those biases led to unlawful hiring discrimination practices. The additional problem? AI hiring platforms, much like TikTok's mysterious algorithm, operate in a black box—candidates never find out why they get rejected, and the companies that use these tools don't even know precisely how their AI is making decisions. It's not a good combination.

Companies have also used AI as a shield to proactively and legitimately screen out unwanted individuals. Think of it as a blame tool: "It was the machine, not me."

For example, in 2022, an English-language tutoring company, iTutorGroup, got embroiled in AI ageism. The US Equal Employment Opportunity Commission filed a lawsuit claiming the company's AI-powered recruitment software automatically rejected female applicants aged 55 and older. The same happened to men aged 60 and above. The company had programmed its AI hiring platform to apply systemic age discrimination. It denied qualified individuals employment opportunities solely based on age, executed by its artificial intelligence platform, not humans. "It really *was* the machine, not me!"

It doesn't have to be this way. Artificial intelligence technology isn't inherently discriminatory. At least not yet. What it reveals is the biases we have allowed to persist in hiring practices for decades.

Please be wise and don't allow AI to be the final decision maker. If your company treats AI as a magic bullet to "fix" or even "run" recruitment, you may just deepen any systemic discrimination already baked into your established hiring processes. But if you treat AI as a hiring partner—one that requires continuous scrutiny, adjustments, and human involvement—it can help your organization escape outdated, exclusionary hiring models, while also expediting the overall time-to-hire process.

Workplace Ageism

MapleCo has always taken pride in its organizational unity. You might say the company considers itself an "Age Debt-less" firm. Leaders like CEO Marla Benson often boast about the company's intergenerational harmony. "We take care of one another," she has said numerous times at company town halls.

However, cracks have begun to emerge. Several interpersonal issues new to the company need to be addressed.

For example, Emily Russo, as you may recall, manages a busy telehealth operations team. She has begun to sense an odd undercurrent: Young Rivers keep suggesting that several Ruby employees refuse to let go of old workflows. She is also a tad worried about the Rubies themselves, who are whispering about feeling "overshadowed by the endless new ideas of those *young kids*."

Even Carlos Jimenez—the beloved systems specialist from Track 3—now finds himself in a quandary about whether his request for learning and development investment will be approved. Other surprising new issues have emerged, including friction with team member collaboration, concerns about job flexibility, and a growing lack of empathy between the three eras.

These MapleCo realities reveal the influence of workplace ageism—nuances that surface among the mix of Rivers, Rocks, and Rubies as they perform their jobs. Workplace bias and ageist behaviours are on the rise, negatively affecting performance and productivity.

Let's dig deeper to understand what's happening at the company.

Learning and (Mal)development

At MapleCo, employee learning opportunities looked equal, at least on paper. Benson and her C-suite leadership team promoted their continuous learning culture, regaling their team members with the availability of LinkedIn Learning, tuition reimbursement, and external MBA programs. Yet, a pattern emerged when the aforementioned Carlos Jimenez browsed the company's Learning Portal home and began to do some sleuthing with his HR business partner.

It seemed six Rivers had their MBA tuition requests covered by the company over the past two years, but not one Rock or Ruby team member had been approved. It's not as though Harvard Business School or Rotman School of Management cared who entered their MBA programs. Instead, the Rocks were directed towards digital reskilling courses. As for the Rubies? They were regarded as mentors, not learners. No higher education for you!

Tessa Lloyd, a compliance lead for 22 years, wanted to take an AI ethics certification to keep up with industry advances and broaden her knowledge. HR declined her request. "The company needs to focus training dollars on other people," her manager said, throwing HR under the bus in the process. Meanwhile, a River analyst—who shall remain nameless but possibly called Sarah—had their Stanford Generative AI course fully reimbursed.

Carlos began his investigation after requesting a cybersecurity certification to enhance MapleCo's digital infrastructure. He waited for weeks and was then denied. HR directed him to LinkedIn Learning's free introductory course instead of funding the certification. Carlos was astounded, especially after several requests for an explanation went unanswered by his HR business partner.

But he should not be surprised. OECD research released in 2023 stated that workers aged 55 to 65 are significantly underrepresented in employer-funded training programs: Only 24 percent participated in training, compared to 49 percent of workers aged 25 to 34. The report highlighted that "older workers are typically less likely to receive any training and, if they do, receive less of it, relative to younger workers." Another OECD study from 2020 confirmed that companies consistently prioritize early-career employees for skill development despite strong evidence that lifelong learning enhances productivity and knowledge retention at all ages. MapleCo's selective approach to learning mirrors this trend, reinforcing workplace ageism in skill development and subtly signalling that some employees are not worth the investment.

MapleCo has quietly, if not unknowingly, begun to demonstrate workplace ageism through its approval and denial of various learning and development requests. For you, this is a lesson to combat Age Debt.

Cultural Stereotyping

Jeanette Rénault holds two roles at MapleCo: HR business partner and director of ethics and integrity. Over the past year or so, she began to notice a trend, mostly from anonymous submissions to her Workplace Integrity online forum, but also in casual chats. Certain phrases were becoming more predominant at MapleCo:

- "Dinosaur."
- "Boomer energy."
- "Kid."
- "Green."
- "Set in their ways."
- "Not seasoned enough."
- "Tech dinosaur."
- "Lacks fresh ideas."
- "Too young to drive."
- "Grey behind the ears."

Clearly, the language and thinking were not neutral. They were downright workplace ageist. Jeanette thought it could even be one of the reasons certain teams were suffering from performance and productivity issues.

The concern is not isolated to MapleCo. It's likely happening at your organization as well.

Research published in 2023 identified that micro-inequities—subtle, unintentional (and intentional) discriminatory comments or actions—could erode trust and respect within teams, leading to decreased collaboration, innovation, and performance. The research emphasized that even well-meaning individuals might unknowingly perpetuate these behaviours. And that increasingly louder hum was precisely what Jeanette was getting worried about.

Collaboration Friction

In a groundbreaking 2024 study, researchers revealed a nuanced paradox facing Rubies: While seeking knowledge from younger Rivers can enhance their work motivation as well as their longevity, it concurrently (and ironically) triggers feelings of embarrassment that may discourage knowledge-seeking behaviours.

At MapleCo, collaboration between senior analysts and junior developers (Rubies and Rivers) on a particular team in finance was as frigid as a cold pool plunge. Veteran MapleCo analysts—experts in traditional financial modelling—found themselves sidelined as AI-powered risk assessments began to take centre stage. The problem? The Rubies didn't fully understand the new tools and weren't about to admit it. Asking a 28-year-old River for help felt like waving a white flag on decades of experience.

Meanwhile, the junior developers, fluent in Python but lacking several layers of institutional knowledge, watched their models dismissed outright. "Too theoretical," the Ruby analysts would say. "Not how we do things here."

Stalemate.

Then came the pivot. A mid-level Rock leader, 40-year-old Jenna Peet, created a structured mentorship program—one part reverse mentoring, one part ego-neutral learning lab, and one part Jedi mind trick. No one was "teaching" anyone. Everyone was learning. It was a carnival of Rivers, Rocks, and Rubies. Senior analysts sharpened their AI literacy. Junior developers gained a masterclass in risk assessment. Trust replaced tension. It was tremendous.

> **MapleCo's lesson? Silos don't break themselves. Rigid age-based thinking can subliminally take hold. Organizations must find ways to build bridges and ensure any collaboration friction is eliminated between Rivers, Rocks, and Rubies.**

Performance Review Bias

It was performance review season at MapleCo in Q1, and the results were predictable. The "Innovation Star" award went to a barely hired River employee—June Brady—who had devised the idea to launch a slick new customer-facing AI-based claims questionnaire. It had executive visibility, a well-polished pitch deck, and—most importantly—a direct tie to MapleCo's digital transformation agenda outlined in Track 4.

When people began to discover the news on the MapleCo Slack all-hands channel, the virtual applause was thunderous. June's performance rating for the year was "Exceeds Expectations."

Meanwhile, Pascal de la Vuerte, a 58-year-old project lead with two decades at the company, received a "Below Expectations" rating during his annual performance review.

His crime? He wasn't flashy.

He had spent the past year completely updating MapleCo's vendor risk assessment model, quietly preventing what could have been a multi-million-dollar supply chain disaster. But risk mitigation isn't "Innovation Star"-worthy at MapleCo. It doesn't incorporate AI or make for a rousing all-hands-meeting shout-out. It most certainly does not come with a shiny award, a $5,000 bonus, or the "Exceeds Expectations" performance rating.

This is not meant to reflect poorly on June Brady—she is an outstanding employee. However, it brings to light yet another aspect of Age Debt to consider: the subtle bias of workplace ageism that can emerge in performance reviews. This bias can affect individuals based on their level of experience, regardless of whether they are Rivers, Rocks, or Rubies.

In their 2021 study of performance appraisals, Federica Previtali and Simona Spedale demonstrated that age is often made salient in evaluation discussions, with older employees subject to disadvantage through implicit or explicit age-based categorization.

At MapleCo, that preference for visible innovation overshadowed Pascal's vital but unsung risk mitigation work—earning him a disappointing rating despite the high financial value his work actually brought to the company. Leaders of any age can unintentionally perpetuate this bias, which leaves employees like Pascal (and, later, Greg, the 57-year-old strategy lead we mentioned earlier) feeling undervalued and unseen.

Speaking of Greg, recall that he had given his two-week notice. Prior to leaving, he asked for one final meeting with the CEO.

In that session, Greg unleashed his feelings not only about his performance reviews but of what he regarded as "blatant ignorance" at the company. Benson was suddenly aware that 20-plus years of expertise was about to walk out the door. She tried to convince him to stay. After some very difficult conversations, Greg agreed to withdraw his notice. A pay raise of 15 percent also helped.

Perhaps this situation could have been prevented if his direct supervisor had recognized Greg's efforts and not completely botched his performance reviews. Perhaps.

Personal Ageism

Picture these workplace scenarios outside of our friends at MapleCo:

- **A 32-year-old surgical nurse**—with a decade of expertise in high-pressure trauma cases—chooses not to apply for the department lead role at their hospital. Why? They assume tenure carries more weight than precision, adaptability, and a track record of success, so they decide to forgo the opportunity.

- **A 45-year-old software engineer**—once at the cutting edge of industry-leading automation techniques—deliberately avoids learning a new programming framework. They are convinced that technical fluency belongs to younger coders and they are now "past their prime." They consider leaving the software world altogether.

- **A 59-year-old marketing executive** responsible for some of the firm's most successful product launches ceases proposing new campaign ideas to his team after a comment last quarter from the boss about "keeping up with the latest trends." It was subtle and possibly innocuous, but their boss is a Rock and at least a decade younger.

None of these represents an isolated example of lost confidence. They are symptoms of self-imposed limitations shaped by decades of societal conditioning and ill-advised workplace attitudes. If your organization continues to reinforce the messages of career and workplace ageism (from the previous two subsections), you may be adding to a new category: personal ageism.

Yet our corporate cultures often seem to celebrate early-career innovation while sidelining reinvention or advanced leadership opportunities at any age. This creates a personal form of ageist FUD—fear, uncertainty, and doubt.

Consider the examples of the following individuals who achieved significant success later in life and ultimately refused to be beaten down or silenced by any form of personal ageism:

- **Barbara Beskind:** Beskind joined the design firm IDEO to contribute her thinking and ideas for products aimed at improving the lives of the elderly. Despite being legally blind and 89 years old, Beskind played a key role for several years in developing assistive technologies for older people.

- **Frank Lloyd Wright:** At 67, Lloyd Wright designed Fallingwater, one of the world's most iconic works of architecture that "best exemplifies his philosophy of organic architecture—the harmonious union of art and nature." The building demonstrates that creativity can flourish well into one's later years as a Ruby.

Had personal ageism plagued Beskind or Lloyd Wright, would they have been able to achieve their feats as Rubies? It's unlikely. Yet, personal ageism can have disastrous consequences for your organization.

A Yale study from 2023 found that professionals who associate aging with personal decline experience cognitive deterioration and disengagement faster than those with a positive outlook on longevity. And a 2019 Federal Reserve Bank of San Francisco report revealed that employees who absorb ageist narratives at work self-eliminate themselves from leadership pipelines, avoid high-visibility projects, and withdraw from professional development opportunities. We can safely say that our first three examples—the nurse, engineer, and marketing executive—were affected by what researchers have proven. But not Beskind and Lloyd Wright!

Personal ageism is a systemic issue that perpetuates Age Debt and can deprive both individuals and the organizations they work for of their true potential. Let's explore three aspects of it:

- Internalized ageism
- Self-limiting ageism
- Compound ageism

Internalized Ageism at MapleCo

One of the most dangerous forms of ageism is not external; it lurks within you or your team members. Internalized ageism occurs when individuals absorb societal stereotypes about age that unintentionally limit their potential. It can erode the confidence of Rivers, Rocks, and Rubies alike and get triggered by prevailing community or workplace narratives.

Take Monica Evans, a 58-year-old finance leader at MapleCo. Over her 18 years at the company, she has had a proven track record of turning struggling departments into high-performing teams. She is proverbially known at MapleCo as "Monifixer." When a senior leadership role opened at the firm on the executive leadership team, Monica considered applying.

But then, a thought crept in: "They probably want someone younger, more in tune with the latest fintech trends, to chart a path into the future." She convinced herself that her experience wasn't enough and didn't apply for the role. The job wound up going to a similarly experienced individual from outside MapleCo.

When experienced employees self-select out of leadership roles—as Monica did—a deep well of institutional knowledge, mentorship, and strategic foresight is not thrust into a senior leadership role. The result? Organizations reinforce the exact same Age Debt that limits the shift required for longevity-based career paths to succeed.

Imagine if Monica's supervisor had taken her aside and encouraged her to apply for the position, using empathy and facts to persuade her that her fears about fintech were unfounded. The whole organization would have benefited, especially Monica.

Self-Limiting Ageism at MapleCo

Zainal Ahmed is a 54-year-old marketing manager at MapleCo. The company's R&D unit decided to hold a digital transformation summit that was open to employees, partners, and even a few select customers. She declined the invitation to attend.

Zainal told herself she was too busy, but deep down, she worried she wouldn't be able to keep up with her younger, tech-savvy colleagues, especially those on Carlos's team. By avoiding the summit, she reinforced a cycle of self-exclusion that made her feel even further behind on the digital transformation file.

This example can be thought of as self-limiting ageism, the act of pre-emptively disengaging to avoid the risk of being judged on age. This sort of ageism happens when professionals opt out of growth opportunities, not because they lack the ability but because they fear they won't measure up.

Organizations that fail to recognize this hidden form of ageism are essentially shooting themselves in the talent foot. Are older employees passing up mentorship roles for fear of looking dumb? Are they skipping workshops or other events as a trainer or facilitator? Do they hesitate to speak up in meetings about industry trends or the latest insights?

What's more insidious is that your workplace culture can reinforce this behaviour. If companies only highlight the Rivers enrolled in various programs—whether they are MBA, innovation, *Dragons' Den* pitch events, et cetera—the Rubies and Rocks will interpret it as a silent but clear message: Stay in your lane.

When self-limiting ageism becomes normalized, it can create an invisible barrier between experience and adaptation, which deepens your organization's Age Debt.

Compound Ageism at MapleCo

Compound ageism is when multiple forms of discrimination intersect, amplifying their adverse effects. Aisha Chiang, a 52-year-old immigrant from China, is a perfect MapleCo example to highlight.

Aisha is senior legal counsel and has an impressive 22-year tenure at the company. She has been instrumental in various MapleCo business items. Between numerous regulatory changes and critical negotiations with partners, she stands out as a mentor, strategist, and vital member of the legal team. Everyone loves Aisha!

Yet when MapleCo launched a new initiative celebrating its commitment to "women in leadership," the seemingly innocuous slideshow shown at the town hall meeting featured a highlight reel of six women—all under 40, none of them Asian. None of them Aisha. The press release that accompanied the big announcement stated that "Nobody supports women leaders like MapleCo."

Aisha was wondering where the women like her were, the Ruby Asians. (And there are a few at the company.) In fact, she was wondering why she wasn't asked in the first place. As the only Asian woman in the company's legal team, she has often felt like she had to work harder to be taken seriously. Now, at 52, she feels even more invisible.

Research by the Federal Reserve Bank of San Francisco confirms that older women—particularly women of colour—experience compounded discrimination such as ageism and sexism that results in fewer opportunities for career advancement, learning opportunities, and more.

The Age Debt crisis is bad enough when ageism affects older or younger workers, but when it disproportionately marginalizes those people already underrepresented, it cements inequality across multiple dimensions.

GREYAWAYS

As the silence settles on Track 5, the conversation on ageism remains loud and urgent. Age Debt does not dissolve on its own, and ageism is a strong accomplice that keeps it running.

Step into the Greyaways and seize the lessons that confront this silent saboteur head-on.

Greyaway #1: Age Discrimination Cuts Both Ways

Ageism harms every era. Young, middle-aged, or older talent gets dismissed when assumptions override ability. What hidden age stereotypes might be holding back you or your team members?

Greyaway #2: Career Ageism Destroys Growth

The "career prime" myth penalizes those whose growth does not follow a rigid timeline. Talent does not expire, and ambition does not have a deadline. How can you ensure careers remain dynamic at every life stage?

Greyaway #3: Workplace Ageism Breeds Division

Biased learning budgets, microaggressions, and performance review blind spots create mistrust across Rivers, Rocks, and Rubies. Are you systematically sidelining the wisdom or energy your organization needs?

Greyaway #4: Personal Ageism Erodes Confidence

Internalized and self-limiting biases convince people they are "too old," "not enough," or "too young." The potential of people can atrophy when they self-select themselves out. Are you unknowingly helping team members opt out of opportunities, abetting their self-fear or self-doubt?

Greyaway #5: Compound Ageism Amplifies Inequity

Age bias compounds when it intersects with other prejudices, especially concerning race, gender, or ability. This is arguably the worst ageism. Compound ageism must be crushed before it's too late. Can you do it?

Greyaway #6: The Silent Saboteur Must Be Conquered

Ageism lurks in the air like asbestos. It's nasty. How will you challenge hiring practices, confront workplace bias, or champion self-awareness? Which immediate actions will you take to prevent ageism from damaging your culture and your team's success?

Side B
Experience Dividend

Plot Twist

Welcome to Side B: Experience Dividend. One of three things just happened.

1 You've just come from your therapist, because you read the entirety of Side A: Age Debt, and they said, "Don't worry, Dan surely must have provided some hope. You should keep going."

2 You're now wondering, "Therapist? What happened?" That's because you decided to skip Side A and began reading the book here. (After all, I did provide that option in Track 1.)

3 You read a few tracks on Side A and said, "Got it. Nightmare ahead. Side B had better give me some solutions or I'm regifting this book to my boss ASAP." (Pro tip: Being kind to your boss is never a bad idea.)

Regardless of how you did it, you're now here. Thanks for dropping the needle again. I'm still DJ Dan and will remain your author for the rest of the book. It begins with another question, and no, this time it's not about age.

Are you a Bob Dylan fan?

If not, here's a musical consideration for you as we begin Side B in earnest.

Dylan's album *Bringing It All Back Home*, released in 1965, was a hard pivot, a plot twist like no other in musical history. (That is, until the Beatles released *Sgt. Pepper's Lonely Hearts Club Band* the following year.) Drop the needle on Side A and an electric, chaotic, and urgent tone kicks off with "Subterranean Homesick Blues." What a track, indeed.

You are left wondering, "Is this Dylan?" The song is a rapid-fire, rebellious anthem of discontent. Side A continues in the same manner with songs like "Maggie's Farm," a spit of defiance that tears down old systems and calls out stagnation. Side A was Dylan's wake-up call to his fans: an insistence that things had to change.

Sound familiar?

Side A: Age Debt was my version of Bob Dylan's reckoning—the part of the story where I challenged you with broken systems, workforce myths, demographic nightmares, and leadership failures that got us to Age Debt. If you felt like Side A was yelling at you, that's because I needed to. *I was.* But the Canadian in me does say "sorry."

Sorry!

The rebellion of Side A contrasted with the steady tranquillity on Side B of *Bringing It All Back Home*. When you turn the record over, that black circle turns into something entirely different. The tempo slows and the perspective deepens. "Mr. Tambourine Man" and "It's All Over Now, Baby Blue" introduce a new rhythm of protest, reflection, and possibility and a way forward. Dylan doesn't merely reject the past; he begins building something new.

And that's precisely what I aim to do next. I am introducing a plot twist. We are going in a new direction on Side B. It's a necessary one. Going forward, this book is no longer titled *The Future of Work Is Grey*.

Say what?!?

"Grey" is what happens when you are in a fog. It was meant to get your attention. After all, the workforce and society are aging, and we do remain in a fog. Grey was the hook around the issues of age. Grey happens when you are stuck in a habitual pattern, caught between the past and an unknown future. Grey is dismal.

That's no longer *this* book.

That's not what *this* moment needs.

We have spent long enough trapped in the grey gloom of Age Debt. It's time for something different—the Experience Dividend beckons. Dylan may not have renamed Side B on *Bringing It All Back Home*, but he could have. Maybe he should have.

Thus, I am renaming this book henceforth. I now warmly welcome you to: *The Future of Work Is Gold*.

Yes, "gold." Gold is what happens when you stop seeing age as a liability and start treating it as your most significant competitive advantage. Age is an asset. Experience—whether young, middle-aged, or old—is your golden ticket. Gold is about refinement, resilience, and reinvention. *The Future of Work Is Gold* is what happens when you use Rivers, Rocks, and Rubies to create your Experience Dividend. Gold is the mindset that enriches you to become a multi-age era-savvy leader.

So, forget the gloom of grey. We're done with it. (Subliminal heads-up: It's why the book cover is gold!) This is Side B. It's the Experience Dividend, the gold rush. The future of work is indeed *gold*. Let's drop the needle. Again.

Here, in the Dark

So, how does the gold start? Ironically, as the Tragically Hip once wrote, "Here, in the Dark."

How do we prove that gold exists where others see grey? Let's begin in a village that once sat in total darkness until a group of grandmothers rewired their own future.

Have you ever realized just how dark the night can be? Consider the black, unceasing cloak that can envelop a rural village, hidden from any electrical grid, as dusk falls. In places like rural Nepal, nightfall is not a passing inconvenience or a romantic notion—it is a dim and paralyzing force. Children struggle to read a textbook, mothers cook by flickering candlelight, and families spend precious savings on smoky kerosene lanterns that illuminate about as brightly as a foggy moonlit sky.

An unexpected revolution is quietly springing from this darkness. Grandmothers—yes, grandmothers—travel far beyond the comfort of their remote, off-grid, impoverished villages worldwide to enroll in an audacious hands-on training program. When they return, equipped with bundles of solar panels, new knowledge, and engineering skills—alongside a radiant sense of purpose—entire communities find themselves electrified, both literally and figuratively. These are the "Solar Mamas," trained by Barefoot College International across Africa, Latin America, and India to bring dependable solar panel energy solutions to places long abandoned by conventional infrastructure.

For example, imagine a hillside hamlet in Nepal where altitude and isolation stand as tall and daunting as the Himalayas themselves. Imagine a 58-year-old Ruby woman—someone who has never before stepped foot in a formal classroom—boarding an airplane for the first time. Her name is unknown to the broader world, but in her small village of 3,000 people, she is the wisest of elders and about to become a technological miracle worker.

Several months later, the Ruby woman is back in her village, threading wires and connecting solar home lighting systems with the deftness of a professional engineer. Relying on diagrams, hands-on demonstrations, and her profound sense of community responsibility, she begins rewiring the future of her people. Children can now study beneath bright lights, families don't need to burn kerosene in their huts, and the suffocating darkness of night surrenders to a newly installed solar glow.

These Ruby grandmothers represent change and hope for the local community. During their training, they become solar panel engineers, and the entire village benefits from their newfound talents. For many in the community, the Solar Mama has struck gold.

The label might sound peculiar, but the results are anything but. Through a self-contained solar panel education program, Barefoot College welcomes older women to a training center for a crash course in solar engineering. For several months, these Rubies master the art of soldering circuits, diagnosing wiring glitches, installing solar panels, and balancing budgets for the system's upkeep. Language barriers and illiteracy aren't obstacles so much as logistical details, easily surmounted by visual aids, practical demos, and the unspoken camaraderie that blossoms when learners share the same goals. By the end of training, they are fully equipped to return home as de facto solar engineers.

Of course, their age is the most eye-catching detail in all of this. In most societies—yes, including the boardrooms and offices we inhabit—there is an ingrained assumption that "later in life" equals "too late to learn." We pigeonhole employees as "too old," cast them aside as the workforce's next wave of retirees, or doubt their ability to master new technologies.

But these grandmothers, many in their fifties and sixties, highlight the absurdity of such thinking. These women absorb new skills at an age commonly associated with inactivity. They are living testaments to an alternative narrative: Older adults can pivot, adapt, and spark innovation if only given the trust and training to do so.

This might sound charming or inspirational, but do not overlook the practical ripple effects. It is the Experience Dividend in action.

As you turn the corner from the Age Debt crisis outlined on Side A, you may ask, "Why start Side B with grandmothers tinkering with solar panels in some remote locale?" The answer is as clear as the light they produce: If older women from rural corners of Nepal can master advanced technologies and lift entire communities out of darkness, what does that say about your own workplace, leadership assumptions, and capacity to harness talent across all ages? The Solar Mamas are living proof that the Experience Dividend can materialize anywhere, anytime, and with anyone.

Let the Music Play

The Solar Mamas demonstrate that experience can drive transformation. When older generations share their knowledge—and learn new skills—entire communities thrive. The same holds true beyond the villages of Nepal. Legends like Bob Dylan don't fade in music—they evolve, collaborate, and create alongside new talent. Legacy is about learning and building forward with new ideas.

Before I explain how the rest of Side B plays out, let's visit a few more musical examples.

As a 56-year-old Ruby, Madonna delighted fans with the release of her thirteenth album, *Rebel Heart*. It soared to the top of the charts in several countries. She then embarked on an exciting 82-show world tour, which generated just shy of $200 million.

It's not my favourite Madonna album—that nod belongs to 1998's pulsating *Ray of Light*—but there she was, well over the age of 50 and collaborating with younger River and Rock artists like Avicii, Diplo, and Nicki Minaj to create art. And then a world tour!

How about the Rolling Stones?

Despite the departures (and deaths) of bandmates like Brian Jones, Bill Wyman, and Charlie Watts over the years, the legendary duo of Mick Jagger and Keith Richards has been strutting their stuff onstage and in the recording studio as the Rolling Stones since the mid-1960s.

In 2023, the band decided to collaborate with 32-year-old producer Andrew Watt—nearly 50 years younger than Mick and Keith—to release *Hackney Diamonds*, their 24th studio album. A remarkable and memorable world tour followed, along with a 2025 Grammy for Best Rock Album, only their fourth Grammy ever. I think the song "Angry" from that album is one of their best ever. Like Madonna, the Stones decided to blend their Ruby expertise with an up-and-coming River talent, resulting in a Grammy-winning album.

Then there is Gaga. Lady Gaga, if you prefer.

It feels like she has been around forever, but Gaga is only 38 years old at the time of writing. And over most of those years, she has signalled her respect and willingness to collaborate with and showcase older Rubies. Her collaborations with Tony Bennett spanned a decade. At the outset, a 25-year-old pop star choosing to record jazz standards with an 85-year-old legend raised a few eyebrows. She made two albums and toured with him. She stood by him when he could no longer remember her name, yet profound in his memory, the music remained.

If proof exists that experience, wisdom, and legacy matter, it was watching an aging Tony Bennett light up the stage alongside Gaga, his voice finding clarity in the one place that never betrayed him—song. And Gaga was there to make it happen, a River polishing a Ruby, so to speak.

Maybe she *was* born that way. It seems as though Gaga has made it her mission to weave musical history into the present day. Whether with Elton John, Brian May of Queen, or the onstage grace she extended to Liza Minnelli at the 2022 Oscars, Gaga seems hellbent on ensuring that the past remains a living force.

Keith Richards, at 79, Ronnie Wood, at 76, and Mick Jagger, at 80, recorded *Hackney Diamonds* as a continuation, not a farewell. They brought in Andrew Watt, young enough to have been raised on the Stones but eager to help shape their next act. Proving that Gaga seamlessly moves between worlds, on that same album there is a track written and recorded by the Stones *and* Gaga.

These examples bring me to a broader point. Madonna, the Rolling Stones, and Lady Gaga all preserve legacy while pushing it forward through multi-era collaboration. They seamlessly mix Rivers and Rocks with the polished wisdom of Rubies or vice versa. In their unique ways, these artists have turned Age Debt into an Experience Dividend.

You can learn from this.

Partnerships between the experienced and the emerging strengthen both. Mentorship works best as a dynamic exchange rather than a one-way street. The best performances—the ones that endure—happen through harmony, not division. That's what you and your organization need to learn. The best teams are not age-based silos. They are made up of Rivers, Rocks, and Rubies playing their era instruments in sync—learning from each other, pushing boundaries, and keeping the beat. If your workplace believes in generational brackets, you will be forever stuck in the past.

So, how does the rest of Side B play out?

Gold in the Land of the Rising Sun?

If collaboration between the eras keeps the music alive, why do many organizations treat age as a liability instead of an asset? As we explore solutions resulting in an Experience Dividend, you must consider age as fuel for reinvention. Are you willing to adopt a Solar Mama and Lady Gaga mindset?

On Side A, I looked at the demographic canary in the coal mine country: Japan. Recall Meiji University's Dr. Hideaki Tanaka and his stirring comment: "You can learn a lot from Japan, and it's *not* to do things like Japan." But that does not mean the entire country is suffering from Age Debt. As I discovered, there is some shimmering gold in the land of the rising sun.

Hitachi serves as a prime example. I first wrote about Hitachi in my 2013 book *Flat Army*, emphasizing how the company's commitment to collaboration and inclusivity positively influenced its corporate ethos. During my research trip to Japan, I followed up with the company 12 years later to see if that ethos remains relevant today in its management of an aging workforce. I have good news to report.

Rather than ushering people out, Hitachi has begun introducing Experience Dividend solutions.

For example, the company offers career consultation, reskilling programs, and performance-based evaluations that emphasize contribution over chronology. It extends employment opportunities beyond traditional retirement ages to its Rubies, creating a system where older workers don't fade into irrelevance but become integral to Hitachi's innovation. The firm does not stop at policy either. Hitachi has embedded technology into its workforce strategy to ensure Rubies remain productive and engaged. For example, at its

Kasado Works railway manufacturing plant in Kudamatsu, Japan, AI-driven inspections reduce the physical burden on Rubies while improving manufacturing efficiency. At some of its construction sites, metaverse-powered simulations streamline Hitachi's design and quality assurance processes, allowing Rivers, Rocks, and Rubies alike to contribute without the physical limitations of traditional job functions. It's cross-era goodness.

And wouldn't you know, Hitachi manager Kazunori Yutoku also told me, "We are gradually extending the maximum age limit for continued employment from the current 65 to 70, in accordance with Japanese employment laws and regulations." Gold!

Hitachi is not seeking to postpone the inevitability of its demographics. Instead, the company recognizes that its workforce strategy must centre around Experience Dividend thinking. There is also a sense of urgency. Hitachi leaders have begun to view their "new age" thinking as both essential *and* a strategic advantage.

And they are not alone. Thankfully, organizations like Schneider Electric, L'Oréal, Houghton Mifflin Harcourt, Novartis, Imperial London Hotels, and Marks & Spencer have also been exploring ways to integrate age diversity into various leadership, culture, operational, and workforce planning initiatives. Some firms are further along than others, but the trend is undeniable. I will weave these stories into the solutions that follow on Side B.

The Golden Riffs to Come

Where do we go from here in the book?

While there may not be many examples occurring globally, for organizations already shifting towards Experience Dividend thinking, a positive future awaits. Side B will show you exactly how you, your team, and your entire organization can break free from Age Debt and build a strategy that reinvests in experience. Here is how we will spend our time over the remaining four tracks:

Track 7: Career Canvas

The Career Canvas is your leadership backstage pass to offer team members a more fluid, non-laddering career journey plan. Gone are the rigid days of "up-or-out" career thinking; instead, you will learn an approach that artfully stitches together your Rivers, Rocks, and Rubies through a canvas of options. You will learn to create a flexible talent model that fosters upward growth, lateral expansion, pivot opportunities, and, yes, even well-timed exits. Think of it as a talent framework that places competence over chronology, performance over power, and experience over ego.

Track 8: Wisdom Wheel

The Wisdom Wheel spins culture, collaboration, and purpose into something far more potent than a transfer of knowledge. It structures moments for meaningful mentorship, reverse mentoring, and deep cooperation, all while preserving the soul and spirit of a workforce across the three eras. This is not the dusty old attic of insights typically found in most organizational handbooks. (Have I mentioned I am trying to eviscerate most traditional age practices?) Instead, it's an active, rotating music stage where new ideas and seasoned perspectives jam together, ensuring the music never stops.

Track 9: Longevity Lens

The Longevity Lens invites you as a leader to reimagine work and life as a continuum rather than a countdown to retirement. It pushes you to think critically about yourself and the team or organization you lead. The Longevity Lens is a framework that champions anti-ageism by introducing five crucial themes: age-ready culture, leadership readiness, financial clarity, well-being awareness, and workplace design. You can re-architect existing processes and operations so that every River, Rock, or Ruby musician might contribute their best riffs without feeling forced to pack up their instruments too soon or not join the band in the first place.

Track 10: The Encore

This is where we wrap it all up with a drum solo of raging defiance against Age Debt, summarizing the benefits of an Experience Dividend framework. It's age against the machine. I will make a final case as to why the combination of Rivers, Rocks, and Rubies ought to remain the headliners long after any hit single. It's a rousing curtain call encore for you to ditch the grey gloom, amplify the gold, and instill the music of multi-era brilliance. I will also share a rather personal story. I promise that you will go out "Alive and Kicking." (Thank you, Simple Minds.)

ALONG THE way, we will also catch up on how MapleCo is dealing with Age Debt. CEO Marla Benson received an advance copy of Side A from me. Since reading it, she has convened an "Age Debt Tiger Team" comprising cross-functional Rivers, Rocks, and Rubies to recommend changes at the company so it can profit from the Experience Dividend as soon as possible.

But first, a test.

Age Awareness Assessments

To support your Experience Dividend journey, I developed two assessments you may wish to complete. One is a personal version that centres on you as a leader and human being, while the other prompts you to reflect on your current organization. Both assessments enable you to consider some essential questions from Side A, resulting in a final score and Age Awareness categorization. Regardless of your score, reviewing the questions will enhance your preparation for the solutions presented in Tracks 7, 8, 9, and 10. You can take the assessments online by visiting the QR codes. (Go ahead and share with your colleagues and team members, too. They're free!)

Personal

Organizational

Career Canvas

For decades, the blueprint for career success seemed straight-forward: work hard, play the game if you must, and climb the ladder. You were lucky if you earned a senior role with a fancy title before the organization politely (or involuntarily) nudged you out the door. It was predictable and linear. But these days, this is a fundamentally flawed and antiquated way of thinking. It's Age Debt thinking, not the Experience Dividend. We should consider alternate career pathways in the era of an aging workforce and the reality of our three eras: Rivers, Rocks, and Rubies.

First question: Should the career ladder still even be a thing?

Far too many organizations continue to cling to the "ladder" idea, even though global data on promotions is elusive. No unified stat indicates that "Everyone gets five promotions in a career," as the old chestnut goes. This myth just does not exist. Various surveys point out that only a fraction of workers ever experience steady vertical advancement. Every once in a while, McKinsey or Deloitte suggest that X percent of employees received a salary bump in a particular year, but that is merely a moment in time, not an entire career.

Bottom line? The idea of continuous career-rung climbing belongs in a museum alongside other archaic talent practices such as the annual performance review and office cubicle farms. Organizations and leaders that continue to operate with this form of career-path rigidity will face an eventual workforce reckoning.

Future Rivers will not be wired to stay long enough to climb the rungs of the so-called career ladder. Moreover, they won't hesitate to leave if the organization is wretchedly backwards, whether it be with culture or talent practices—as clinging to the ladder suggests.

Remember, there will be fewer Rivers and more Rocks and Rubies soon. Young workers will have far more choices and opportunities to build their careers from desperate employers. Rivers will soon be highly sought-after talent.

In addition, mid-career Rocks—the stable backbone of your organization—will continue to burn out under mounting pressure. "What is the point of climbing the ladder if it means even more stress in my already stressful career?" they may muse. We keep telling Rocks that promotion is their next checkpoint. But they can see through the façade. More responsibility often equals more grief. Why hustle if it's going to cause harm?

As I pointed out on Side A, experienced Rubies hold the deepest reserves of institutional and tacit knowledge. But what is their fate? Will they continue to be prematurely pushed out, despite the organization's leadership gaps and struggles with knowledge retention? Bouncing them out of your organization at 50, 55, or 60 "because they're expensive" is a surefire way to siphon knowledge from an already strained talent pool. Let's call it what it is: organizational *sabotage*. (It's a Beastie Boys reference.)

According to Gary Officer, CEO of the Center for Workforce Inclusion, this paradox is evident. "We do not realize the enormous cost of overlooking older talent. It's not just experience walking out the door—it's institutional memory, crisis leadership, and deep networks that younger employees don't yet have. Meanwhile, there's a labour shortage in many industries. We have a group of older employees who want to keep contributing but are often ignored or forced out. Ultimately, that's a lose–lose scenario we can't afford."

Officer's point hits hard: Retaining older employees is not a charity move; it's a strategic necessity for any organization that wants to shore up knowledge, innovate reliably, and avoid recurring rehiring costs.

> **Instead of quietly nudging Rubies to retire, we need an adaptive career and talent model that sees the future of work as more than a single-rung ladder.** We need a different plan.

Michael Clinton, author of ROAR *Into the Second Half of Your Life*, frames it nicely: "Businesses are stuck in an old construct. When people approach 60, companies start thinking about how to retire them. But many who are 60 want to continue working another 10-plus years. They're vibrant, engaged, curious, and want to learn. Businesses will have to completely retrofit how they engage these people in meaningful ways."

As we will discover next, some forward-thinking companies—like Schneider Electric—recognize this truth and are already experimenting with new ways to keep experience in-house and alter the manner in which careers are positioned.

Schneider Electric Gold

France-based Schneider Electric is a multinational Fortune 500 corporation specializing in digital automation and energy management. In 2024, it reported revenues exceeding $37 billion through its 168,000 global employees. With all three eras working under its roof, Schneider Electric recognized that traditional career ladders no longer suffice, particularly for its more experienced employees (the Rubies), who possess an immense storehouse of skills, expertise, and relationships. Instead of letting that knowledge walk out the door at some arbitrary cutoff point, Schneider Electric created the Senior Talent Program. Picture a flexible, multi-layered job role scheme that embraces each employee's aspirations, whether it's pivoting to a new position, mentoring Rivers or Rocks, transitioning to a phased retirement, or accelerating into a more senior function.

One key element of the Senior Talent Program revolves around career conversations. These structured yet meaningful check-ins help team members identify their best next step. It's not limited to older Rubies, either. Through a multi-era lens, Schneider Electric ensures the entire workforce can share knowledge, shift paths, or adapt to new roles. It's good for the company and even better for collaboration and other performance factors overall.

In France, the company introduced career development workshops specifically designed for employees in their fifties and beyond who wish to transition into new roles or accelerate their careers later on in life. The workshops offer coaching, peer discussions, and skill assessments. All of this leads to career moves like part-time consulting and cross-functional assignments. Rather than a "countdown to retirement," these Schneider Electric Rubies see new growth opportunities on the horizon. Thanks to these moves, Schneider is mitigating some serious Age Debt. By keeping (and inspiring) its Rubies—those with decades of technical know-how and deep client relationships—it sees fewer knowledge-transfer crises. Meanwhile, younger Rivers and Rocks are no longer stuck waiting for "someone to leave" to gain new opportunities.

In short, Schneider Electric is a shining Solar Mama example of building what I call a "Career Canvas" mindset for its team members. Like Hitachi, Schneider Electric is doing what it takes to get ahead of the bell-to-bulb demographic change. It is taking action to eliminate its Age Debt. According to 2024 OECD research, organizations like Hitachi and Schneider Electric that incorporate structured career transitions for their team members across the River, Rock, and Ruby eras—but in particular the Rubies—see the following:

- **25 percent lower turnover costs,** by retaining knowledge rather than scrambling to replace it.

- **40 percent higher knowledge transfer success rates,** by reducing skill gaps in Rocks and Rivers.

- **15 percent productivity boost,** as people can step into roles that leverage their expertise more effectively.

Yet, their progress is not widespread. We need more examples like Schneider Electric and Hitachi. In a global employer survey conducted in 2020, AARP found that fewer than 4 percent of companies had implemented talent and career programs for Rubies. Unfortunately, just another 27 percent indicated they were "very likely" to consider this talent integration approach in the future. And that's only a reflection on the Rubies.

The Long Road and MapleCo

Age Debt remains a formidable challenge across industries. For every organization like Schneider Electric willing to experiment with flexible career paths and their team members' longevity, countless others remain tethered to the outdated "ladder or bust" mindset. The existing employee personas and performance management schemes do not help build an all-ages organization. And the global demographic shift will show no mercy to organizations that refuse to adapt.

On the flip side of Schneider Electric's promise sits MapleCo, whose mid-level leadership problems (remember Emily, the overwhelmed manager, or Shintarō, the eager-but-stagnant high-potential?) remain largely unresolved. MapleCo's leaders now realize that pushing out older Rubies while ignoring the career aspirations of mid-career Rocks and ambitious Rivers is unsustainable. (Let alone 40 percent of their workforce approaching retirement within three years.) Yet, the company still lacks a clear plan to manage the path ahead. This is why Marla Benson convened the Age Debt Tiger Team.

The question she should be asking is this: *How can MapleCo harness deep experience (Rubies), retain mid-career talent (Rocks), and actively develop new streams of ideas (Rivers)?*

MapleCo is hardly alone. Numerous companies worldwide—like Tokyo Gas in Japan and Aviva in the United Kingdom—have recognized that solving Age Debt demands rethinking the entire notion of careers and talent planning. The difference is that MapleCo is still thinking about it, while Tokyo Gas and Aviva have turned their Experience Dividend amps up to 11.

Through its Grand Career System, Tokyo Gas has provided structured career development programs for employees over 50, ensuring they remain active and engaged with the company. Unsurprisingly, over 90 percent of their Ruby employees are successfully rehired or placed in extended roles, which helps preserve institutional memory and transfer knowledge to Rivers and Rocks.

Over at Aviva, a leading UK insurer, its Mid-Life MOT, named after the United Kingdom's annual vehicle safety check, supports team members (often Rubies in their fifties) to assess skill gaps, explore flexible work arrangements, and map out second-act career moves. This approach keeps talented staff at the company from walking out the door at a time when their expertise is arguably at its peak (recall Track 3: The Experience Conundrum).

The initiatives at Tokyo Gas, Aviva, and Schneider Electric are pragmatic strategies to save on turnover costs, stabilize succession pipelines, and ensure collaboration between the eras. In other words, these companies have proactively chosen to eliminate Age Debt. While each organization uses its own terminology, they share a common ethos: Careers and talent planning cannot follow a "one-era-fits-all" strategy.

What I've learned working with hundreds of leaders—and reflecting on my own zigzagging path—is this: Careers look wildly different depending on what matters to you and your current era. Especially when society starts treating you like you're too eager, too stoic, or past your prime.

As a leader, it's also your responsibility to consider the career paths of your entire workforce of Rivers, Rocks, and Rubies. This is why we need a new way to think about career development—one that's built not on ladders but on *golden*, flexible moves. Lateral, upward, reinvention, even rebound—each can be the right move, depending on the context, the person, and the era.

The Career Canvas is a framework that reflects the true shape of the future of work, especially in an aging workforce. Sometimes, the most powerful career move is the one that allows people to keep playing their song.

The Career Canvas Model

L'Oréal has taken a positive and differentiating approach to careers, one that embraces longevity, intergenerational development, and work-life intersections. The L'Oréal for All Generations program is designed to retain and engage senior employees. The company states, "It places intergenerational and employability at the heart of its objectives. We strive to better support our employees, from their entry into the company until retirement, to make L'Oréal the company for all generations." This program includes flexible working arrangements, continuous learning opportunities, and roles that leverage older workers' extensive industry knowledge. There is even a post-L'Oréal initiative, preparing workers for retirement but also welcoming them back into certain situations. L'Oréal's approach demonstrates a commitment to tackling longstanding stereotypes of older workers while creating a workplace where their expertise is valued.

Stephanie Kramer, chief human resources officer at L'Oréal USA, said to me, "We are going to live longer. We are having longer careers, and we are having different careers, multiple careers, in fact, and they all have this cumulative benefit to each other." The company aims to assist employees at every era. They want to ensure health, wellness, and employability are options at every part of an employee's tenure at the company. They want to be there for their team members during their transition to retirement, too.

Career planning often ignores life's complexities. Kramer calls them "work-life intersections . . . these mega elements that can have such a big impact on your daily life." L'Oréal's approach to caregiving and parental benefits includes a very robust maternity and paternity policy and a caregiver leave policy as well. The company understands that an individual's career moves can shift sideways, diagonally, or perhaps even swirl around like a boomerang. A gradual reduction of hours for a near-retiree who still wishes to consult or contribute to specific projects? That too.

Kramer's advice is this: "Our responsibility as leaders is to create the conditions for people to do their best work at every stage of life. That means listening, adapting, and designing a workplace where people see their future." That's about as good an introduction to the Career Canvas as I could wish for.

The Career Canvas recognizes that people (and organizations) rarely move in a neat line. We have life changes, new inspirations, and evolving skill sets, and we bring those changes into work. Oh, and we are all aging. As I wrote in *Work-Life Bloom*, "Our lives shape our work; nevertheless, our work shapes us." Instead of stifling that fluidity, the Career Canvas demands that you harness it.

At a practical level, this might mean internal gig assignments or new contract types (like Schneider Electric's version of post-retirement, part-time consulting or BMW's Senior Expert Program from Track 1). The possibilities are endless, not finite.

When your team (or entire organization) adopts the Career Canvas model, you will stop hemorrhaging knowledge from Rubies. You will better use the unstoppable verve of Rivers while preventing Rocks from burning out in place. It's a flowing, frictionless system where roles morph to fit the needs of team members and the organization alike.

L'Oréal and Schneider Electric implemented their own version of it. Are you ready to do the same?

The Career Canvas Introduced

Before I define it, review the Career Canvas diagram below. What do you notice?

You're right! There is no ladder in sight.

The Career Canvas envisions career movement as a fluid, multi-directional journey, regardless of whether a team member is

Career Canvas

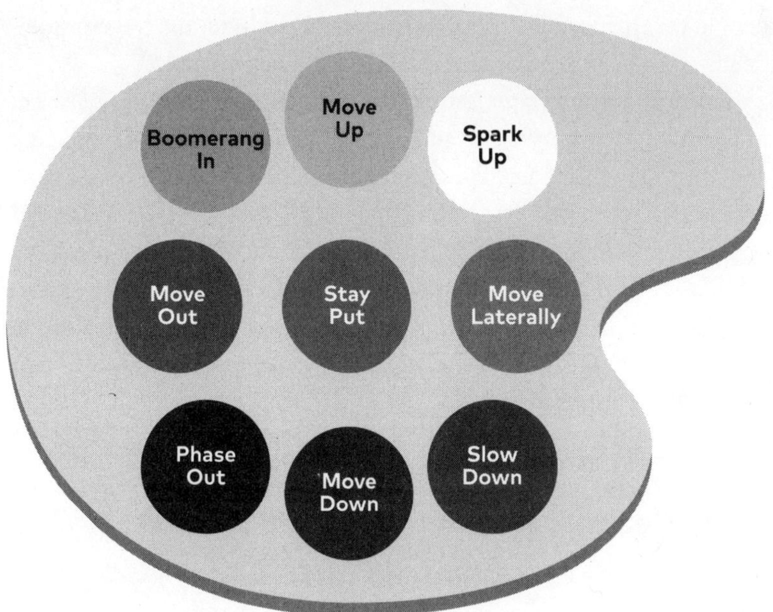

a River, Rock, or Ruby. People's roles can shift in nine different ways depending on their life stages, career aspirations, and performance profiles. It may be temporary or permanent. Some team members may want to ramp up, some may seek fewer responsibilities, others might pivot laterally, and a few may need to step away altogether, by choice or involuntarily.

The Career Canvas is not about forcing everyone to "move up" or "move out." It is not solely about laddering, shipping out, or shipping up to Boston, for that matter. Instead, it provides a varied tapestry of possibilities that accommodate each person's evolving aspirations while ensuring your organization retains knowledge, stabilizes talent pipelines, and addresses Age Debt head-on. It becomes a refreshed way to assess and actualize your overall talent plan.

Envision an artist's canvas: It is a flexible space where they can paint in layers, change direction, or add new textures at will.

Similarly, a team member's career can unfold, adapt, or even circle back after a break or retirement. The Career Canvas respects that people rarely move in neat lines. Instead, individuals have unique needs shaped by family, finances, health, and passions.

Think about Bill Gates. After leaving his post as CEO of Microsoft in 2008, he took his wealth and began using his Ruby wisdom at his eponymously named philanthropic foundation to help millions of people. He remained on as chairman at Microsoft for six years and still today provides occasional coaching to the current CEO, Satya Nadella. Whether a team member is a top talent or not, if they see an opportunity to experiment or temporarily lessen their commitments without needing to quit entirely or simply stay put, this results in an Experience Dividend for you.

> **As a leader, you should always have at the ready the following question: What career move—if any—sets my team members up best now and in the future?** That's where the nine potential moves of the Career Canvas come in.

The Career Canvas Defined

You can think of the Career Canvas as being played in five major and four minor keys. Composer Paul Hindemith called the minor key a "clouding of the major" scale. Similarly, certain moves on the Career Canvas may seem less flashy than a big promotion. Yet, they can keep an employee engaged or reinvigorated while their life circumstances shift, making your team stronger and more adaptable.

The Career Canvas's minor keys fit Hindemith's assessment because they are a subtle clouding of the major moves. But all nine Career Canvas moves are of equal importance if you want to achieve the Experience Dividend.

First, let me define the five major and four minor moves. Then I will discuss how to apply them.

Major Moves

Stay Put: A deliberate choice for a team member to remain in their current position without expanding their responsibilities or title. Whether it involves a River still in learning-and-development mode, a steady mid-career Rock, or a seasoned Ruby, the choice to "stay put" is a respected and positive Career Canvas stance at the organization.

In sum: An intentional commitment to continue in one's current role.

Move Up: A permanent full-time shift to a position with broader leadership or skill responsibility. It suits a forward-charging River who seeks fresh challenges, a mid-career Rock ready to leverage deeper expertise, and a well-seasoned Ruby eager for an expanded influence.

In sum: A proactive decision to expand responsibility, scope, and organizational impact.

Move Down: A conscious reduction in scope or seniority, *not* a demotion. It benefits a mid-career Rock or a seasoned Ruby who must balance new personal priorities to ensure a deliberate realignment rather than a retreat. They remain full-time employees.

In sum: A recalibration of workload and focus without abandoning one's career aspirations or remuneration level.

Move Laterally: The shift to a comparable role at the same seniority level. It may attract a River seeking wider exposure, a Rock aiming to broaden skill sets, or a Ruby who craves renewed perspectives.

In sum: A strategic sidestep that cultivates cross-functional insight, collaboration, networking, skills advancement, and diverse growth.

Move Out: A planned or unplanned exit. For a River, Rock, or Ruby, this could be departing on a high note, a deliberate choice that can preserve goodwill and open doors for a future boomerang return. Or the employee could be involuntarily exited from the organization due to poor performance or organizational headcount reductions.

In sum: A definitive departure that sees the team member no longer employed at the organization.

Minor Moves

Phase Out: A gradual easing of hours or responsibilities over months, quarters, or years. This appeals to Rubies who still enjoy contributing but prefer less than full time or mid-career Rocks seeking a gentler slope into new personal or professional phases.

In sum: A softer runway out of the organization that sustains institutional knowledge while adjusting to life changes at an even pace.

Boomerang In: A return to the organization—by boomerang—after having stepped away. Rivers, Rocks, or Rubies can rejoin with established credibility, bridging familiar processes, institutional knowledge, culture, and previously established relationships.

In sum: A savvy reunion after time away that delivers instant cultural fluency and renewed value for everyone.

Spark Up: A time-bound expansion of scope on a high-visibility project, short-term rotation, or apprenticeship. It can even test the readiness for Move Up or Move Laterally opportunities. It might suit an ambitious River, a mid-career Rock, or a hungry Ruby, assessing and confirming the capacity for different roles and responsibilities.

In sum: A short-term leap towards a broader scope, with ample room to resume baseline duties if needed.

Slow Down: A temporary reduction in workload or schedule, distinct from retirement. A mid-career Rock might juggle elder- or childcare, a driven River might pause for additional studies, or a Ruby may need to recharge after intensive commitments. It can also include a 3- to 12-month career break or sabbatical when someone needs an unpaid break from work.

In sum: A measured break that balances personal priorities with the option to return to full pace later (unique from a Phase Out opportunity).

The Career Canvas Applied

Despite its nine potential career moves and robust flexibility, the Career Canvas remains deceptively simple at its core. So where do you start as a leader? The key is to treat the Career Canvas not as a guitar solo but as part of an album of career discussions. Here's how:

Build Culture and Conversations with Openness

- The nine major and minor career moves should be openly discussed as part of your team's culture. It's not a once-a-year career chat but an organizational or team norm used to build your Experience Dividend culture.

- When you meet a team member for one-on-one meetings or when there are team sessions, you should always present the nine options as equally valid. A quick, high-visibility initiative (Spark Up) can be an excellent litmus test for someone pondering a more significant leadership role. Meanwhile, a Move Down might be the perfect solution for a burnt-out Rock juggling personal stress. If Stay Put is the call, emphasize that it's not a silent status quo but an active choice.

- Conversations like these feel more open because team members will see the wide range of possibilities that the Career Canvas allows—and it permeates your culture, becoming an organizational norm in how you conduct an Age Debt–free team.

Keep Time Frames Short and Fluid

- The Career Canvas works best if you routinely revisit where team members stand. It can't be a conversation that happens once every Summer Olympics.

- A Rock might be all in for a short Spark Up or Move Laterally shift, only to realize a Move Out could surface in a year. This fluidity is healthy, not chaotic.

- By scheduling more frequent check-ins, you can catch attitudinal or desired professional changes earlier. The Career Canvas model is dynamic, like your team members' lives.

Align Moves with Organizational Needs

- Yes, the Career Canvas is about professional growth. However, your organization also has urgent skill gaps and demographic concerns.

- What if a wave of older Rubies plan to retire soon, and you need them to share knowledge via a phased approach? What if several team members need upskilling? What happens next if a slew of new hires just do not pan out?

- Use the Career Canvas to match your institutional priorities—failing to do so makes the framework a one-sided and biased tool.

Embed It Across the Culture

- Treat the Career Canvas like a day-to-day culture staple, not an HR annual event or policy.

- Highlight examples of past successes. Discuss the opportunities that exist as a team or unit (or across your entire organization).

- The faster your team's culture adapts to Career Canvas thinking, the more "normal" it becomes for all leaders and team members to understand the benefits of pivoting, slowing down, or temporarily shifting roles.

What is the big payoff with the Career Canvas? As a leader, you develop a multi-directional career ecosystem in which Rivers, Rocks, and Rubies all find their natural pace and place, which ultimately helps to eliminate many of the Age Debt factors from Side A.

The Career Canvas Marketplace

Having embraced the Career Canvas and its nine major and minor moves, ask yourself one more key question: How can my team's culture adopt this Career Canvas mindset?

One way is through the Marketplace. Think of it as an internal "career board" where team members from every era—Rivers, Rocks, and Rubies—can browse opportunities for short rotations, spike assignments, permanent roles, or skill-building opportunities. You can build it, buy it, or use discussion forums in products like Microsoft Teams, Slack, Workvivo, Google Groups, and others to make it happen.

Bottom line? It's not meant to be complicated. When done right, it can eliminate the "managerial gatekeeping" that tends to stifle cross-functional development and collaboration, regardless of your organization's size.

The Marketplace also removes the hoarding mindset that so often derails organizational culture. Instead, team members can propose a unique project, test a Move Laterally pivot before making it permanent, or try out a Spark Up assignment to gauge readiness for a bigger career leap. It should become the place to define the rationale of all nine career moves. The Marketplace is also the ideal spot to highlight case studies of people who have boomeranged back into the organization or the policies around a Phase Out transition to retirement.

It can also be where you define (and endorse) the importance of Move Laterally, Slow Down, and Move Down roles and assignments. Examples and case studies are great ways of making them real and inspiring others to build their own moves, too.

MapleCo and CrossPaths

An example from MapleCo serves as proof of concept for the Career Canvas Marketplace.

One of the Age Debt Tiger Team recommendations was to launch an in-house platform called "CrossPaths," encouraging managers to post real business needs and issues. It was partly a job board but also an online Career Canvas mecca. There were tips, information, internal gigs, case studies, and even an online discussion board dedicated to careers at the company.

In a recent example, Harjeet Singh, a marketing manager who was super stressed and needed some analytics assistance, posted a three-month Spark Up for someone to join their team. A mid-career Rock named Zoe Wenzel not only took on the Spark Up gig that Harjeet posted—after receiving permission from her manager—but also discovered a new facet of work after the assignment. Zoe was re-energized during her short-term assignment, which led to some great discussions with Harjeet about a permanent role. She was hired onto the team full-time after her stint was completed.

In the end, a Spark Up short-term gig turned into a permanent Move Laterally situation for Zoe. She had been a little bored in her previous role but was now so happy to be continuing her career at MapleCo.

Meanwhile, Zoe's former leader, Timothy Walker, had already seen the writing on the wall. Timothy had a hunch that Harjeet's opportunity would eventually be too good for Zoe to pass up on a full-time basis. He reached out to Mia Till, a Ruby who had left MapleCo three years earlier, wondering if she might be interested in returning.

Mia had spent the last three years at Oracle, so Timothy figured she might yearn to return to the friendly confines of MapleCo. He was right! Mia gave a four-week notice period and happily came back to MapleCo with open arms.

One Spark Up assignment not only opened a Move Laterally pathway for Zoe but also directly enabled a successful Boomerang In move for Mia.

Marketplace Outcomes

A Career Canvas Marketplace can accomplish several vital outcomes:

- First, it normalizes multi-directional movement, so you do not have to tread water waiting for that rare top-down assignment to shuffle roles.

- Second, it fosters a culture of transparent skills exchange. The Marketplace boosts collaboration and knowledge retention by showcasing the actual tasks that need doing.

- Finally, it becomes an open communication tool that directly (and indirectly) endorses career movement between the eras. It also helps people understand that not all careers go up—they can move laterally, be reduced, go away and come back, or even go down.

> **One final consideration:** If you believe your organization is too small to implement an online Career Canvas Marketplace, don't fret; the spirit and beliefs remain the same.

When you adopt these concepts as a team cultural norm—when your team members start to see the Career Canvas not as an HR ideology but as a living, breathing engine of career fluidity that supports everyone's success—you are well on your way to eliminating

Age Debt and profiting from an Experience Dividend, regardless of team or organization size. And again, these concepts can easily be applied using free or low-cost options. You just have to get creative.

The Marketplace—a transparent internal career development ethos—enables all nine Career Canvas moves, from Spark Up assignments to Phase Out transitions. It's your team's career fluidity hub.

The Career Canvas in Action

An example of the Career Canvas in action can be found at Houghton Mifflin Harcourt (HMH), a global leader in education publishing based in Boston. The company launched its LEAD Connected rotation program to rid itself of enterprise-wide career stagnation for its older workers. The program offered top Ruby performers Spark Up and Move Laterally opportunities where they could step into roles far removed from their usual domains. For example, senior product managers immersed themselves in operations, while other Rubies bravely took charge of new equity and inclusion initiatives—something they had no previous experience with. Remarkably, instead of their performance waning, it flourished. Once-bored executives were suddenly having the time of their lives, thriving doing something new.

These unique immersion experiences through the LEAD program enhanced the Rubies' agility, and the program graduates went on to become some of HMH's most sought-after leaders, some attaining Move Up positions. The key lies in a deliberate, well-structured push beyond past comfort zones. It requires risk-taking with the right type of culture reinvention.

Here are a few more exemplars of companies like HMH embracing the concepts introduced in this track:

- **British Columbia Lottery Corporation (BCLC):** BCLC implemented a version of the Phase Out concept where team members—once approved by their leader—can stagger their retirement by combining a portion of their pension with a set number of workdays per week over 12 to 24 months. The Phased Retirement Program, or PRP, permits team members to ease their transition into retirement at roughly the same full-time wages. At the same time, the organization benefits from their skills, contributions, and knowledge transfer until they retire fully.

- **Mayo Clinic:** Like BCLC, the Mayo Clinic, a leading nonprofit academic medical centre, offers a phased retirement program. Recognizing the value of their experienced physicians and healthcare professionals (Rubies), the Mayo Clinic allows them to gradually reduce their work hours and responsibilities over a defined period. This allows for knowledge transfer and mentoring of younger staff (Rivers and Rocks) while providing the Rubies with a smoother transition into retirement.

- **UK Civil Service:** The UK Civil Service's "Returnships" target individuals who have taken career breaks, offering training and support services to re-enter the workforce. This aligns with the Boomerang In element of the Career Canvas, where organizations can tap into a diverse talent pool of previous employees. It is also an example of hiring individuals outside your organization into the Move Laterally or Move Down categories.

- **Michelin:** France-based Michelin's Job and Career Management agreement was an improvement to the company's approach to internal mobility and end-of-career policies for its 16,000 employees. Instead of forcing team members onto one upward track, Michelin fosters open, multi-directional moves, from short cross-functional stints to phased retirement options. Personalized career partners help workers in sensitive roles identify new job pathways, while newly created positions must consider internal candidates first. By bridging skill upgrades, job transitions, and flexible retirements, Michelin shifted how it views its Career Canvas.

GOLDEN NUGGETS

We have shifted away from Side A Greyaways in favour of Side B Golden Nuggets. How refreshing! Here are your Career Canvas Golden Nuggets from Track 7:

Golden Nugget #1: Careers Are a Canvas, Not a Ladder

Scrap the rigid-rungs thinking. The Career Canvas envisions multi-directional moves—up, sideways, phased, down, or even boomerang—so your team members can paint novel paths and your organization can harness intergenerational talent.

Golden Nugget #2: Institute Major and Minor Career Moves

Five "major" career options—Stay Put, Move Up, Move Down, Move Laterally, and Move Out—plus four "minor" ones—Phase Out, Boomerang In, Spark Up, and Slow Down—offer your team members a choose-your-own-adventure approach to role transitions.

Golden Nugget #3: Short-Term Assignments Spark a Fuse

Spark Up mini-rotations, apprenticeships, and short-term gigs allow Rivers, Rocks, or Rubies to test-drive new responsibilities on a short timeline. It's the perfect proving ground before anyone leaps head-first into a new role.

Golden Nugget #4: Boomerangs Are Da Bomb

Concerning the future of work, talent will become a highly prized commodity. You should give ample consideration to welcoming back retirees and once-employed former team members into your team.

Golden Nugget #5: Design Transitions to Safeguard Knowledge

Any of the nine moves—even a Move Out—can be harnessed if you consider the necessity of preserving institutional memory. A Phase Out retirement, Move Laterally assignment, or even Slow Down job reduction can be a preventative knowledge-retention action. (More in Track 8: Wisdom Wheel.)

Golden Nugget #6: Team Culture Is the Career Fuel

The Career Canvas thrives under an operating culture that normalizes open conversations, zero stigma around "non-traditional" career arcs, and frequent check-ins. If your team members sense they are allowed to pivot, they will.

Wisdom Wheel

The year was 2009. The Black Eyed Peas were crushing it with their hit single "I Gotta Feeling." Coincidentally, I also *gotta feeling* when I discovered something happening at work. It was a feeling of wisdom that I had not anticipated.

I was about a year into my new role at TELUS as the organization's chief learning officer. We had introduced a homegrown tool called Habitat Video, which enabled team members to create and post user-generated videos within the organization's firewall. It functioned much like YouTube, but it was private and exclusive to TELUS. In 2009, this was well ahead of its time.

What I did not foresee was how two crafty Rubies would turn their roles into a dynamic example of mentoring, collaboration, knowledge capture, renewal, and purpose, all through video distribution.

I'd be lying if I said I had proactively considered using Habitat Video as a means for older team members—with decades of experience—to use a digital camera or camera-enabled smartphone to record parts of their job and share with other team members. Their recordings felt less like instructional content and more like an archive of working lives, precisely what Studs Terkel honoured in his book, *Working*, where he observed, "Most of us . . . have jobs that are too small for our spirit." But they did it anyway. No prompt. No playbook. All purpose.

These seasoned telecommunications field technicians took it upon themselves to record short lessons and share them on the Habitat Video platform. They might be up a telephone pole talking circuitry, in language that was foreign to me but seriously useful to many others. They could be at a central office—where phone lines from subscribers connect to the local loop—explaining faults, wiring intricacies, troubleshooting methods, and complexities that only experience can teach.

When my team figured out what they were up to, we highlighted their contributions, gave them better cameras and training, and urged other Rubies in field roles to share *their* unique, hard-earned knowledge on Habitat Video.

I was 38 years old at the time, a mid-management Rock. Denise and I were frenetically tending to our young goats (remember, kids!), who were six, four, and two at the time. I bring this up, why? Here I was, supposedly in charge of leadership development at TELUS as a Rock, learning invaluable lessons about wisdom transfer from the very Rubies I was meant to be helping. Yet, back then, I was somewhat illiterate—if not an Age Debt subordinate—regarding the concept we will explore in this track: *wisdom*. More specifically, I hadn't even considered the importance of the capturing, sharing, and mentoring of wisdom.

I'm reminded of Charles Handy, the British organizational thinker, who once wrote: "To learn anything other than the stuff you find in books, you need to be able to experiment, to make mistakes, to accept feedback, and to try again. It doesn't matter whether you are learning to ride a bike or starting a new career, the cycle of experiment, feedback, and new experiment is always there." It was those two TELUS Rubies who taught *me* a lesson.

I would not make that same mistake today as a 54-year-old. In part, that's because I am now a Ruby. But whether you are a River, Rock, or Ruby, it is also why I urge you to think hard about what will be unpacked in this track. Don't be ignorant like I was as a Rock.

> ## Wisdom is to the Experience Dividend what oxygen is to fire.

Alas, without intentionally capturing, nurturing, and renewing wisdom within organizations, Age Debt will increasingly resemble a harmful virus if left unchecked, impairing your organization's potential and stifling your Experience Dividend.

Mentors on the Railway

Germany's Deutsche Bahn implemented a wisdom transfer philosophy like that one at TELUS—except they did it deliberately, at scale, and with foresight.

Picture a sprawling rail and transit operation with thousands of employees, from platform coordinators to locomotive engineers to drivers. At DB Cargo—a subsidiary of Deutsche Bahn, where about half of its roughly 19,000-strong workforce is over 50 and more than a third are 55 or older—an aging demographic is no mere footnote. Naturally, these seasoned Rubies hold the kind of institutional expertise that you simply cannot replicate overnight. They are the workforce equivalent of chart-toppers who keep the hits coming year after year.

As retirements loomed, DB knew it could not simply hire replacements overnight. Shunting locomotive drivers or wagon inspectors possess specialized, on-the-ground expertise accumulated over decades. The company proactively built a forward-looking strategy, blending digital forecasting (think a DB-specific Career Canvas) with deep, person-to-person mentorship, knowledge sharing, and collaboration. For starters, DB implemented a workforce-planning system that could look five years ahead to pinpoint precisely when and where Rubies might exit the organization. They drew a giant map of all the "experience hot spots" that enabled them to mobilize new hires in advance or cross-train mid-career Rocks to step into critical roles. It's an example of how the Career Canvas from Track 7 can also be used as a strategic bond to wisdom, knowledge, and intelligence.

At the same time, the company established a structured path for successors and invited both prospective leaders and technical specialists to enter a multi-year development track. This involved formal training, but more crucially, it paired them with Rubies—folks who, for decades, had tested the resilience of everything in these highly technical roles, from overhead lines to locomotive engines. This mentor program became key. Many of the Rubies helped their designated younger successors troubleshoot equipment issues and guided them through the minutiae that rarely appeared in any standard guide. Think of it as an homage to the "tacit knowledge" problem I highlighted in Track 3: The Experience Conundrum. All kinds of DB Rubies leaned into mentoring relationships with their River and Rock mentees, meeting weekly to share tips, discuss curveballs from the field, or plan site visits that put textbook lessons into gritty, real-world settings. The entire process the company implemented ensured that the intangible street smarts of their invaluable Rubies remained in-house.

In addition, DB invested in cross-generational teaming—think clusters of Rivers, Rocks, and Rubies who work together to tackle operational challenges while learning from one another. This arrangement meant older staff did not simply fade out; they became the cultural and learning glue that linked DB's past and current operations to its evolving, technology-forward future.

In short, DB has been flipping the script on its demographic headwinds, turning the looming retirements of so many seasoned Rubies into a springboard for tomorrow's workforce. It did not want to suffer from Age Debt and instead turned a potentially nightmarish situation into an Experience Dividend using wisdom transfer as a key tool. Deutsche Bahn strategically turned demographic realities into opportunities by proactively engaging Rubies in mentorship and capturing their critical wisdom. Instead of facing Age Debt, DB converted looming retirements into an Experience Dividend.

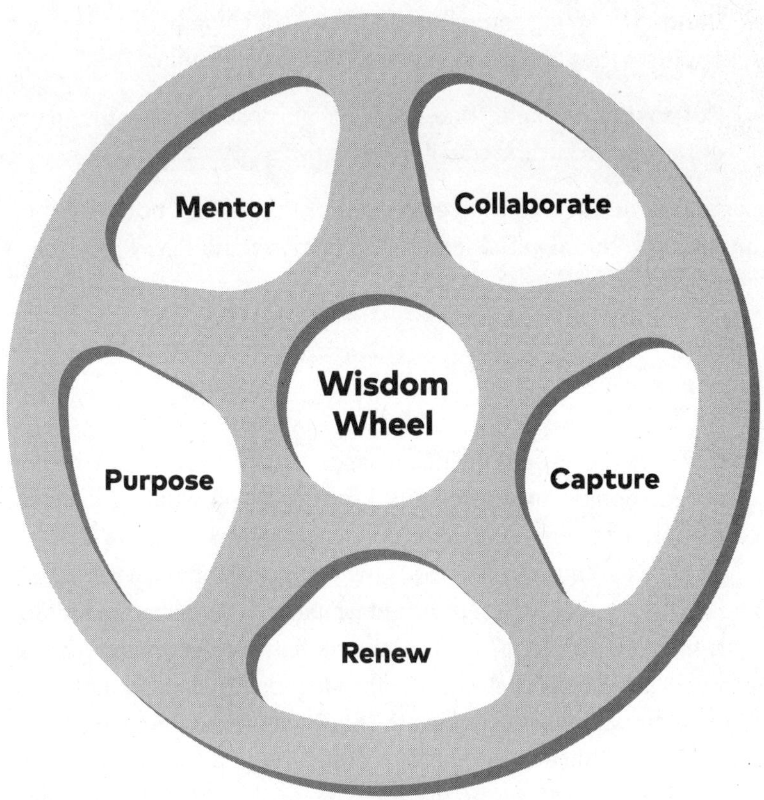

Now is a good time to introduce the Wisdom Wheel, the key tool of Track 8.

The five components of the Wisdom Wheel—ideally used together—form the nucleus of an inter-era wisdom construct, defined as follows:

- **Mentor:** Nurturing deliberate, cross-era learning between Rivers, Rocks, and Rubies.

- **Collaborate:** Fostering intentional, team-wide sharing across Rivers, Rocks, and Rubies.

- **Capture:** Systematically preserving critical institutional knowledge before it leaves the organization.

- **Renew:** Enabling continuous individual development and growth opportunities equally for Rivers, Rocks, and Rubies.

- **Purpose:** Leveraging one's sense of purpose for meaningful wisdom generation and transfer.

Let's look at each of the components. I'll explain not only their importance but also the leadership tactics that align with each. I gotta *wisdom* feeling. Do you?

Mentor

I never thought I would include a positive story about Jack Welch in one of my books. I never thought I would attend a Billie Eilish concert either, but here we are. Sometimes, guitars do fly.

There was a buzz back in 1999 when professionals in the people and culture space, like me, learned what CEO Welch had mandated with his General Electric (GE) leaders. Usually, my stories about "Neutron Jack" refer to the dark side of leadership. For example, also in 1999, he was caught cooking the books (again!), and GE was fined $50 million. This was on top of GE agreeing to pay $147 million to settle lawsuits that accused the company of illegally collecting debts in that same year. Read David Gelles's fantastic 2022 book, *The Man Who Broke Capitalism*, to really get a handle on the ways of Welch.

However, there was one aspect in which Welch was arguably ahead of his time. In 1999, he turned GE's mentoring model on its head. Welch famously required hundreds of senior GE leaders—including himself—to seek out younger mentors to help navigate the digital revolution. The year 1999 was the peak dot-com era. Amazon had started to take serious flight with its online bookshop. Google entered the picture with its search engine. Other players like Alibaba, SurveyMonkey, and eBay arrived. It was, in a word, *wild*.

Welch saw what was happening and, to his credit, made an organizational mentoring change. Picture a seasoned GE VP, a Ruby of corporate wisdom, learning dot-com fundamentals from a

24-year-old River fresh out of college. Welch's mandate transformed GE's digital fluency over a couple of quarters. It highlighted an essential truth that remains painfully overlooked by many leaders today suffering from Age Debt: Wisdom travels in more directions than merely top-down.

Mentorship, when intentionally structured, is one of the keys to the Experience Dividend. It unlocks the latent knowledge of experienced Rubies while harnessing the innovative thinking of younger Rocks and Rivers. But let me be clear: Reverse mentoring—as this version is often called—is not only about young workers instructing older ones. In Experience Dividend organizations, the most effective mentoring flows in *all* directions.

Novartis, a Swiss multinational pharmaceutical corporation, has embedded this balanced exchange of wisdom in its culture. Through its ZOOM@Novartis initiative—a formal collaboration with the University of Basel—the company systematically pairs seasoned executives with young doctoral researchers for reciprocal mentorship. Senior leaders offer guidance on career advancement, networking, and industry navigation while simultaneously gaining direct exposure to cutting-edge scientific research. The ZOOM@Novartis program enables young and older participants to exchange knowledge equally, creating a new partnership that improves the skills of everyone involved.

> **On a practical note, the company's structured approach directly confronts a stubborn component of Age Debt:** the assumption that young workers must quietly "wait their turn" to meaningfully contribute.

Novartis actively dismantles this barrier by establishing mentoring as a two-way dialogue, reinforcing that wisdom—like experience—is cumulative and never confined to a single age bracket.

In France, Sodexo has taken a slightly different yet equally meaningful route. Known for its food services, facilities management, and hospitality amenities, this global company with almost half a million employees set out to address the digital skill gaps within its senior leadership rank. Like Novartis, Sodexo implemented an intentional reciprocal mentoring program. Young, digitally fluent employees began guiding senior leaders on everything from collaborative platforms to data analytics tools. In return, senior leaders passed down nuanced industry insights and contextual know-how.

Helen Hirsh Spence, founder of Top Sixty Over Sixty, a firm aimed at transforming the narrative of aging from negative to positive, argues for blended mentorship models like these. "Organizations have an untapped resource within their walls," she told me. "They simply haven't fully leveraged the power of intentional mentorship to transfer critical knowledge and wisdom between generations." She points to mentorship's role in generating an Experience Dividend—transforming wisdom from an aging workforce into a tangible competitive advantage.

I recommend three practical tactics to embed the "mentor" component of the Wisdom Wheel into your organization:

- **Formal mentor pairings:** Explicitly pair Rubies and Rocks with Rivers in structured, bidirectional mentorship relationships. Clearly outline mutual learning goals, scheduled interactions, and accountability to ensure effective, ongoing wisdom exchange. Within the TELUS MBA program I run for the organization, students are paired with graduates of the program in a "buddy mentor system" that allows for a range of Rivers, Rocks, and Rubies to intermix and learn from one another.

- **Short-term rotations and Spark Up assignments:** Embed short-term rotational assignments, what I call "Spark Up assignments," into your Career Canvas Marketplace (detailed in Track 7).

For instance, Rubies might temporarily embed themselves within digitally fluent teams to gain hands-on experience with emerging technologies. Rivers or Rocks, conversely, could rotate into more senior and seasoned teams to absorb critical institutional insights. Does your organization have a rotational shadow executive leadership team or executive board of governors made up of Rivers where they participate to learn? Can you institute an apprenticeship program so Rivers can work alongside a Rock or Ruby? These intentional experiences build mutual understanding, enrich skills, and normalize intergenerational collaboration. (See next subsection.)

- **Mentor Moments via Career Canvas Marketplace:** Expand (or launch) the Career Canvas Marketplace to include short, informal "Mentor Moments." Team members can offer or request short mentoring opportunities on specific skills or topics. This approach democratizes wisdom-sharing, removes hierarchical stigma, and keeps the knowledge flow fluid, accessible, and immediate between all team members regardless of level, title, or seniority.

Even if your organization does not have a Career Canvas Marketplace, these mentorship ideas can still be contemplated. Implementing them can transform mentorship from a reactive afterthought—or not a thought at all—into a strategic organizational asset to combat Age Debt. Whether reverse or traditional, mentorship can genuinely break down your age silos while building on the Experience Dividend.

Intentionally weaving mentorship into the fabric of your organizational culture will help create an organization where wisdom is continually and inclusively shared (and renewed) between Rivers, Rocks, and Rubies.

Collaborate

Collaboration, a pivotal component of the Wisdom Wheel, acts like the master orchestra conductor that unlocks your team's capacity to innovate and execute together across all age spectrums. It's the whole symphony.

As we have just learned, mentoring is essential, but you will not see its full power unless there is an underlying culture of collaboration, one that promotes Rivers, Rocks, and Rubies—in the words of former Ford and Boeing CEO Alan Mulally—"working together."

Maybe you are a leader who hangs one of those awkwardly absurd "Collaboration" posters in a meeting room and wishes for it to happen. But you know as well as I do that a true collaborative ethos requires much more intentionality. This is especially true as we strive to rid ourselves of Age Debt.

Let's revisit BMW, an organization that has deliberately woven collaboration into its working DNA across all eras. As part of its approach to sustaining an experienced but future-ready workforce, BMW ensures that many of its new projects bring together young team members with strong tech competencies alongside veteran colleagues who have lived through multiple generations of vehicle design and manufacturing processes.

"Our management style is to build small teams intentionally," explained Konstanze Carreras-Solé, director of diversity, equity, and inclusion at BMW Group headquarters in Munich. "Whenever we have a project, we try to combine younger, less experienced people— particularly those with strong technical competencies—with older, experienced employees. This approach creates a win–win situation by effectively combining fresh digital knowledge with longstanding expertise on our work teams. We see collaboration work well in these situations."

Part of BMW's collaboration magic lies in connecting knowledge among these distinct age groups. A Ruby with 30 years of engineering background might team up with a fresh-faced River who only recently joined the company. Maybe a Rock team member—

perhaps someone with 10 or 15 years of BMW product management experience—steps in to help keep everything on track. The organization believes that a multi-eras composition of Rivers, Rocks, and Rubies is good for business outcomes. If vehicle sales are any indication, their strategy seems to be working. Since 2009, BMW's global automobile sales have risen from roughly 1.3 million units annually to over 2.5 million.

The triad collaboration approach between Rivers, Rocks, and Rubies demonstrates how BMW continues to drive transformation while simultaneously respecting the company's storied automobile engineering heritage. They have discovered that ideas fuse faster and more effectively when you intentionally set the stage for cross-ages conversations—be it in automotive design, supply chain innovation, or technology integrations. Recall from Track 1 BMW's Tom Allemeier, a member of the company's Senior Expert Program, where he continues his passion for automobile design—but relinquished his team-leader role—by collaborating with younger Rock leaders and River team members on future designs.

So if collaboration is essential for realizing the Experience Dividend, why do organizations still find it challenging to get it right? One reason is that genuine cross-ages collaboration requires leadership teams to move beyond a box-checking mentality ("We have a cross-functional project team, check!") to an immersive system in which tasks and priorities rely on—and benefit from—cross-age interaction. When that starts to happen, people organically lean on each other's strengths. Mixing people of different age brackets is no longer an issue because it becomes a team or organizational norm.

The following tactics can help you galvanize River–Rock–Ruby collaboration into a day-to-day reality:

- **Intentional unit or team composition:** Ensure your overall team composition intentionally reflects age diversity. If your broader organizational units lack a balanced representation of Rivers, Rocks, and Rubies, everyday interactions will remain segmented by age. A balanced mix of the three eras in regular team structures promotes cross-age collaboration, establishing a foundation to dissolve Age Debt issues naturally, if not subliminally. It may take time to transform, but it's at least worth keeping in mind as you plan for talent additions and subtractions.

- **Purposeful project-team composition:** When forming temporary or project-based teams, try to intentionally integrate Rivers, Rocks, and Rubies. This could be cross-functional or just from your team or unit. As a leader, you should explicitly state why generational diversity is strategically valuable for the project's objectives. This purposeful integration signals that cross-era collaboration is intentional and essential for success.

- **Multi-age project charter:** If you are launching a project, at kick-off, explicitly outline in a concise charter the value each persona from the eras (Rivers, Rocks, and Rubies) might bring to the initiative. The charter sets expectations around mutual respect and interdependence, reinforcing the explicit necessity of cross-era collaboration from day one of the project. It also subliminally points out that the team will not tolerate any form of ageism. (Recall Track 5: The Silent Saboteur of Ageism.)

- **Co-op placements:** When young up-and-coming Rivers, still in college or university, are placed in an organization as interns to gain experience, there is goodness all around. It's a symbiotic relationship where the students benefit because they get real-world experience before graduating while making connections with experts. The organization benefits by involving more youth with fresh perspectives and new ideas. (Plus, it's just the right thing to do.)

- **Wisdom exchange sessions:** Schedule regular "Wisdom Exchange" sessions between team members. These brief collaborative sessions allow team members from each persona to share insights and lessons learned. Encouraging these cross-era dialogue sessions demystifies the idea that only Rubies are wise. Furthermore, it allows Rivers and Rocks to ask questions of the Rubies that they might not otherwise have a chance to.

- **Rotational meeting facilitation:** Whether it's a team or project meeting, try to rotate facilitation leadership across the personas, ensuring each group—Rivers, Rocks, and Rubies—gets to experience shared leadership responsibilities in these meetings. This intentional rotation can cultivate an appreciation of diverse perspectives and promote more open dialogue. It's another way to solidify cross-era collaboration as a team or organizational norm.

However, none of these tactics will be effective if your corporate culture is still mired in territorial, Age Debt thinking. If the team perceives knowledge sharing as a loss of power, collaboration will struggle. Conversely, if your organizational culture fosters curiosity, embraces constructive debate, and celebrates the achievements of a multi-generational team, it will establish the right conditions for collaboration to flourish. Individuals will view inter-era collaboration as a means of personal growth and team goal achievement rather than as a burden. It's 1985's Live Aid on steroids.

When you integrate collaboration into your culture in a genuine and era-friendly way, it does not matter if you are building premium automobiles in Munich, launching a new iPhone in Cupertino, or revamping a facilities-management process in Versailles. The result will be the same: good performance plus a synergy that propels your teams beyond artificial silos of age and tenure. Inter-age collaboration is yet another tactic to future-proof your team and organization.

Capture

If "mentor" and "collaborate" are essential strategies for reducing Age Debt, then "capture" is the mechanism that preserves all that knowledge before it exits the company.

Let's briefly return to CEO Marla Benson at MapleCo. You'll remember Benson's pivotal decision to establish the Age Debt Tiger Team. She inherently and rightly understood that without structured knowledge-capture processes, MapleCo would eventually lose decades of institutional wisdom whenever a Ruby retired. The tiger team's analysis and report confirmed her suspicions. There were no "capture" programs or processes whatsoever at MapleCo.

Organizations such as MapleCo have historically faced challenges regarding this crucial aspect of capturing wisdom. Many firms consider it an afterthought instead of a strategic necessity. Guy Wallace, a performance analyst and knowledge management expert, expressed this bluntly to me: "Organizations repeatedly overlook the structured effort required to preserve deep institutional knowledge. Without deliberate processes, critical tacit expertise vanishes overnight."

Dr. Richard Clark is a renowned cognitive psychologist specializing in knowledge transfer and cognitive task analysis. He offered me a similar warning: "Capturing knowledge can't be casual or incidental. It demands intentional methodologies to ensure vital expertise—the kind earned through decades of real-world experience—does not disappear quietly."

I witnessed this intentionality first-hand at TELUS, when those two Ruby technicians began recording and sharing their telecommunications knowledge through Habitat Video. Except it wasn't company policy—it wasn't something even I was thinking about; the two team members just took it upon themselves. Let me turn the microphone over to a more systematic example that demonstrates the full power of intentional knowledge capture.

Tata Chemicals, an India-based multinational company with nearly 5,000 employees and $2.5 billion in annual revenues, is known for industrial chemicals and crop nutrition solutions. Its structured knowledge capture endeavour has become nothing short of an organizational obsession. The company recognized the critical risk associated with losing decades of specialized know-how as Rubies retired and other employees were left wondering how to perform certain job tasks. Tata Chemicals collaborated with their sister firm, Tata Steel, to launch an integrated approach designed explicitly to capture and disseminate critical tacit knowledge. Tata's approach is multi-layered and comprehensive:

- **Storytelling and memoirs:** Employees nearing retirement are systematically interviewed by Tata's Knowledge Management team, and their experiences—including critical safety insights, production techniques, and troubleshooting—are captured through structured storytelling. These insights are documented into what they call "memoirs," which are then carefully archived and shared broadly across Tata Chemicals.

- **Performance dialogues:** Regular yet brief daily check-ins between team members explicitly document real-time challenges, solutions, and lessons learned. When an issue is resolved, the findings are recorded in a structured internal repository accessible to future generations of employees.

- **Know More Booklets and Knowledge Nuggets:** Tata produces concise, focused documents ("Know More Booklets") and brief, practical one-page summaries ("Knowledge Nuggets") to capture and distribute key improvements and innovations. These small formats break down the firm's critical institutional knowledge into easily digestible and immediately applicable insights for the broader workforce.

Tata Chemicals' wide-ranging and intentional approach is precisely what the capture component of the Wisdom Wheel advocates. It recognizes knowledge capture not merely as preservation but as a strategic asset that strengthens organizational resilience and adaptability, transforming the risk of Age Debt into a tangible Experience Dividend. Here are three practical tactics you should consider implementing:

- **Wisdom exit interviews:** Don't settle for a single exit interview when someone is about to leave the building. For example, establish a six-month structured exit process for any Ruby in a critical role after they announce their retirement. Schedule regular monthly knowledge-capture sessions to aggressively document their tacit knowledge and context-rich expertise. Use elements of cognitive task analysis to ensure critical skills and processes are not lost. The use of artificial intelligence will do wonders in the capture of such cognitive tasks. The Phase Out option from the Career Canvas is also a good thing to implement.

- **Role capture:** Establish short, focused wisdom capture sessions where Rocks and Rubies explicitly document specific technical skills, process nuances, client or partner insights, problem-solving strategies, and anything else critical to their roles. It's a great time to use artificial intelligence to capture and sort. Unlike mentoring—which fosters mutual relationships—these sessions are intentionally transactional and documentation-driven, clearly aimed at creating durable and reusable records of institutional knowledge know-how. Deutsche Telekom Shared Services Europe, for example, implemented its "TTS," a digital performance-support platform that enables employees to capture, document, and share task-specific knowledge within their daily workflow to ensure expertise is preserved and accessible long after they depart.

- **Digital wisdom archive:** Establish a centralized, easily accessible wisdom archive within your organization's current collaboration platform. Think of it as an online wisdom library. Following Tata's example, fill this digital archive with diverse formats— videos, narrated workflows, how-to booklets, concise instructional summaries (Knowledge Nuggets), and memoirs. It should also contain stories of past successes and failures. If you don't have a collaboration platform, Google Workspace and Dropbox have free options for you to consider.

Capturing wisdom is as critical as bringing an amp to a gig. It is that serious as a tool to combat Age Debt. No amp, no sound. No capture, no future. In doing so, you are safeguarding decades of experience, reducing unnecessary learning curves, and creating an organizational memory accessible to all eras.

Capture at MapleCo

Back at MapleCo, Marla Benson stared at the Age Debt Tiger Team's report. The company had no capture strategy whatsoever. It was a face-palm moment—not quite as bad as a Boeing airplane door popping open mid-flight, but close.

Rather than waiting for the Age Debt iceberg to strike, Benson set a clear tone from the top, introducing what she called Maple Staples—a three-pronged knowledge-capture framework rooted in deliberate, practical action.

First, Benson initiated a company-wide wisdom audit. This identified the MapleCo team members' institutional knowledge using cognitive task analysis (CTA). Think of CTA as organizational archaeology: a structured, rigorous interview technique that systematically extracts critical yet hidden expertise from retiring Rubies and current Rocks and Rivers who possess deep knowledge. It was a strategic move to capture decades of experience, and MapleCo used artificial intelligence to assist with the process. Read any of Dr. Richard Clark's work on CTA to get up to speed.

Next, Benson formalized intentional knowledge handoff sessions, pairing team members with one another. The sessions captured deep, contextual, tacit knowledge and various wisdom across personas. The Ruby to Rock and River sessions were instrumental.

Finally, Benson launched Maple Stories, an internal video-sharing platform that allowed team members to visually record stories, practical skills, insights, and other knowledge bits in accessible, reusable segments. It was a massive success across the company.

Through the Maple Staples action plan, Benson became more at ease while also making one thing abundantly clear to her teams: Capturing wisdom was not a feel-good exercise. It was an essential organizational culture strategy, designed to ensure MapleCo's future did not walk out the door.

What will you do to capture your team's wisdom?

Renew

Some bands tour endlessly, coasting on yesterday's hits, their setlists predictable and stale. Radiohead isn't that band. Album after album, the Oxfordshire quintet has deliberately evolved, risking reinvention over nostalgia. I may be biased, but I believe this is partially why they have remained relevant for so long while other bands settle comfortably into repetition. Even the band members' side projects are unique. For example, Thom Yorke and Jonny Greenwood's band the Smile ventures into sonic segues that will make your head spin.

Your organization's depth and breadth of wisdom will encounter a similar challenge. You must consider your team's ongoing renewal needs and a thoughtfully integrated strategy to strengthen the organization's intelligence across all personas.

Think about *who* in your workforce gets renewed, but also *how* they get developed.

Innovation grows stale fast without intentionality. If you keep relying on yesterday's greatest hits, your organization risks becoming the corporate equivalent of 3 Doors Down: repetitive and predictable. (Unless, of course, 3 Doors Down is your jam, in which case, please, no hate mail!) Unfortunately, organizations often invest resources exclusively in developing Rivers, assuming that Rubies (and even Rocks) already possess sufficient knowledge or that the funds might be a wasted investment.

Simon Chan, founder and CEO of Adapt with Intent, a firm focused on innovation at the intersection of longevity, work, higher education, and retirement, puts it bluntly: "Some of the brightest, most adaptable people I know are people who are 50-plus, and they're craving to learn. The idea that you can't teach an old dog new tricks is a really dated concept. There is a beautiful opportunity for learning, both for older and younger adults."

Jeanette Leardi—a social gerontologist, educator, and author of *Aging Sideways: Changing Our Perspectives on Getting Older*—has spent years studying how our society misinterprets the concept of age. She offers a complementary point to Chan: "Most older adults are incredibly adaptive. They've been adapting their whole lives. The idea that they can't learn or change is not only wrong but also insulting."

Both Chan and Leardi nail it, and Prudential Singapore provides a practical example. Prudential Singapore is one of that country's leading life insurance companies, with nearly $53.3 billion in funds under management. Rather than quietly ushering seasoned Rubies out the door, the company eliminated its mandatory retirement age and intentionally reinvested in those who chose to remain. It designed targeted training programs—digital skill-building, financial advisory updates, and modern customer-engagement practices— explicitly tailored to renew the skills of experienced employees while also benefiting younger Rivers and Rocks. Prudential Singapore invested deliberately because it recognized the demographic reality it faced and saw the strategic advantage of continuously renewing skills across all personas, including its Rubies.

In 2021, Paris-based Atos took a similarly proactive approach. Realizing it had 21,000 employees aged 50-plus, the $17 billion global IT consulting firm decided to invest in them intentionally rather than letting them walk out the door. Atos implemented personalized training and development programs, empowering seasoned team members to identify their own skill gaps and select courses and programs aligned with their career goals.

Both Prudential Singapore and Atos offer compelling evidence: Renewal isn't just a matter of fairness; it's a strategic necessity to combat Age Debt. So, what tactics should you consider implementing as a leader to ensure that your team members renew?

- **Learning and development investment audit:** Many organizations assume they invest in learning equitably, but the data typically reveals otherwise. I recommend conducting a thorough learning and development (L&D) investment audit. This process dissects how learning and development resources—money, tools, time—are allocated across your workforce. You might discover an imbalance where most resources funnel to early-career Rivers, while mid- or late-career Rocks and Rubies receive the leftovers or none at all. The fix becomes an intentional rebalancing act. Consider establishing a quarterly or annual personal dashboard that outlines precise L&D spend per persona (Rivers, Rocks, Rubies) across your team or unit. Think of it as a financial statement that balances L&D opportunities with your talent.

- **Growth sprints:** Where apprenticeships require an extended commitment, growth sprints can pack intense skill-building into shorter, high-energy bursts. Over a short period (e.g., four to eight weeks), participants can dive into a targeted topic and finish with a tangible outcome, such as a project prototype or a revised process. During the burst, naturally, they are learning. You may also consider combining the Spark Up idea of the Career Canvas with the growth sprint. Imagine a Ruby from operations, a Rock from HR, and a River from product design coming together to solve a pressing business need. They leave with sharper skills, an expanded network, and fresh insight into cross-organization problem-solving. These sprints deliver a focused and invigorating dose of ongoing renewal across eras.

- **Encore apprenticeships:** Imagine a short-term internal apprenticeship of three to six months where a seasoned team member picks up a skill in a new or emerging field. Perhaps it's AI-enabled customer support, sustainability analytics, or data visualization. During this apprenticeship, the Ruby partners closely with a River or Rock with the relevant expertise. Encore apprenticeships shatter the myth that only young talent can learn new tricks. When Rubies show they can adopt skills in next-gen domains, it preserves their wisdom, keeps them engaged, and sets the tone that renewal is for all. On the flip side, the River or Rock mentor learns a thing or two from that veteran's deep institutional context and crystallized intelligence, forging cross-persona synergy.

Purpose

Do you have a favourite song from one of your much-loved artists that features another musical act? I'll go first with three of my faves:

- "Under Pressure" by Queen (feat. David Bowie)
- "He Got Game" by Public Enemy (feat. Stephen Stills)
- "I Love It" by Icona Pop (feat. Charli XCX)

It's the "feat." part that I'm interested in for this final component of the Wisdom Wheel: purpose. This final portion features a unique, sonically hip treat for you—an exceptional bonus or hidden track, if you will. May I introduce you to... *The Future of Work Is Gold (feat. The Purpose Effect)*

I published a book in 2016 titled *The Purpose Effect: Building Meaning in Yourself, Your Role, and Your Organization.* Since then, the concepts of purpose and meaning have been central to each subsequent book. Surprise! This book is no different.

When we mash up purpose with wisdom—both the generation and transfer of wisdom—you might say it parallels a musical collaboration. Each individual's unique sense of purpose can amplify the collective wisdom. Just as great collaborations elevate music, a clear purpose deepens the authenticity and strategic value of wisdom.

In *The Purpose Effect*, I introduced three types of purpose: personal, role, and organizational. Personal purpose is fundamental to how an individual perceives the concept of wisdom, whether generating or sharing it. The impact of one's wisdom might also be influenced by whether someone is currently a River, Rock, or Ruby.

I defined personal purpose through three key criteria:

- **Develop:** Evolving your personal values
- **Define:** Clarifying your identity and intentions
- **Decide:** Aligning your actions with meaning

When you develop, define, and decide your personal purpose—when you continuously evolve what matters most, clearly understand who you aim to become, and align your daily actions accordingly—it can help to become a foundational layer of meaningful wisdom generation and transfer.

Importantly, your personal purpose is never static. It evolves and is shaped by whether you currently identify as a River, Rock, or Ruby. Recognizing how purpose alters across your era stages helps you understand how and when to amplify wisdom.

That's why *The Future of Work Is Gold (feat. The Purpose Effect)* is a catchy way to assimilate all components of the Wisdom Wheel as a leadership tool. In this section, we'll explore how personal purpose evolves through one's River–Rock–Ruby career-eras continuum, influences wisdom generation and sharing, and integrates with the other four Wisdom Wheel components.

Chip Conley, author and founder of the Modern Elder Academy—the world's first midlife wisdom school—defines wisdom as "metabolized experience shared with others." I have my own take, one that connects directly to purpose: *Wisdom is when your purpose is expressed, experienced, and exchanged.*

What does this mean in practice?

- **Expressed:** Purpose gives clarity to your intentions, making your wisdom both credible and meaningful to others.

- **Experienced:** Purpose shapes your experiences, which then influences your insights and personal growth towards wisdom.

- **Exchanged:** Purpose ensures that wisdom is not kept to yourself—when shared intentionally and meaningfully, it can create a lasting impact.

When I sat down for dinner in March 2025 with Henry Mintzberg of McGill University—arguably one of the GOATs of management thinking—he shared an insight that deeply resonated with me. He suggested that organizations not only help themselves but also provide significant benefits to society by intentionally employing Rubies. When older team members are asked to actively contribute their wisdom, these Rubies get the opportunity to instill purpose and meaning in their lives. This engagement offers cognitive, social, and physical benefits, which can slow down or even prevent various forms of decline. There is a clear societal advantage to this outcome, as hospitals, care centres, and families may not need to confront issues that could arise sooner.

Research directly supports Mintzberg's sage point. In 2024, through a landmark 28-year prospective study, Florida State University researchers proved that a higher sense of purpose positively impacts cognitive health. Specifically, for every standard deviation increase in purpose among adults aged 63 to 70, there was approximately a 20 percent reduced likelihood of dementia measured 8 to 17 years later. Moreover, in that same study, researchers proved that higher purpose scores predicted significantly slower declines in episodic memory and mental status, suggesting that purpose directly sustains cognitive vitality later in life.

> **Integrating purpose with wisdom is more than a corporate culture party trick; it demonstrates that you genuinely care for your team members.** It enhances their professional contribution and personal well-being, and it benefits society at large. Purpose for the win—again!

But purpose-driven wisdom is not just about Rubies. Let's not forget the Rocks and Rivers. Every career persona can contribute uniquely to wisdom generation and transfer:

- **Rivers:** Purpose through *curiosity*—sharing new ideas and insights.

- **Rocks:** Purpose through *reliability*—sharing pragmatic thoughts and solutions.

- **Rubies:** Purpose through *reflection*—sharing more profound and proficient wisdom.

By aligning each era's purpose definition with the Wisdom Wheel components, you can see how it might help in the exchange of wisdom, the crux of this track:

- **Mentor:** Personal purpose enriches mentoring relationships and ensures that wisdom conversations are meaningful and relevant.

- **Collaborate:** Personal purpose ensures that any organizational, team, or individual exchanges are complemented by wisdom.

- **Capture:** Personal purpose helps capture authentic, relevant, timely, and actionable wisdom.

- **Renew:** Personal purpose drives your continuous development in the pursuit of growing wisdom.

With the conceptual groundwork now laid, it's time to get practical. Let's explore two tactics that I believe will help you assist your team members as they leverage purpose as a strategic catalyst for wisdom generation and exchange.

The Declaration of Purpose

Encourage every individual—River, Rock, or Ruby—to craft their own personal purpose statement—a declaration. You should take this action as well. Invite team members to succinctly reflect on the following:

- **Develop:** How have my personal values evolved, and what more is needed?

- **Define:** How do I describe my sense of self—who I am?

- **Decide:** How do I want to be known by others, now and in the future?

Next, have each team member articulate a concise, meaningful Declaration of Purpose—ideally, no more than two lines. In over a decade of working with leaders and teams on purpose, I have found this simple act profoundly clarifies individual clarity and confidence. With a clear definition of purpose, the creation and exchange of wisdom become natural extensions of everyday actions.

For context, my own Declaration of Purpose is this: We're not here to see through each other; we're here to see each other through.

The Purpose Pulse Check

Building directly from the Declaration of Purpose, the Purpose Pulse Check is a quarterly or self-defined regular practice designed to sustain purposeful wisdom alignment and relevance. Regularly prompt your team members with two targeted questions:

- **Current alignment:** What recent insight feels most meaningful for you to share with the team right now?

- **Strategic application:** How would sharing this insight specifically benefit your colleagues, our team, or the broader organization?

CONSISTENTLY USING these two tactics reinforces the integration of purposeful wisdom across all career personas, supporting practical execution across the other four Wisdom Wheel components: mentor, collaborate, capture, and renew. It would be wise to ask yourself these questions as well.

GOLDEN NUGGETS

"As I Wind Down the Pines" of the Wisdom Wheel (if you know, you know), here are the essential Golden Nuggets from Track 8 to help you put wisdom into action for you and your team.

Golden Nugget #1: Wisdom Is Oxygen

Wisdom is like oxygen—remove it, and your team will suffocate. If you are not intentional about wisdom capture, generation, and transfer, there will be an inevitability of Age Debt in your future.

Golden Nugget #2: Mentoring Is a Two-Way Street

If you think mentorship is solely about older Rubies lecturing to younger Rivers, you have missed the point. Mentorship is golden—the mutual exchange of insight, curiosity, and knowledge, regardless of who sits on either side of the interchange.

Golden Nugget #3: Wisdom Loves Company

Collaboration is not about forcing different personas into a room to pretend they get along. To collaborate is to ensure Rivers, Rocks, and Rubies are engaged in purposeful dialogue, where each persona understands the value of exchanging wisdom.

Golden Nugget #4: Capture Wisdom Before the Goodbye Party

If you wait until your Rubies announce their retirement to begin capturing their wisdom—or after an unexpected River or Rock resignation notice—you are committing leadership malpractice. Put systems in place so wisdom stays put, even if your team doesn't.

Golden Nugget #5: To Renew Is to Be Wise

You must constantly think about how your team members can continuously learn, reflect, and interact with one another, as this is the essence of wisdom. And wisdom is not static. It has to be renewed incessantly, remaining omnipresent in its relevance.

Golden Nugget #6: Purpose Is the Drumbeat of Wisdom

Wisdom without purpose is like Pearl Jam without Eddie Vedder. When your team members are clear on their personal purpose—what drives them, shapes them, and moves them, the beat that anchors their every song—the wisdom they share becomes strategically meaningful, authentic, and indisputably impactful.

Longevity Lens

B**ack at MapleCo,** CEO Marla Benson and the Age Debt Tiger Team have begun laying the groundwork for the Experience Dividend, but significant Age Debt challenges remain.

Initiatives being implemented from within the Career Canvas (like their talent and career marketplace, CrossPaths) and the Wisdom Wheel (Maple Staples, for knowledge capture and sharing) have helped build adaptive career pathways while facilitating essential knowledge exchange. But Benson knows it is not enough. Without addressing longevity—the third vital pillar of the Experience Dividend triad—their transition out of Age Debt risks stalling.

Imagine Coldplay releasing their greatest hits album and omitting the crowd favourite "Clocks." It would never happen. You would feel as if something was missing. Let's consider "Clocks" as similar to the idea of longevity. This is why the Longevity Lens is an essential track from the Experience Dividend. Is your organization underestimating—if not misjudging—its multi-dimensional longevity challenges? This could prove to be a costly mistake.

So, what is the Longevity Lens?

The Longevity Lens is an organizational framework that proactively establishes conditions for Rivers, Rocks, and Rubies to thrive at every age and stage. It is based on the understanding that an organization's workforce will age over time and encompass a wider age range. It addresses five crucial aspects of age in the workplace:

culture, leadership, financial clarity, well-being, and workplace design. It outlines what leaders must do differently to promote and adopt longevity. I define the Longevity Lens as follows: workplace conditions that enable every age to thrive.

Look no further than Westpac, Australia's oldest bank, for signs of what to do. It didn't earn its longevity badge by accident. Faced with over 20 percent of its workforce surpassing the 50-year age threshold, Westpac launched an integrated set of initiatives to embed longevity into its organizational culture. Their strategy was both cohesive and humane. The bank's overarching longevity program—50PLUS—was no token gesture. For example, team members who approached traditional retirement ages were offered phased retirement pathways (similar to those mentioned in Track 7 at BCLC and the Mayo Clinic). These provided thoughtful transitions for long-tenured Rubies that respected both their institutional wisdom and their personal ambitions. The bank also introduced tailored "Create Your Future" workshops in partnership with specific career-transition experts. The workshops helped guide older team members through critical discussions and considerations—finances, health, identity—so they could define their next act clearly and confidently.

What else? Westpac decided to focus on well-being. For example, flexible leave arrangements, including an innovative "grandparental leave" program, recognized that caregiving may not end when children move out. Furthermore, resources such as the Eldercare Kit provided tangible support for stressors faced by Westpac team members who might be juggling eldercare responsibilities. Even Westpac's physical and digital work environments received an age-conscious overhaul. Through the launch of its "Design for Dignity" charter, Westpac revamped physical workspaces to improve accessibility, comfort, and ease of use. It conducted ergonomic assessments and launched digital tools that boosted productivity and team member satisfaction.

The results? Westpac reported significant improvements in overall employee engagement and an increase in their Organisational Health Index, which placed them in the global top quartile in 2024.

While these figures also reflect broader cultural initiatives, Westpac's integrated approach to longevity—including well-being programs and age-inclusive leadership training—shows the difference a proactive approach to longevity can have on an organization. The firm's foresight shows that organizational success and employee longevity are deeply intertwined.

The concept of retirement is in the midst of a complete transformation. The old script—learn, work, retire—no longer applies. Lynda Gratton and Andrew Scott, writing in *MIT Sloan Management Review*, describe a multi-stage life, one defined by reinvention, learning, and evolving purpose over time. Some Rivers are starting earlier, while others are delaying the commencement to full-time work. Rocks are adjusting midstream in the messy middle, while many Rubies wish to stay employed long past 65; sometimes by choice, often by necessity. The Longevity Lens helps organizations respond to this changing dynamic with tactics tailored to the new expectations of a rapidly changing workforce.

Longevity Lens

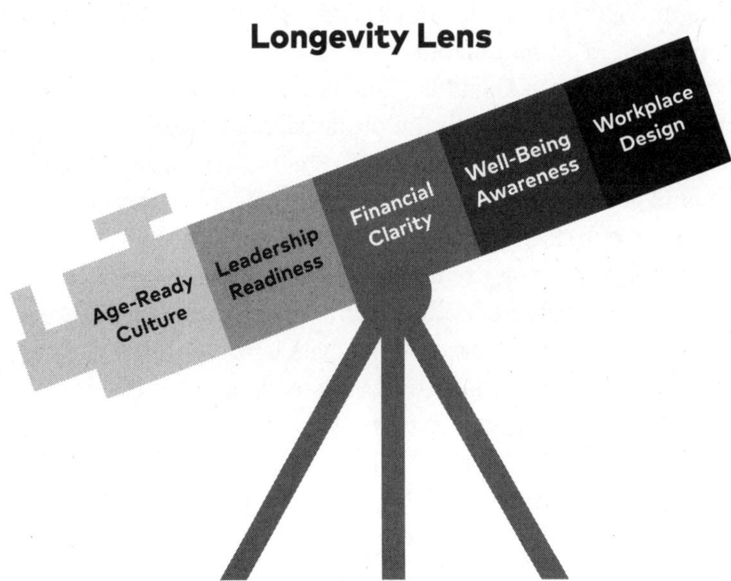

The Longevity Lens has five essential components:

- **Age-ready culture:** Are your organization's values, behaviours, and processes inclusive of all ages, to harness the strengths of Rivers, Rocks, and Rubies?

- **Leadership readiness:** Are you equipping team members and leaders so they can effectively lead and operate from an age-positive perspective?

- **Financial clarity:** Are you offering financial planning education and information to reduce anxiety during key River–Rock–Ruby–Retirement stage transitions?

- **Well-being awareness:** Are you addressing your team members' physical, emotional, and mental health in the context of age-related matters?

- **Workplace design:** Are you adapting your organization's physical and digital work environments to accommodate age-related differences?

In Ralph Waldo Emerson's 1841 classic essay "Circles," he writes, "People wish to be settled; only as far as they are unsettled is there any hope for them." He adds, "Life is a series of surprises. We do not guess today the mood, the pleasure, the power of tomorrow, when we are building up our being." Emerson suggests something profound here: Continuous evolution and discomfort are central to growth and purpose.

Leaders must recognize that their role is to create environments where every River, Rock, and Ruby is supported through each phase of their evolving careers and even in their lives. That's why the Longevity Lens is imperative. Your team members want you to genuinely care about their journey. This mindset is at the heart of the Longevity Lens.

Remember, everyone ages—including you.

Leveraging the Longevity Lens is a vital aspect of the Experience Dividend triad. With the Career Canvas and the Wisdom Wheel, it completes the trilogy. Organizations, teams, and leaders that understand and apply its five longevity principles will sustain long-term success while implementing a vibrant, thriving, purpose-driven, and all-ages workplace.

Paying homage to another Coldplay greatest hits album classic, the Longevity Lens will indeed "Fix You" to become a longevity leader. As Emerson suggests, let's get "unsettled" with the first component: age-ready culture.

Age-Ready Culture

The MapleCo Age Debt Tiger Team is still trying to figure out how to embed longevity into the organization's cultural fabric. They know it's essential, but they're not quite there yet. The challenge for you and your team is the same: *How will age inclusivity be incorporated into all aspects of your culture?*

Age-ready culture is straightforward. You must integrate age inclusion into the everyday fabric of your workplace norms, communication processes, and operational practices to ensure the entire spectrum of your Rivers, Rocks, and Rubies is equally valued. All without the trope of boxing people into generations. Age diversity should be as natural as breathing. No symbolic gestures, ageist language lurking in memos, or perfunctory attempts at inclusion—just a seamless tapestry of Rivers, Rocks, and Rubies working together.

So, how do you build an age-ready culture? Four practical tactics will embed age inclusivity firmly within your organization's cultural DNA.

Promote Age-Inclusive Language

Remove any age bias from your organization's vocabulary and daily interactions. Ageist language—such as references to "digital natives," "fresh perspectives," "generations," or calling Rubies "old school"—creates unnecessary and unwanted division.

Review your enterprise-wide collateral—communications, educational materials, handbooks, and so on—to ensure all of it is age inclusive. Make the necessary modifications if it seems out of touch. Review your digital strategy and processes, be it your intranet, collaboration platform (e.g., Slack and Teams), or email habits, and look for tone-deaf language across the age eras. Launch training programs that sensitize team members and leaders to age-related communication and collaboration biases. Help them learn language and behaviours that value experience across all ages. Include examples of extended careers, phased retirements, mentoring instances, boomerangs, and returnships—many of the components from the Career Canvas—in your training programs and various corporate communications.

While the Career Canvas is a fluid model of age-neutral role changes, it does not cover ageism in the recruitment cycle. Another task is to assess and modify how your organization promotes and recruits talent. Are your current approaches disregarding one era over another?

For example, Imperial London Hotels struggled to attract workers after the pandemic. As with many hotels globally, its employee population dropped from over 1,200 workers to only 125. The company revamped job descriptions in its employment ads to attract older candidates. The hotel replaced words like "energetic" and "vibrant" with more inclusive language, such as "experienced" and "customer focused." This led to a higher recruitment of Ruby workers.

Sandra Nunes, head of people and development at the family-run hotel, said, "I realized that more mature people could be the answer to our prayers, but I had to change minds internally first because young people have always been the mainstay of the hospitality trade."

Words matter, and so does your culture. Make yours inclusive, intentional, and impactful.

Codify Multi-Persona Leadership Competencies

While age-inclusive language is a good first step, it's a bit like when a band performs a soundcheck before a concert. Without the soundcheck, you're unsure how the band will sound that night. The next logical step—the actual concert in this analogy—is to codify multi-era competencies into your existing cultural leadership framework.

Age inclusivity demands clear expectations and standards. Leadership models typically detail competencies or attributes like strategic thinking, innovation, and collaboration, but age inclusivity seldom appears as an explicit criterion. In my research, I have not encountered a single organization that codifies multi-era competencies into its leadership model.

> **One simple suggestion: Change this.**
> **Clearly outline multi-persona leadership competencies.**

For example, how will leaders demonstrate support for phased retirements, equitable mentoring opportunities, or other facets of the Career Canvas and Wisdom Wheel if age-impartial thinking is not ingrained in your leadership culture?

To combat such a plight, leaders should integrate age-related competencies directly into their leadership model. You might even take it a step further and add it to your developmental reviews. Leaders who consistently demonstrate inclusive management across age lines—such as successfully integrating Rubies into mentoring programs or developing Rivers and Rocks via targeted learning—will provide their career and the organization with a great outcome.

A 2024 study across Belgium and the United States revealed several benefits of age-inclusive leadership competencies in organizations, providing an interesting corollary to my point. When a well-defined and integrated age-inclusive leadership competency model is actioned, it will create a host of positive organizational outcomes, such as increased employee motivation, enhanced engagement, and better intergenerational connections. The researchers also discovered that when leaders are expected to manage age diversity, organizations achieve better retention, morale, and collaboration within age-diverse teams.

Age inclusivity should become overt within your organization's leadership model. In the process, it will reinforce the cultural expectations of an Experience Dividend mindset.

Implement Age-Inclusive Hiring Practices

The example at Imperial London Hotels also provides a clue about your hiring and promotion practices. If you know the talent age range is shifting—and your River talent pool will eventually decrease—you should systematically revise your hiring and promotion processes, focusing on removing all explicit age biases, including those that lurk beneath the surface. Revising your language is the first step; the second is rethinking your hiring and promotion behaviours.

For example, consider shifting to blind hiring processes, where you evaluate candidates based purely on skills and achievements without clues about age. Ensure that your recruiters (and you, as a hiring manager) actively seek diverse age profiles, debunking myths around "overqualification" or limited innovation capacity among older Rubies. Retrain your managers so they don't exclude Rivers or Rocks from consideration because they think they are too young or underqualified. While younger hires may not have role competence, they may have transferrable skills and a high aptitude for learning that you are overlooking. Implementing blind hiring practices can significantly reduce age-related biases. This approach fosters inclusivity by focusing on capability rather than chronology.

In addition, you should review your promotion criteria and processes. Too often, implicit age biases exclude Rivers from leadership roles because of perceived inexperience. Similarly, delaying or preventing promotions for Rocks and Rubies under the misguided assumption that they are "already at their peak" or "past their prime" is unwise. Develop clear, age-neutral competencies and performance indicators to ensure promotions focus solely on capability, skills, achievements, and potential, regardless of age.

Age Diversity Recognition

Age diversity can thrive and flourish when your organization celebrates it intentionally. Rather than a once-a-year generic recognition strategy—planting a tree because someone hit a 10-year milestone is nice but insufficient—regularly spotlight contributions from Rivers, Rocks, and Rubies. Publicly recognize prominent examples that emphasize the ongoing contributions of Rivers and Rocks and the lasting wisdom, insights, or deliverables of Rubies. Include, not exclude!

This may be an even easier tactic to achieve when you sponsor the rollout of an open platform. For instance, UK-based aerospace company Rolls-Royce Holdings implemented various initiatives to promote inclusion across its entire workforce. In one called Being Like Me, team members could share personal stories on one of the company's collaboration platforms. By sharing their stories, team members openly reveal their backgrounds and individual circumstances. This improves understanding among the firm's River, Rock, and Ruby colleagues.

You might consider implementing a similar approach in your organization. You could also introduce different initiatives—such as a regular "people spotlight" session or dedicated segments within existing team meetings—to share stories of team-member successes (or hiccups) across all age brackets. When your celebrations and recognitions become regular, authentic, and integral to your cultural norms, age diversity will transform from mere rhetoric into something you've always done.

Measure What Matters

Management legend Peter Drucker once wrote, "Work implies not only that somebody is supposed to do the job, but also accountability, a deadline and, finally, the measurement of results—that is, feedback from results on the work and on the planning process itself." MapleCo took Drucker's words to heart.

The tiger team recommended launching an online dashboard called Maple Metrics that tracks age diversity in recruitment, promotion, and retention criteria. Leaders are now tasked with reviewing their talent data segmented by River, Rock, and Ruby talent brackets. (Team members self-classify their persona, by the way.) MapleCo has also decided to link age diversity to performance reviews to drive accountability further. Leaders who effectively manage age inclusion earn credibility; those who overlook it will face difficult performance evaluation conversations in the future.

The launch of Maple Metrics is helping longevity remain front and centre and a business priority, not an aspirational ideal. It may also be a tactic that you consider for your team or organization.

Embedding an age-ready culture is the first step. You must be willing to make changes, manage them, and measure your performance. Hold others accountable. However, culture alone cannot sustain the Longevity Lens. As a leader, you need to step up, as do the leaders you may be leading on your team. Let me explain what to do next.

Leadership Readiness

Much like your organization, MapleCo must ensure that leadership readiness is addressed at three distinct levels for the Longevity Lens to materialize:

- **Macro:** Clear commitments from senior leadership

- **Meso:** Equipping mid-level leaders with explicit Experience Dividend actions

- **Micro:** Frontline actions that reinforce an age-inclusive workplace

Only deliberate leadership readiness across these three levels will make the Longevity Lens a sustainable component of the Experience Dividend. Let's first address a few macro considerations.

Macro Senior Leadership Considerations

If senior leaders believe the Longevity Lens emanates from an HR handbook, your efforts are already sunk. Longevity leadership requires clarity from the top. Executive leadership teams, executive committees, and boards need to own longevity publicly. Consider the Commonwealth of Massachusetts.

In 2021, the state, which encompasses vibrant areas such as Cape Cod, Plymouth, and Cambridge, faced the stark reality of a rapidly aging public sector workforce. Fast-forward to 2022. Massachusetts became the first state government in the United States to be certified as an Age-Friendly Employer. Through several public engagements, the governor at the time, Charlie Baker, publicly reinforced the administration's intentional stance towards workforce longevity. Baker insisted that the certification was critical to the Commonwealth's strategic agenda. That same philosophy continues. The Commonwealth's Age-Friendly Massachusetts Action Plan "serves as the state's multiyear plan to make the Commonwealth, as a whole, more age-friendly."

The Massachusetts example illustrates why clarity around longevity at senior leader and board level is crucial. Your senior executives and board members (if you have them) should consider several macro-level commitments:

- **Longevity commitments:** Require the CEO and senior executives to publicly articulate longevity goals. The objective is to reinforce age inclusivity as a strategic priority rather than a meek HR initiative.

- **Board-level accountability:** No different than, for example, the finance sub-committee, include age-diversity and longevity goals as a standing agenda item at board meetings—at least one per year—to ensure board oversight for strategic progress.

- **Executive-level metrics:** Incorporate longevity indicators—such as age-diverse hiring, retention of Ruby employees, and leadership development programs—into executive targets and performance evaluations. You may even consider linking senior compensation and career progression to these outcomes.

- **Transparent reporting:** Share the organization's longevity progress and challenges with your stakeholders both within and outside the organization. This will underscore senior leadership's accountability and reinforce your organizational commitment to the Experience Dividend.

With clear senior-level commitments and explicit board oversight, longevity can shift from an abstract aspiration into a concrete strategy. After all, leadership starts at the top.

Meso Mid-Level Leadership Considerations

While the C-suite, senior executives, and board provide the Longevity Lens's rhythm, your mid-level Rock and Ruby leaders sing the melody. Without these leaders taking a key role, your Experience Dividend risks becoming background music. The dreadful kind: Muzak.

Marla Benson realized rather quickly after the tiger team presented their Age Debt findings that not only did longevity lack senior-level commitment—it had never been discussed at a board meeting, for example—but MapleCo's mid-level leaders did not fully understand their pivotal role either. The solution depended on embedding the Career Canvas and Wisdom Wheel principles into their daily managerial playbook. MapleCo began equipping mid-level Rocks and Rubies with clear guidance and retraining directly rooted in these two foundational frameworks. Benson greenlit the introduction of a targeted education program, Mind the Gap, which articulated the roles leaders were expected to fulfill.

Post-training, mid-level leaders began using CrossPaths, MapleCo's internal Career Canvas Marketplace, to transparently post gigs, short-term Spark Up assignments, and Move Laterally opportunities.

This empowered Rocks and Rubies to operationalize senior leadership's vision by facilitating a multidirectional career movement and intentionally matching MapleCo talent with evolving business needs. Leaders were also instructed to leverage Maple Staples—a Wisdom Wheel initiative—by proactively capturing institutional wisdom from soon-to-retire Rubies through structured mentoring and wisdom exchange sessions. The mandate was clear: Integrate wisdom sharing into everyday leadership practices so essential knowledge was not exchanged accidentally or informally but systematically.

Consider the following tactics for your mid-level leaders:

- **Anchor expectations to the Career Canvas:** Equip mid-level leaders to regularly use your internal job marketplace (similar to CrossPaths) to promote fluid, multidirectional career moves for Rivers, Rocks, and Rubies alike.

- **Operationalize the Wisdom Wheel:** Hold mid-level leaders accountable for systematic use of the Wisdom Wheel, emphasizing structured mentoring (mentor), intentional collaboration (collaborate), deliberate wisdom capture (capture), and continuous growth and development opportunities (renew).

- **Embed age-ready culture practices:** Ensure leaders champion age-inclusive communication practices while confronting and actively removing biases that might discourage Rivers, Rocks, or Rubies from contributing in meaningful ways. Mind the gap!

Only when mid-level leaders understand and own their responsibilities within the Career Canvas and Wisdom Wheel frameworks can the Experience Dividend be accomplished. It is your role—and that of all leaders leading other leaders—to make it happen.

Micro Frontline Leadership Considerations

Suppose senior executives and board members provide the rhythm to the Longevity Lens, and mid-level leaders sing its melody. Sounds good; but we still need individual contributors and frontline leaders to play the part of longevity harmony singers. This happens through daily micro-actions that repel various ageism factors. Without it, the

Experience Dividend could remain a wishful organizational aspiration. A terribly off-key song, even.

MapleCo's Age Debt Tiger Team recognized that lasting change requires simple yet intentional behaviour changes among frontline team members. The team recommended launching a toolkit named Everyday Age, which outlines tangible actions that any team member—including frontline leaders—could incorporate to combat ageism. For example, frontline leaders were instructed to initiate brief monthly Age Dialogues with their Rivers, Rocks, and Rubies—short, focused conversations to uncover specific developmental or team integration opportunities aligned directly with the Career Canvas. These dialogue sessions were a 10- to 15-minute segment inserted into a team's typical group meeting sequence. The frontline leaders were also taught how to amplify lesser-heard voices, including drawing Rivers' perspectives during meetings or inviting Rubies to share their historical insights from similar projects or past challenges. Individual contributors also received guidance on addressing subtle age biases that emerge during daily interactions. For example, team members received scenario-based, 60-second micro-learning video modules sent to their mobile phones called Bias Breakers to help them recognize their unconscious age biases in everyday interactions. The MapleCo L&D team introduced Perspective Pairings as part of CrossPaths: informal monthly 30-minute meetups that paired Rivers, Rocks, and Rubies to build empathy and dispel misconceptions rooted in age differences.

Consider implementing the following micro-level leadership actions:

- **Intentional check-ins:** Coach frontline leaders to hold regular, structured "age dialogues" tailored around Career Canvas opportunities to foster multidirectional career growth and open discussion.

- **Bias-spotting training:** Equip frontline leaders and individual contributors with practical skills to recognize and address age biases through micro-learning moments and coaching opportunities.

- **Mentor and collaborate moments:** Reinforce the Wisdom Wheel principles by intentionally embedding mentoring exchanges and collaboration opportunities into team practices so cross-generational wisdom flows more naturally and not by chance.

Only when longevity actions become part of everyone's daily rhythm will one's leadership readiness genuinely move from aspiration to reality.

Next up is the oft-overlooked longevity aspect of financial clarity.

Financial Clarity

One of my most loathed corporate phrases is "do more with less." I reserve a special frown for CFOs and other senior executives who invoke the term in an attempt to cut costs but increase performance. It rarely works.

The phrase takes on a troubling new relevance when viewed through the Longevity Lens. People are living longer (*Hooray!*) but are financially ill prepared for it (*Boo!*).

> **Without proactive steps, many Rivers, Rocks, and Rubies will face the daunting reality of stretching insufficient savings across increasingly lengthy retirements. Age Debt is terrible, but Age Death is worse. Therefore, I say, "Death to 'Do more with less'!"**

If you recall from Side A, there are myriad financial issues that workers are grappling with, be it inadequate retirement savings, the rising cost of living, and so on. How did it get to this? That's a fab question, and the full answer is not the purpose of this book. But if you wish to cash in the Experience Dividend, I am pretty passionate about how leaders and organizations must step up and help fill this financial clarity gap.

The following tactics should be considered:

Teach Financial Fluency

Stop pretending young Rivers magically become finance savvy the day they leave campus and knock on your organization's front door—physical or virtual. Universities and colleges do not teach this life skill. Instead, embed financial literacy into onboarding and your early talent development programs. You might even consider a voluntary financial fluency training module. Equip your Rivers from day one of hiring to navigate their financial future—so they don't drown later when faced with real-life costs like housing, caregiving, and retirement planning. A financially fluent River becomes a confident, loyal Rock and eventually a well-prepared Ruby. (Even if they don't stick with you forever.)

Personalized Tools

No one wants to face the sobering reality of retirement alone. Even irreverent rock'n'roll legend Billy Mack learned that lesson in the classic holiday film *Love Actually*. Provide interactive planning tools backed by reputable partners that let Rocks and Rubies visualize their personal financial trajectory. Think of it as Apple Maps for retirement planning. You may even partner with a bank or credit union. The goal is not to scare your employees; it's to help them make informed financial decisions and eliminate nasty surprises as they face down life's curveballs.

Normalize Financial Check-Ins

Instead of awkwardly tapping around financial topics (like at an eighth-grade school dance when the slow song comes on), encourage your frontline leaders to integrate financial discussions naturally. For example, regular "clarity conversations" can be brief, casual check-ins, ensuring Rocks and Rubies are not secretly stewing in financial anxiety. You could even extend these to Rivers if you think that would be helpful. It's not to pry or moonlight as a financial advisor. It's simply a connection point so that the team members know, first, that you care and, second, how to find more reliable resources not named you.

Offer Practical Financial Mentorship

Formalize financial mentorship opportunities within your Wisdom Wheel model to connect Rivers (and Rocks) with financially savvy Rubies (and Rocks). This is a mentorship chance with a practical, personal, and economic twist. Just imagine one of the conversations in Canada: "Hey, how'd you figure out that RESP [Registered Education Savings Plan] thing again? Do I really care about saving for my kid's university tuition now?" Rather than vague platitudes, financial mentorship conversations become real, tangible exchanges of financial life lessons learned—sometimes the hard way—so your younger talent can avoid painful financial potholes down the road. (And, in the example of RESPs, get free money from Canada's federal government.)

Targeted, Just-in-Time Financial Learning

Let's be honest: A generic lunch-and-learn won't solve your team members' financial anxieties. Instead, personalize short, relevant financial-learning modules tailored explicitly to significant life milestones—first home, parental leave, caregiving, approaching retirement, and so on. Deliver this targeted learning via mobile-friendly videos or quick micro-learning nudges directly aligned with each career stage or situation on your version of the Career Canvas. Because one-size-fits-all financial education is like a one-hit wonder—quickly forgotten and rarely helpful.

And finally, why am I worried enough about financial clarity to include it in the Longevity Lens? Enter Exhibit A via the World Economic Forum: "By 2050, there will be 2.1 billion people over 60 years old, and most people globally will outlive their retirement savings by between 8 and almost 20 years." I urge you to be equally anxious.

Well-Being Awareness

Organizations give themselves their own version of a Grammy by sending out well-being surveys, installing beanbag chairs, offering EFAP (employee and family assistance program) packages, or announcing a "mental health awareness day" like Bell's "Let's Talk" campaign. But ask team members from those organizations whether they have explicitly been questioned about how their menopause experience or chronic health conditions affect their productivity or if caregiving stress is keeping them awake at night. The answers start to become foggier than the pyrotechnics at a Nickelback concert.

When I was in my twenties and thirties—even my forties—I never really knew what a colonoscopy was. I mean, I knew *what* it was, but I had no idea what it entailed. If you're younger than 50, why should you? Going into my first colonoscopy appointment, after I had figured out what it was, I was as nervous as I'd been at my first high-school dance. That apprehension started about two weeks before the procedure. Did it affect my performance at work? Undeniably.

When my infinitely better half, Denise, was diagnosed with menopause, a host of wellness issues outlined by the doctor began to make sense (e.g., hot flashes, insomnia, fatigue, mood swings, brain fog, anxiety, extra impatience of her husband). Did it affect her performance at work? Undeniably.

Well-being tied specifically to age-related issues needs a rethink across the River, Rock, and Ruby spectrum. Generic organizational wellness programs and openness continue to fall short when faced with life's messy realities, such as menopause or an upcoming colonoscopy. And there are a host of additional issues to consider concerning a team member's well-being, such as mid-career stressors stemming from increased workload and burnout or even the anxiety young Rivers face when financial pressures stack up. (See "financial clarity" from the previous subsection.) It's time for leaders to act.

For example, on the topic of menopause, Marks & Spencer (M&S) got specific—and serious—about this vital but oft-overlooked wellness issue. Since over 70 percent of their UK workforce are women and, according to M&S HR director Sarah Findlater, 70 percent of them will experience menopause, the company decided not to settle for blanket wellness webinars. Instead, they fostered a supportive environment through a large Menopause Network, a founding partnership with GenM, and a dedicated microsite offering resources and tips. The company also gave managers explicit guidance on flexible scheduling tailored for symptoms such as insomnia and fatigue.

Remember Aviva, that leading UK insurer? Way back in 2018, the company recognized that it had an aging workforce to contend with: Nearly a third of its 17,000 employees were over 45. Concerned about losing critical experience and skill sets, Aviva launched its Mid-Life MOT. This structured initiative provides mid-career employees with a reality check around wealth, work, and well-being, helping them to rethink their futures and improve financial and wellness clarity. The check-ins help Aviva's mid-career Rocks take stock—getting them to open up about their financial, career, and wellness realities. With seminars, one-to-one financial planning sessions, and plenty of digital tools at hand, the Mid-Life MOT creates clarity instead of confusion. Aviva recognizes that such conversations can feel awkward, but because the company has normalized these reviews, it not only extends the careers of its team members but also sharpens its competitive edge with a healthier, wiser, multi-generational workforce.

These examples from M&S and Aviva are strategic moves that acknowledge age-related realities head-on. Well-being isn't a once-a-year checkbox. It must be regarded as an ongoing commitment to address the very specific, nuanced, and evolving health needs that directly impact every River, Rock, and Ruby you lead. It is going to help your bottom line, too.

If you have not yet started, this is a great moment to reflect:

How well does my organization understand age-specific well-being, and what steps am I taking to address it?

Consider the following tactics to kick off that meaningful and necessary conversation.

Caregiver-First

Adopt a "caregiver-first" policy. Such an act recognizes the unique challenges faced by mid-career Rocks, leaders and individual contributors who are often forced to juggle the responsibilities of raising their children while caring for aging parents. The policy offers caregiver-friendly work adjustments, specialized leave options, and direct managerial support to ease the caregiving burden. The ultimate goal is to help lower the stress and burnout that often comes with this Sandwich Generation balancing act.

Hilton's "Care for All" initiative is a perfect proof point. It equips team members to handle their caregiving challenges by providing straightforward, actionable resources, from podcasts and articles to online learning. Hilton also backs this with dedicated leave policies, caregiving concierge support, and (impressively) focused manager training. The company's approach signals to its individual contributors and leaders that looking after young children or elderly parents is integral to organizational culture.

Recharge Days

What if you were to authorize a "recharge day" that team members can use as they see fit? Some firms already have such a scheme—known as "well-being days"—but if your organization doesn't, you could institute it on your own, outside of HR. The day (or days—I recommend three per year) allows team members across all age groups to proactively focus on preventative wellness activities, such as annual screenings like colonoscopies, wellness checkups, fitness assessments, and mental health days. Maybe someone wants to use it to take their child to their first day of school or move them into their university residence. Whatever the case, and unlike typical PTO or sick leave, these recharge days highlight your proactive approach to well-being while directly tackling age-sensitive health and well-being needs.

Menopause-Specific Accommodations

Given that the Menopause Foundation of Canada's 2022 research revealed that over 75 percent of working women felt that their employer was not supportive of menopausal conditions, it's time—once and for all—to launch a menopause-specific policy. Ensure the policy includes accommodations that allow women to opt for flexible scheduling, temperature adjustments, or remote work arrangements when they experience symptoms that impact their wellness. In doing so, you demonstrate genuine empathy for those navigating this noteworthy life transition and, at times, considerable health impact.

Much like the groundbreaking example of M&S, in 2022, HSBC UK also launched a policy focused on menopause that offered several layers of support, including temperature-controlled workspaces, flexible hours, and comprehensive training on menopause awareness. The bank's actions decreased menopause-related absenteeism and boosted workplace morale while increasing organizational understanding of menopause-related health challenges. You can do the same.

Team Wellness Norms

There is no book I have written where the concept of "team norms" does not appear. This one is no different. I urge you to collaboratively establish team wellness norms, guidelines that define clear expectations around work hours, response times, and after-hours communication. For example, teams might agree to norms like "No email responses after 6 pm," "Mandatory 15- or 30-minute breaks between meetings," "No texts on weekends," and designated "meeting-free-afternoon Fridays." Whatever the team wellness norms are, your job is to quarterback and remember to incorporate age-sensitive considerations, such as flexible breaks for chronic-condition management or accommodating midlife health screenings. Establishing explicit team wellness norms will foster accountability and respect for your Rivers, Rocks, and Rubies' diverse health needs.

Reality Checks

Implement structured, confidential reality checks separate from performance reviews. These are periodic conversations designed to provide a safe, judgment-free space for team members to discuss personal and professional challenges related to age and life stage: caregiving responsibilities, health transitions, mid-career stress, age-related anxieties, or anything in between. You may choose to have the discussion yourself with a team member, or a professional could be hired as part of the idea.

For instance, at the request of their younger River team members, Synchrony Financial offered team members across the age spectrum regular access to confidential, onsite therapy sessions. Employees use the sessions as proactive check-ins, allowing them to openly discuss wellness and mental health issues before these affect their productivity or well-being. The program significantly alleviated stress-related challenges and absenteeism.

Similarly, at MapleCo, the Age Debt Tiger Team piloted a Reality Check-In launch with the finance team. They brought in a registered psychologist once a quarter whose job was simply to make themself available for open, private dialogue. The conversations—where several young Rivers, mid-career Rocks, and older Rubies disclosed previously hidden stressors—led the leaders of finance to create a few personalized accommodations, resources, and flexible work arrangements for certain team members. Marla Benson is considering expanding the pilot company-wide next fiscal year.

Workplace Design

Foreseeing Japan's demographic crisis, Toyota recognized its aging workers brought irreplaceable craftsmanship but would soon impose physical limitations on the company's traditional assembly lines. In response, the company launched its Super Skill assembly line, a re-engineered workspace for Ruby workers. The company's changes included gravity-assisted tools, adjustable workstations, and ergonomic seating (raku-raku chairs). Toyota made these modifications to decrease the potential physical strain experienced by older Rubies on the lines. The adjustments aimed to prevent possible injuries, too. In addition, the company paired these physical adjustments with simplified digital interfaces and accessibility enhancements to ensure that its older workers encountered fewer technological barriers. Toyota's Super Skill strategy permitted its Rubies—some returning through boomerang roles (remember the Career Canvas)—to continue contributing their invaluable skills and craftsmanship to the company. They got to continue earning a paycheque while transferring some of their wisdom to Toyota's Rocks and Rivers.

I think of the Super Skill initiative as a mashup of Tracks 7, 8, and 9, seamlessly aligning with Toyota's broader goal of enhancing workplace conditions while preserving essential technical expertise and not degrading its overall productivity. It's Toyota's response to a question they and other forward-thinking organizations have grappled with for some time, though many more still neglect the challenge entirely.

> **The question is simple:** How can leaders operationally, physically, and digitally design workplaces that proactively address the distinct needs of Rivers, Rocks, and Rubies?

Effective, age-inclusive workplace design requires intentional leadership—both behavioural and policy-driven. Here are three tangible tactics you can implement immediately.

Structured Flexibility

The location where one's work is conducted—especially if it involves knowledge work rather than frontline, customer service, or manufacturing roles—will always be a source of contention between employer and employee. During the pandemic era, many knowledge workers demonstrated to their employers that they could do their work effectively and efficiently from a distance, yet conflict continues to shape the narrative.

But every microphone needs a microphone stand to function "Fully Completely." As Gord Downie, lead singer of the Tragically Hip, proved repeatedly onstage, one is not as effective without the other. Thus, employers and employees must find common ground for the music to be heard. Whether team members are Rivers, Rocks, or Rubies, to insist on an "always remote" work policy is ludicrous. Likewise, employers cannot expect their employees to be satisfied with an "always onsite" model either. Where's the common ground? Study after study proves that flexibility in where one performs the work profoundly impacts longevity, health, and performance. Structured flexibility must become foundational to truly benefit your Rubies—but also to be inclusive with your Rivers and Rocks. You should not offer a 100 percent remote work policy nor mandate 100 percent of a team member's time in the office.

German chemicals firm BASF implemented structured flexibility globally across all production and office teams. Among other policies, it offers customizable part-time and phased retirement schedules designed with older employees' health, caregiving, and personal obligations in mind. It also provides a combination of onsite and remote options. The company publicly acknowledges that "Compatibility of work and private life requires flexible working models." One of the keys for BASF was to make structured flexibility transparent, accessible, and culturally normalized rather than a special arrangement granted reluctantly.

Leadership Considerations

- **Policy-based:** Develop explicit guidelines that outline available flexible arrangements, clearly articulating eligibility criteria and scheduling options for Rivers, Rocks, and Rubies.

- **Developmental:** Leaders should openly advocate and demonstrate flexible work practices, routinely communicating flexibility as integral to organizational or team effectiveness, not just a specialized accommodation.

Ergonomics

Whether your team members work on a production line or in a cubicle, the physical workspace can positively or negatively influence their well-being and productivity. This is particularly true for Rubies, who may not be their sprightly selves from years past. If your workplace overlooks ergonomic conditions, this will worsen health issues and likely diminish performance. Conversely, a thoughtfully designed workspace will enhance comfort for any team member while reducing injury risks. That is why Toyota took the steps it did.

In a detailed 2023 study, researchers assessed how innovative ergonomic design interventions could support older Rubies. They employed advanced motion-capture technology (e.g., Xsens suit) and simulation software to conduct their research, and analyzed the differences in physical strain between younger Rivers and older Ruby employees while performing routine tasks across various roles. The findings were illustrative. Older Ruby workers exhibited a higher ergonomic risk than their River counterparts across most factors when adjustable furniture, anti-fatigue flooring, clearer visual signage, and reduced physical demands were not used. The study also showed that certain ergonomic adjustments reduce injury risks, lessen employee absenteeism, and enhance productivity for Ruby workers.

Leadership Considerations

- **Policy-based:** Establish an annual ergonomic assessment to identify and alter age-related workplace design risks. Implement the recommendations once the results are in.

- **Developmental:** Leaders should actively engage in ergonomic evaluations and training sessions, openly endorsing ergonomic principles as integral to sustained employee health and organizational effectiveness. At a minimum, leaders must support the results of the ergonomic assessment and help bridge the gap.

Digital Inclusivity

Far too often, digital transformation ideas and innovation overlook older workers. Organizations that pour money into launching shiny new platforms or digital widgets but neglect to ask if experienced team members find them intuitive or usable are essentially singing into an unplugged microphone.

In 2024, the OECD released a study that showed that older workers struggle unnecessarily when an organization unleashes newly minted digital tools on employees. Their struggles were not due to a lack of ability, but rather because interfaces and training programs failed to reflect their specific Ruby needs. Intuitive design, simplified navigation, and built-in help features are good practices for any user but sometimes, in particular, for Rubies. The study suggested tailoring digital training programs for older workers' learning preferences. But that's more of a reactive step. Leaders and organizations need to understand the importance of digital inclusivity. Leaders must be proactive and involve Rubies in the evaluation of digital tools from the beginning. Well before launching any new tool, tailored adoption training should also be rolled out to Rubies.

Leadership Considerations

- **Policy-based:** Implement clear and mandatory digital standards that emphasize simplicity and usability. Follow this by supporting ongoing, tailored digital training programs explicitly designed for Rubies. Regularly engage older workers so they can proactively evaluate any proposed new digital tools or platforms.

- **Developmental:** Leaders should openly embrace digital inclusivity, participate personally in training, and reinforce digital fluency as a standard expectation for everyone.

Bonus Longevity Factor: Technology and AI

You may now be wondering, "Thanks for the deep dive into the Longevity Lens, Dan, but I think you forgot something: technology and artificial intelligence." Well, just like that classic Billy Joel song, "You May Be Right."

While there are five key components to the Longevity Lens, you may have noticed from the metaphorical diagram earlier in the track that a telescope was included. No telescope can operate without a lens, and no lens can function without a casing filled with widgets and gadgets. In other words, technology (and AI) will inevitably wrap themselves around all five key components of this book's Longevity Lens recommendations. (This will also happen to the Career Canvas and Wisdom Wheel.)

There is, however, an elephant in the room, and it originates from Gordon Moore, co-founder of Intel. Moore's Law, as he proposed, is the idea that computing power doubles roughly every two years, reshaping technology and organizational strategy along the way. With Moore's Law as a metaphor, it's almost useless for me to propose any technology or artificial intelligence solutions to combat Age Debt when technological change is so rapid. I began writing this book in early 2024, and it was published in the spring of 2026. The pace of technological change has been Moore's Law on steroids during that time, particularly with AI. Any attempt to provide you with specific technology or AI-based tactics within the River–Rock–Ruby spectrum would be rather embarrassing.

Rest assured, it's my belief that all of us—regardless of age—will eventually be working a lot closer with technology. Whether it's through digital twins, robot assistants, AI agents, or concepts not yet invented (or released), technology and artificial intelligence will need to be a River–Rock–Ruby consideration for all leaders. However, there are a few leadership tactics I do want to encourage that get you thinking about how technology might impact the Rivers, Rocks, and Rubies under your direction.

Sanity Checks, Not Vanity Checks

AI isn't a miracle, it's a tool. However, too many leaders roll out tech upgrades like a new album launch: glitzy and hyped, while forgetting the human audience. Before chasing shiny new tech, conduct "sanity checks." Get brutally honest about how AI and any new technology will affect your Rubies' dignity, your Rocks' workload, and your Rivers' ambitions. If technology steals our humanity rather than amplifies it, your job as a leader is to question it and, if in doubt, stop it. Prioritize solutions that elevate the employee experience and our foundation in humankind.

Age-Proof Your Tech Roadmap

Tech roadmaps are often fantasy novels—futuristic, exciting, and, for the most part, fiction. Instead, design your roadmap explicitly for an aging workforce. Stop treating your Rubies as tech passengers; give them the steering wheel or, at a minimum, a seat in the car. Proactively integrate their input into tech decisions and map how each new AI tool will realistically impact Rivers, Rocks, and Rubies differently. Age-proofing your roadmap prevents tech-driven chaos and avoids another round of expensive regret. As MapleCo did, add it as a component to your Age Debt Assessment.

Stop Blindly Trusting AI and Other Future Technology

AI and tech evangelists at the annual CES Conference in Las Vegas love jargon, but you do not have that luxury. Your role isn't to hype technology; it's to scrutinize it. Build genuine AI and tech futures literacy among your teams, actively questioning whose interests these algorithms and widgets serve and whose they ignore. If new technology sidelines the irreplaceable wisdom of your Rubies or discounts your Rocks' loyalty, you are walking into the wrong concert hall. Maintain healthy skepticism. Blind trust in technology typically ends badly—just ask Theranos.

GOLDEN NUGGETS

You have probably realized by now that you cannot wish the Longevity Lens away like an annual performance review meeting. It's here for good. Either you deliberately shape the conditions so Rivers, Rocks, and Rubies thrive at every age and stage or you stumble headfirst into Age Debt. Here are seven Golden Nuggets from Track 9.

Golden Nugget #1: Age Inclusivity Is a Cultural Imperative

You can't build an age-ready culture with good intentions alone. You must embed intentional age inclusivity into your organizational DNA—language, behaviours, processes—until every River, Rock, and Ruby instinctively senses they matter equally.

Golden Nugget #2: Leaders Must Walk the Longevity Talk

Senior leadership must visibly champion longevity as a strategic priority—publicly and emphatically. But that won't hold water unless mid-level and frontline leaders translate those declarations into day-to-day actions, integrating longevity into how they coach, manage, and develop their teams. Longevity leadership is a band, not a solo artist.

Golden Nugget #3: Financial Clarity Is No Rarity

Financial uncertainty must move from mild concern to existential dread for Rivers, Rocks, and Rubies alike. It's your role to proactively normalize financial conversations, provide relevant learning, and deliver accessible tools so your people can turn their looming anxieties into clear-eyed confidence. If you are not helping your team see around the financial corner, you are failing to lead fully.

Golden Nugget #4: Well-Being Isn't Generic

Your team does not need another vanilla wellness program. Team members crave and need genuine recognition of their unique age-driven health realities. Menopause, eldercare or daycare stress, and midlife wellness concerns are not distractions; they are central productivity factors that must be addressed intentionally and unapologetically.

Golden Nugget #5: Workplace Design Reflects Your Organizational Truth

If your physical and digital workspace fails to account for the tangible, evolving needs of your Rubies (and, by extension, Rivers and Rocks), it exposes your organizational naïveté. Thoughtful ergonomics, structured flexibility, and digital inclusivity are not perks; they are essential design principles.

Golden Nugget #6: Measure … or Else

Fact: You cannot manage what you do not measure. If longevity is a priority, your metrics need to scream it, including factors like age diversity in recruitment, promotion fairness, and retention analytics. Hold yourself and your fellow leaders publicly accountable. Another fact: When longevity becomes visible, performance improves.

Golden Nugget #7: Comfort with Discomfort Defines Longevity Leadership

Leaders who understand that their role is to continuously evolve the conditions for team members at every persona stage will elevate longevity from a burden to a competitive advantage. If you are perpetually comfortable, you are likely getting longevity wrong. Be unsettled, stay unsettled, and lead accordingly. Get comfortable being uncomfortable with the Longevity Lens.

The Encore

The **"Grey to Gold" concert is almost over.** The wild cheering has brought me back onstage for one final song, "The Encore." When I sat down with a good friend, outstanding author, and one of the world's greatest thinkers, Canadian Roger L. Martin, to get his thoughts on this book and the Age Debt predicament, as usual, he was thought-provoking: "Organizations recognize the aging workforce challenge. They see it clearly. Yet they lack the tools to meaningfully respond. It's like the drunk searching for keys under the streetlight because that's where the light is, even if the keys aren't there."

I took his feedback as a challenge. Leaders and organizations now need to find their keys.

None of the solutions to Age Debt described on Side B—notably the Career Canvas, Wisdom Wheel, and Longevity Lens frameworks—matter unless you and your team agree to take the microphone and start singing a "new age" tune, like "Everything in Its Right Place" by Radiohead. It's all a colossal waste of time otherwise. Why? Age Debt will remain gargantuan and detrimental unless you do something about it. Aging populations, declining birth rates, and emerging skill gaps will inevitably and negatively affect your workforce productivity, culture, innovation, and, if applicable, profits.

Those three frameworks are your keys. Stop fumbling with them and step into your streetlight.

I cannot stress this enough: This is your "age *age*." Taylor Swift may prefer to call it the "age era." It might even become a full-blown "clim*age* crisis," as I mentioned in Track 1. Your inheritance of Age Debt, however, is entirely avoidable.

On Side A, I outlined several arguments regarding Age Debt. Allow me to reintroduce the main ones one last time:

- **Bell-to-bulb workforce reality:** Organizations built for a bell-shaped demographic (the consistent and expected flow of young Rivers eventually replacing older Rubies) are structurally unprepared for tomorrow's bulb-shaped reality: fewer young team members and a growing number of veterans at the top. This mismatch will disrupt workforce planning and team cultures for decades to come.

- **Tacit knowledge erosion:** Organizations underestimate the detrimental impact of tacit knowledge loss when seasoned Rubies and Rocks depart without intentional capture and transfer. This expertise cavity will slow innovation, inflate costs through unnecessary relearning, and leave significant gaps in critical organizational and team competencies. Tacit knowledge loss is your organization's version of unplanned corporate dementia.

- **Mid-management mayhem:** Mid-level Rock leaders have become increasingly overloaded, sandwiched by tending to aging parents and their own parenthood plights. They are subsequently emotionally, mentally, and physically burned out as they fill the void left by departing team members and their wisdom. Meanwhile, they must hire, train, and integrate inexperienced replacements. Moreover, many of these mid-level leaders take on the extra work themselves. Increased stress and reduced productivity levels are inevitable outcomes of these mid-management mayhem scenarios.

- **Age-based short-termism:** Organizations that frequently adopt a cost-centric myopic mindset—leaders that disproportionately target older, higher-paid Rocks and Rubies in budget cuts—will feel preventable operational pain. Such short-term thinking results in the easily avoidable high cost of losing institutional wisdom, let alone the inevitable scouring to replace the knowledge and productivity when things fall apart.

- **Leadership vacuum:** Leadership vacuums will appear at various organizational levels—not just the C-suite—when experienced Rocks and Rubies exit prematurely or unexpectedly. Organizations tend to overlook wisdom holders who have historically operated without formal leadership titles. When these team members exit—many of whom hold critical tacit knowledge—various client relationships and internal processes are negatively affected. It also obviously decreases the potential for mentorship, social learning, and knowledge transfer between colleagues.

- **The silent rage of ageism:** While often invisible, ageism remains widespread and deeply ingrained in your organization's culture. Ageist biases and generational memes shrewdly undermine your team's effectiveness. It does nothing for morale because ageism diminishes trust and cooperation across the River, Rock, and Ruby spectrum. This silent saboteur incapacitates the Experience Dividend, and it occurs in all age-related directions.

Longevity Pressures

Retirement itself is no longer a fixed finish line. Social realities and longer lifespans—as well as low levels of retirement savings—will continue to push people to remain in the workforce. Living longer, though positive, will significantly challenge traditional organizational structures, retirement plans, succession strategies, talent development, and overall career management for individuals *and* organizations.

I opened the book by paying tribute, twice, to the Roman philosopher Cicero. It is fitting that I should close "The Encore" with another nugget from his timeless wisdom. Cicero once observed the following: "The shifts of fortune test the reliability of friends."

Your organization—and indeed, your leadership skills—will be tested by the shifting and inevitable realities of Age Debt. Cicero's "friends" are your Rivers, Rocks, and Rubies. They are the invaluable human capital within your workforce. When you embrace your colleagues as indispensable allies rather than liabilities, you transform Age Debt from a crisis into the promise of the Experience Dividend.

The choice Cicero hints at is crystal clear: Squander the wisdom accumulated within your team and organization or harness it to illuminate a better path forward.

> **You've found your keys—but how you use them in the light matters.** It's the Experience Dividend versus Age Debt, where strategic wisdom can triumph over entrenched ignorance.

Of course, *your* leadership and that of *your* team will determine whether your Experience Dividend future merely survives or courageously thrives.

Speaking of which, it is time to check in one last time with our favourite health tech firm, MapleCo, and the final notes of their Age Debt to Experience Dividend journey.

MapleCo: Summary Snapshot

You can't hide from demographic reality. Not for long, anyway.

As we've learned from MapleCo throughout this book, their story—much like yours—is likely a tale of Age Debt. But will it be one of the Experience Dividend, too? Let's recap MapleCo's plight.

When Marla Benson took the stage at that senior leadership retreat a few years ago, the room wasn't exactly brimming with hope. Instead, the air was thick with dread, nervous glances, and the unspoken understanding that their long-ignored Age Debt bill was finally due. Benson put it bluntly: MapleCo had been built on the backs of experts and veterans who had quietly kept things humming along for decades. Many started as Rocks—and a few were Rivers—but now a large portion of the staff were Rubies. The problem? Over 40 percent of those Rubies were eyeing retirement within three years. Three years! That's an organizational blink-of-an-eye, and MapleCo was caught flat-footed.

It was not simply a retirement wave, either. MapleCo faced a tsunami of tacit knowledge loss with little strategy to capture or even slow it down. Remember when Allison Carter packed up her 30-year career into a cardboard box? The company didn't just lose a senior leader—they lost a repository of priceless know-how. Her retirement alone blew a multi-million-dollar hole in client revenue, which you would think might have raised some Age Debt alarms. But MapleCo kept hitting the snooze button despite the Beatles' "Help!" blaring over the speaker.

Do you recall the mid-level Rock story of Emily Russo, who was left to pick up the slack and the pieces of the Rubies that had left the firm? Retirements and departures decimated Emily's team. It left her running on fumes, near burnout. The team did hire a few fresh faces, young Rivers eager to make their mark, but the onboarding was haphazard, and the mistakes began to pile up. The team's missed step in compliance cost MapleCo over $300,000— no small potatoes, even for them. Emily was left to play firefighter instead of leader, and she burned out faster than an Eddie Van Halen guitar solo.

Then there was Shintarō Takahashi, one of MapleCo's brightest Rocks. Takahashi was ambitious and motivated yet quite stuck. His problem? He found himself banging his head on a career ceiling that several Rubies were inadvertently blocking. There was no career advancement plan, just frustration. Shintarō saw himself as a future leader, but MapleCo was subliminally telling him to find that future elsewhere.

Of course, it wasn't all unintentional neglect. Subtle ageism was baked right into MapleCo's culture.

Do you remember the story of 58-year-old Pascal de la Vuerte and the kind of institutional memory you can't buy? His performance reviews were slipping, not because he was ineffective but because his role involved behind-the-scenes crisis prevention—hardly the flashy innovation the leadership team were rewarding. Or what about Carlos Jimenez, the beloved systems specialist, passed over for cybersecurity training because someone in HR said, "He might struggle with new tech." Those biases were embedded deep enough in the organization to remain unnoticed until it was almost too late.

During Benson's inquiry into various Age Debt issues, she also realized something: "Our talent pipeline of young team members considering MapleCo as a career option is meek." The company had become known as the place where careers were more about stability and safety than invention and excitement. Young potential River hires—talented in AI, analytics, and innovation—were not even considering the company for a job. MapleCo's traditionalist workplace image had become a recruitment liability. "Don't go to MapleCo—it's stale."

The firm had become a complex web of structural oversights, subtle biases, leadership stagnation, and outdated practices. MapleCo's Age Debt had gone from quietly accumulating a deficit to loudly demanding repayment, and fast.

The time had come for MapleCo to face the music—pun intended—or risk losing the very rhythm that had once defined them. Enter the Age Debt Tiger Team.

MapleCo: The Age Debt Tiger Team

When MapleCo finally stared Age Debt squarely in the eye, Marla Benson knew half-measures would not cut it. It was no longer enough to sound the alarm; the company needed a strategic intervention. Enter the Age Debt Tiger Team. Benson's rationale in creating it was clear: The team would not be another committee graveyard filled with good intentions, fancy PowerPoint decks, and zero follow-through.

As you may recall, Benson started by making the problem visible. The tiger team's first mission was to fully acknowledge the firm's demographic reality. MapleCo may have been built for a bell-shaped workforce, but its age profile was shifting rapidly to a bulb-shaped one. The company knew fewer younger Rivers were flowing into the organization, and its Rubies and Rocks stacked heavily towards the top. This "bell-to-bulb" realization was now openly being discussed and communicated alongside its aging workforce reality. (Recall that over 40 percent of the company's Rubies were near retirement in the next three years.)

With their demographic reality now firmly on the setlist, MapleCo next got tactical. First, they took to heart the Career Canvas concepts from Track 7.

The tiger team launched CrossPaths, a new internal talent marketplace where leaders post real, meaningful internal opportunities—actual career moves, not just role vapourware. They didn't stop there, either. Spark Up assignments—short-term, cross-functional projects and initiatives—became a quick hit, allowing Rivers to broaden their skills. It also gave Rocks like Emily Russo an escape valve from burnout. As for the Rubies, it was a chance to stay engaged without jumping ship on new and exciting MapleCo opportunities outside of their regular jobs.

Next, structured career conversations became the norm, not an exception. Team members finally had explicit discussions about lateral moves, development, and growth—not just vertical promotions.

MapleCo started openly valuing "zigzag" careers, signalling that linear ladders were no longer their default thinking. Boomerang In examples were welcomed back with (mostly) open arms, and several Move Down role shifts occurred.

In addition, the tiger team attacked one of the core Age Debt issues head-on: the loss of tacit institutional knowledge. Under what I called the Wisdom Wheel in Track 8, MapleCo rolled out Maple Staples, a deliberate and structured knowledge-capture process. Ruby employees nearing retirement were being paired intentionally with younger Rocks and Rivers. It was not just an informal exchange. Instead, the Rubies systematically documented critical know-how through structured mentorship sessions, cognitive task analyses, intentional rotations, and—most notably—the wildly successful Maple Stories. The launch of Maple Stories—an internal video platform showcasing practical wisdom and candid insights from team members across all personas—drove home the intellectual capital that resided in many of its current Ruby employees.

But Benson knew more had to be tackled. Enter Maple Metrics, part of the Longevity Lens framework I introduced in Track 9. MapleCo started to track recruitment, promotions, and retention numbers by persona demographics. It made age diversity visible, actionable, and impossible to ignore. Leadership accountability became a front-and-centre conversation because MapleCo made longevity a critical component of its talent and culture strategy.

To ensure the concepts stuck, the tiger team recommended embedding many of its longevity ideas into the fabric of the company's culture. MapleCo launched focused training on age-inclusivity—no cringe-worthy modules, but candid workshops like the Everyday Age toolkit, structured Age Dialogues, and experiential sessions called Perspective Pairings, where team members shadowed other colleagues for half a day once a year. The company did not want to simply discuss inclusivity; they wanted to practice it openly and explicitly.

By the time the following year's leadership retreat rolled around, MapleCo may not have been fully cured of Age Debt, but something was unquestionably different. Benson's tiger team had made serious inroads. There was now a clear structure for addressing its Age Debt, real solutions were yielding results, and cautious optimism replaced dread. Sure, a few skeptics remained at the leadership and team member levels, but it was getting harder to argue with the success.

However, Marla Benson clearly understood that this was just the beginning.

MapleCo: The Experience Dividend Realized

Benson knew a few tracks remained unfinished on MapleCo's *Experience Dividend* album.

CrossPaths, Maple Staples, and Maple Metrics were strong leadoff songs changing the age game, but a few gaps lingered, especially after the tiger team's deep dive. For a truly complete album, MapleCo had to push further.

The tiger team was inspired by Goldman Sachs' successful Returnship program—a structured internship designed to help skilled professionals re-enter the workforce after lengthy career gaps. MapleCo launched Encore Pathways, targeting people who had not worked in the previous five years or more. Anywhere.

Encore Pathways offered tailored onboarding, mentorship from experienced colleagues, and customized skill-enhancing workshops over a 16-week period. After graduating from their Encore Pathways stint, many of these Rubies and Rocks, who had stepped away for caregiving, wellness breaks, or life sabbaticals, joined MapleCo in meaningful full- and part-time roles.

Encore Pathways was a big hit. The initiative also successfully brought back a few former MapleCo employees through Boomerang In situations via the company's Career Canvas model. MapleCo realized that their Encore Pathways program participants possessed a deep level of transferrable skills and backgrounds that greatly benefited the company's culture, productivity, and innovation. In the words of a hiring manager, "Hiring them was a no-brainer."

But despite this success, MapleCo still faced what Benson privately dubbed the "Takahashi problem," where talented Rocks were stymied by mid-career ceilings due to limited senior-level opportunities.

Enter MFlex, inspired by Unilever's innovative U-Work model—a flexible employment structure combining project-based internal assignments with guaranteed benefits and security, thus a corporate-sanctioned freelance model. As Unilever describes, "U-Work gives employees the freedom and flexibility associated with contract roles with the security and benefits typically linked to regular employment." At MapleCo, MFlex permitted senior Rocks and Rubies to take on specialized internal gigs, effectively dismantling career roadblocks and opening fresh leadership pathways for ambitious Rocks like Shintarō Takahashi. It was win–win. MapleCo even allowed team members the opportunity for side hustles. So long as it did not affect their roles inside the company, as part of the program framework, team members could hold a secondary gig outside the MapleCo doors. MFlex was an even bigger success than Encore Pathways.

Still, Benson and the tiger team recognized that recruitment needed even more creative thinking. Taking cues from several organizations that offer apprenticeship programs explicitly designed for older workers—individuals over 50 pursuing second (or third) career journeys—MapleCo established NextChapter Apprenticeships. NextChapter quickly emerged as an unexpected gem. Within months, midlife apprentices joined MapleCo, bringing enthusiasm, adaptability, and surprisingly fresh perspectives exactly where the company needed them most. Although limited initially to five apprentices as a pilot, MapleCo is already preparing to double that number next year.

Benson felt energized by the distinctiveness of these programs. NextChapter differed from Encore Pathways. The former focused on apprenticeships for people seeking an immediate career shift, while the latter targeted individuals wanting to return to work after extended breaks of five years or more. Meanwhile, MFlex completely reshaped workplace dynamics by providing flexibility yet stability through internal and external contract gigs in ways MapleCo had not imagined previously. Yet Benson knew MapleCo could still push further and do something genuinely groundbreaking.

Beyond the tiger team's recommendations, she remembered a conversation she had had with a friend and their enthusiastic description of Stanford University's Distinguished Careers Institute. Stanford's program helps seasoned Rubies transition to meaningful roles that focus on social impact, innovation, or knowledge-sharing as they near or enter retirement. It puzzled her that no corporate equivalent existed. US-based higher education institutions—including Stanford but also Harvard, Notre Dame, the University of Chicago, and the University of Connecticut, among others—seemed to be cornering the nascent market. Seeing a unique opportunity, Benson decided MapleCo should take the lead. She launched their own corporate version: Second Act.

Carefully curated for senior Rocks and Rubies—both from within MapleCo and externally—Second Act participants immerse themselves in purpose-driven projects, internal innovation initiatives, post-work professional development discussions, and meaningful community engagement after retirement. It was part programming, part dialogue, part planning. Second Act quickly gained positive prestige. Even better for the company, they turned it into a revenue-generating venture through paying customers. Why let Stanford and other universities have all the fun? Given that MapleCo is a health company at its core, Benson felt it would be a great way to position the company as an industry leader in post-retirement health. The company leverages its extensive network of corporate partners and clients, making marketing Second Act straightforward and attractive. (In fact, once word got out, business partners practically lined up at MapleCo's doors—turning Second Act into an innovation hub and profit centre rolled into one.)

By the time the next senior leadership retreat arrived, the age transformation at the company was undeniable. Dread had vanished. Palpable excitement had top billing. As Benson stepped onto the stage to discuss MapleCo's evolution from Age Debt to Experience

Dividend, the atmosphere in the room was vibrant, almost electric. You could practically hear the MapleCo leaders' crowd buzzing with excitement, reminiscent of when the Beatles took the stage of *The Ed Sullivan Show* in 1964. Okay, it might not have been that type of vibe, but there was undoubtedly a hum in the air.

MapleCo was no longer threatened by the demographic bell-to-bulb shift. They had harnessed their situation to transform MapleCo into an even better organization. After a long journey, they could confidently claim that MapleCo was no longer burdened by Age Debt. Instead, they had reinvented themselves *because* of it. They were demonstrating *and* benefiting from the Experience Dividend. Benson was so proud.

Closing up her time at the podium, Benson smiled the cheekiest of smiles, knowing she had one more thing to broadcast into the mic.

She announced *her* retirement.

Well, not really. Although Benson was indeed stepping down as CEO, she also revealed she was set to take on a new challenge. Benson was about to become the new chair of the MapleCo board *and* the new executive director of Second Act. Marla Benson, the Ruby, could not have been happier.

Building, Not Breaking, Bridges

One final strum of the guitar.

If you are a fan of languages, especially Welsh and Latin, you will know that my last name translates to "broken bridge." Pontefract comes from the Welsh word *pont* (bridge) and the Latin word *fractus* (broken). When you smash the two together, in English, it translates to "broken bridge."

These days, Pontefract is a lovely town in Yorkshire, England. The black licorice Pontefract Cakes made in the region are delectable, but I digress. Pontefract the town gets its name from a historical event in 1069, when a bridge on the River Aire was destroyed—possibly by Viking rebels or Anglo-Scandinavian insurgents—to thwart the progress of ruthless strategist William the Conqueror. Over time, the name evolved from "Ponte Fractus" to "Pontefract."

The ongoing and self-deprecating joke over my career is that I have been trying to be the opposite of my last name. Instead of breaking bridges, I'm trying to *build* them.

Unsurprisingly, my aim for this book was to build a bridge. I hope you agree that I built a bridge between

* bell-shaped demographics to the pending bulb-shaped future;

* the foolhardy concept of generations to Rivers, Rocks, and Rubies; and

* Age Debt and the Experience Dividend.

We also crossed other bridges, from outdated views on careers, wisdom, and longevity to new, refreshed, age-neutral ones. I hope I built those bridges sturdy enough for you to consider traversing them one day in your leadership career.

But the final bridge I want to build (and cross) in this book is mine: the Pontefract Bridge. It's one that takes you through my career as a River, Rock, and Ruby.

One ordinary Wednesday evening in the fall of 2018, I was upstairs in my bedroom, folding laundry, my mind wandering, when my iPhone buzzed. Texts are a routine pulsating sound, easily ignored, but I instinctively paused mid-fold this time for some reason. Something felt different. That quiet, subtle vibration would trigger everything you now hold in your hands.

I glanced down at my phone. The text read, "We need to discuss funding."

A chill began to run quietly through my veins. I had spent enough years inside corporate walls to instantly decode *that* message. It's a digital harbinger, some corporate kismet in disguise.

My full-time role at TELUS—my carefully and strategically built corporate Rock identity—was about to change and be repurposed due to a budget reallocation. A few gentle, polite texts (we were all Canadian, after all) on a quiet evening suddenly shifted my world.

My identity pivoted while my career trajectory was being rewritten in the blink of a pixel.

Weirdly, eventually, and perhaps counterintuitively, I became grateful.

Maybe that's strange. But it felt like I had been preparing subconsciously for this moment for a long time. Years prior, as I mentioned earlier in this book, I had written and declared my purpose: "We're not here to see through each other; we're here to see each other through." Standing beside my half-folded laundry, I realized that Declaration of Purpose had quietly anchored me for precisely this moment—when certainty evaporates and raw vulnerability is all you have left.

But life—and bridges, apparently—can surprise you.

Amid that uncertain, gaping pause, another message appeared right away. The executive on the other side of those texts carefully yet poignantly opened a different door.

They wanted me back—not as a full-time Rock leader anymore, but as a boomerang fractional Ruby.

They greatly appreciated my contributions and recognized the value in my insight, experience, and the relationships and ventures I had built over the previous 10 years. While the budget was being shifted away from the small venture I had passionately nurtured for the prior half-decade, my professional bridge seemed intact, valued, and respected. I was to continue running the TELUS MBA— something near and dear to my heart—and go from solid Rock to key Ruby member within another unit at TELUS.

So, there I stood, pants and shirts half-folded, thrust suddenly into solopreneurship—something I had secretly considered but never entirely embraced—with an anchor client that had just happily led me into my Ruby era.

As I listened to my three young children playing outside in the backyard—Were they juggling knives? Eating dirt? Painting each other with turpentine? It hardly mattered—I felt the world beginning to shift beneath my feet. A series of messages in the most mundane setting had reshaped my entire identity in a matter of minutes.

Maybe you've been there too, standing at life's invisible pivot points, feeling the unsettling yet exhilarating sensation of identity suddenly untethered from title, role, or security. For me, that Wednesday evening became a fundamental redefinition, a reclaiming of something I had not realized I had quietly lost somewhere along the way: *my age*. In the reflection that followed, I saw my entire career laid out clearly along the River–Rock–Ruby continuum. That was how—and when—this book began to take shape.

As a River leader, I had often thought leadership meant exhibiting certainty and strength rather than doubt or vulnerability. Today, I would tell my younger River self that uncertainty is a strength, not a weakness, and empathy always outweighs pugnacity. While looking in the rearview career mirror, it has become clear to me that every leader must recognize that each of their team members travels their own River–Rock–Ruby journey.

Age and stage matter,
but only if the leader acts as such.

If I were to apply the Career Canvas framework from this book to my River leadership era 25 or so years ago, I would suggest it taught me that every person—young, mid-career, or seasoned—needs intentional, humane conversations about their distinct work and life needs. I had desperately wanted to Move Up, but not everyone does. In fact, many people desire lateral or fractional roles. I wish I had understood sooner that leadership is less about providing answers and more about genuinely exploring questions alongside my team, however young or old they may be. I received some fine Ruby mentorship guidance, but I would bolster my mentor pool five times if I could.

By the time I entered my Rock leadership era—about 17 years at SAP and then TELUS—I had grown significantly more confident in my leadership abilities. Yet in hindsight, I still made several Age

Debt mistakes. I could have done much better to foster an Experience Dividend culture.

Ultimately, becoming a Solopreneur Ruby was an inevitable transition that continues to reverberate with new drumbeats each day. That transition taught me the following:

Every Ruby is a polished Rock shaped gently over time by the flow of their River.

Wherever you are on your career continuum, remember this: Everyone around you is travelling the same River–Rock–Ruby journey. It's inescapable and precisely why understanding each other's work (and life) stage matters deeply. Long live the eras tour! (Thank you, Taylor.)

Remember my first question: *How old are you?* (Go ahead, say it loud and proud.)

The Career Canvas, Wisdom Wheel, and Longevity Lens concepts from this book are not just frameworks but leadership-age tools of empathy and intentionality. They should remind you, as a leader, to see beyond your own age, enabling you to actively help others cross their bridge more effectively and generously.

Perhaps your own bridge feels shaky, wood splintered, or broken right now—career uncertainty, personal fears, quiet questions about your professional worth or legacy. I have stood on that bridge, guitar in hand, and felt those exact emotions. If this book has shown you anything, I hope it's this: Every broken bridge is not an ending but an invitation—a concert ticket to repair, rebuild, reconnect, and embrace your Age Debt vulnerability so you can turn it into an Experience Dividend. In the end, perhaps your Age Debt-to-Experience Dividend leadership journey is simply a series of bridges you build, repair, strengthen, and cross. Maybe the irony of my surname has always been beautifully fitting.

Pontefract—a broken bridge—is precisely the reminder I needed.

Our strongest age bridges are built not from unbreakable materials but from the pluck, compassion, and humility we summon to make it over towards the side of the Experience Dividend. Perhaps a broken bridge can become your most potent and enduring song.

As always, thank you for reading. May you lead through "Courage" and "Grace, Too."

Pontem firmissimum amor facit.

(Love makes the strongest bridge.)

Acknowledgements

acknowledge and respect the traditional territories of the Lək̓ʷəŋən Peoples, known today as the Songhees and Esquimalt Nations, on whose land much of this book was written. I also recognize the Lək̓ʷəŋən and W̱SÁNEĆ Peoples, whose historical and ongoing relationship with this land continues to this day.

This book is dedicated to Steven Hill, Lorna Shapiro, and Brian Reid—three Rubies who continue to teach me new ways to think about work, life, love, and laughter. Thank you!

There were four unique blocks of people who helped bring *The Future of Work Is Grey* to life. I am indebted and grateful to each of them.

First, to the early readers. After the research phase was largely completed, I put out a call to my *Pontefractions* Newsletter Community, asking if anyone wanted to join me for the alpha writing phase. To my surprise and delight, 55 people signed up; even better, 30 provided actual feedback. That's 55 percent—I'll take it. (They didn't even get paid!) Thank you so much to my early readers: Alejandra de la Torre, Brandi Matheson, Caroline Hackney, Christopher Evans, Chuck Hamilton, Claire Pontefract, Dave Galloway, Deanne Repski, Debra Nave, Don Loney, Dorothy Paukste, Eric Moeller, Grant Harris, Greg Lowe, Jason Barr, Jeff Fried, Jennifer Torres, Jessica Benedet, Joe Dicianno, Karina Maneely, Michele Buckley, Natalie Morris, Nick Hixson, Prashant Agrawal, Robert Lennox, Rose Kattackal, Sean Riordan, Sharon Summerfield, Stan Vanneste, and Trish Ward. Your feedback was instrumental.

Second, several people were generous enough to let me badger them with questions, interviews, emails, texts, and other forms of contact to get to the root of the topics in this book, as well as for promotion purposes. My sincere thanks to: Tom Allemeier, Konstanze Carreras-Solé, Simon Chan, Dr. Richard Clark, Leanne J. Clark-Shirley, Michael Clinton, Maureen Wiley Clough, Dr. Amy C. Edmondson, Haruki, Christian Jerusalem, Stephanie Kramer, Jeanette Leardi, Roger L. Martin, Mehmet, Henry Mintzberg, Gary Officer, Dr. Hiroshi Ono, Jun Saito, Bradley Schurman, Helen Hirsh Spence, Ellen Taaffe, Dr. Hideaki Tanaka, Guy W. Wallace, Avivah Wittenberg-Cox, and Kazunori Yutoku.

Third, to the "special ones," thanks for being in my corner with check-ins, hugs, whisky, dinners, lattes, digital drop-ins, and overarching concern for my masochistic book-writing pursuits over the past three years: Michael Bungay Stanier, Chris Labonté, Mark Komlenic, Liane Davey, Roger L. Martin, Mark Colgate, Henry Mintzberg, Rebecca Kirstein Resch, Adam Kreek, Ehren Lee, Kelsey Trigg, Eric Termuende, Silas Brownsey, Keith Keating, Ron Carucci, Keven Fletcher, Bryan Acker, Ruth Gotian, Mitch Joel, Kevin Jones, Matthew Wood, Stephen Lamb, Ami Barnard-Bahn, Kiran Mohan, Shakeel Bharmal, Josh Blair, Glain Roberts-McCabe, Pete Johnston, Malcolm Crow, Phil LeNir, Daniel Hughes, Matthew Gould, members of the Thinkers50 posse as well as 100 Coaches, Larry Pontefract, Jane Borutan, Adam Pontefract, Michelle Pontefract, Zoe Pontefract, Nicole Till, Roy Till, and Mia Till.

Fourth and finally, to the Page Two family. While you may be my fourth publisher, you have treated me with warmth, grace, and camaraderie as though we have been working together for a decade. As MBS said, "Why did it take you so long?" You sure know how to make a guy feel special. Thank you Jesse, Trena, Tass, Peter, Scott, Kendra, Taysia, Leslie, Felicia, Mary, Jenny, and everyone else across the spine. You are so fab.

Why "colour" and not "color," you the reader asks? Elbows up, eh?

On the matter of AI—*yes*, it was used. All types: Perplexity, NotebookLM, Gemini, Fuel iX, ChatGPT, Grammarly, QuillBot, and even Canva AI to sketch a few things. (Granted, Grok was a no-go before *or* after the Nazi stuff.) I've never used an AI research assistant before or an artificial writing sparring partner akin to an always-on substantive editor. AI helped me in many ways, although it was also prone to errors and hallucinations. One excellent example was my use of Google's Notebook LM podcast feature, which was a great way to instruct the hosts to find holes in my arguments. Hearing your writing being torn to shreds by AI hosts while wearing AirPods during a cycling ride is humbling, to say the least.

To those who have terminated me, doubted me, overlooked me, ridiculed me, shafted me, usurped me, aged me, shunned me, blocked me, or fibbed to me, I just want to say thank you. It's your past behaviour that motivates me not only to be a better human but also to avoid becoming like you. You may occasionally live rent-free in my head, but please know that I'm making a living off of you, which significantly offsets the cost.

Much love to my goats, as always—Claire, Cole, and Cate. May you always feel golden as you enter your grey days. Thank you for the love and laughs. Luv, Daddio.

Denise: I feel like we're entering the "ruby" era of our relationship. And you know what? That feels so good. Let's have a dance party. Again. Table One for the win! xxx

Notes

Track 1: Drop the (Age) Needle

p. 7   *Psychologist Raymond Cattell first conceptualized:* Raymond B. Cattell, "Theory of Fluid and Crystallized Intelligence: A Critical Experiment," *Journal of Educational Psychology* 54, no. 1 (1963): 1–22, doi.org/10.1037/h0046743.

p. 7   *Later researchers described fluid intelligence:* Erlend J. Brevik, Rune A. Eikeland, and Astri J. Lundervold, "Subthreshold Depressive Symptoms Have a Negative Impact on Cognitive Functioning in Middle-Aged and Older Males," *Frontiers in Psychology* 4 (2013): 309, doi.org/10.3389/fpsyg.2013.00309.

p. 7   *Subsequent research further emphasized:* Paul B. Baltes, Ursula M. Staudinger, and Ulman Lindenberger, "Lifespan Psychology: Theory and Application to Intellectual Functioning," *Annual Review of Psychology* 50 (1999): 471–507, doi.org/10.1146/annurev.psych.50.1.471.

p. 7   *Researchers Christian Grund and Niels Westergaard-Nielsen:* Christian Grund and Niels Westergaard-Nielsen, "Age Structure of the Workforce and Firm Performance," *International Journal of Manpower* 29, no. 5 (2008): 410–22, doi.org/10.1108/01437720810888553.

p. 9   *Research has shown that generational differences:* Emma Parry and Peter Unwin, "Generational Differences in Work Values: A Review of Theory and Evidence," *International Journal of Management Reviews* 13, no. 1 (March 2011): 79–96, doi.org/10.1111/j.1468-2370.2010.00285.x.

p. 11   *By 2030, one in five Canadians:* Statistics Canada, "Population Projections: Canada, Provinces and Territories, 2023 to 2073," *The Daily,* June 24, 2024, www150.statcan.gc.ca/n1/daily-quotidien/240624/dq240624b-eng.htm.

p. 11   *The 2024 birth rate plummeted:* Akshay Kulkarni, "Canada Records Its Lowest Fertility Rate for Second Year: StatsCan," CBC News, September 30, 2024, cbc.ca/news/canada/british-columbia/canada-lowest-ever-fertility -rate-1.7338374.

p. 12   *By 2032, Americans aged 65:* Richard Fry and Dana Braga, "Older Workers Are Growing in Number and Earning Higher Wages," Pew Research Center, December 14, 2023, pewresearch.org/social-trends/2023/12/14/older-workers-are-growing-in-number-and-earning-higher-wages.

p. 12   *Those aged 55 to 64:* Kevin S. Dubina, "Labor Force and Macroeconomic Projections Overview and Highlights, 2022–32," *Monthly Labor Review*, Bureau of Labor Statistics, September 2023, bls.gov/opub/mlr/2023/article/labor-force-and-macroeconomic-projections.htm.

p. 12   *Europe's working-age population:* Wido Geis-Thöne, "Working Age Populations Develop Differently in Europe: An Analysis of Demographic Structures in the 27 EU Countries," IW-Report No. 38, German Economic Institute, October 14, 2021, iwkoeln.de/en/studies/wido-geis-thoene-in-europa-entwickeln-sich-die-bevoelkerungen-im-erwerbsfaehigen-alter-unterschiedlich.html.

p. 12   *By 2030, 22 percent of the UK population:* Office for National Statistics, "National Population Projections: 2021-Based Interim," January 30, 2024, ons.gov.uk/peoplepopulationandcommunity/populationandmigration/populationprojections/bulletins/nationalpopulationprojections/2021basedinterim.

p. 12   *With a birth rate of only 1.2 children:* Nippon.com, "Japan's Fertility Rate Drops to New Record Low," June 12, 2024, nippon.com/en/japan-data/h02015.

p. 13   *With a birth rate of 0.75 children:* Julian Ryall, "South Korea Records Birth Rate Rise," DW News, January 10, 2024, dw.com/en/south-korea-records-birth-rate-rise/a-71812274.

p. 14   *In 2025, even Goldman Sachs wrote:* Jan Hatzius, Joseph Briggs, Kevin Daly, Johan Allen, Sarah Dong, and Megan Peters, "The Path to 2075: The Positive Story of Global Aging," Goldman Sachs Economic Research, May 20, 2025, goldmansachs.com/insights/goldman-sachs-research/the-path-to-2075-the-positive-story-of-global-aging.

p. 15   *In the United States, for example:* Vanguard, "Saving for Retirement," November 6, 2024, investor.vanguard.com/investor-resources-education/retirement/savings.

p. 15   *The median for all retirement savings:* Aditya Aladangady, Jesse Bricker, Andrew C. Chang, et al., "Changes in US Family Finances from 2019 to 2022: Evidence from the Survey of Consumer Finances," Board of Governors of the Federal Reserve System, October 2023, doi.org/10.17016/8799.

p. 19   *By 2030, the manufacturing sector:* NAM News Room, "2.1 Million Manufacturing Jobs Could Go Unfilled by 2030," National Association of Manufacturers, May 4, 2021, nam.org/2-1-million-manufacturing-jobs-could-go-unfilled-by-2030-13743.

p. 19   *The United States is projected to need:* Tanner Bateman, Sean Hobaugh, Eric
Pridgen, and Arika Reddy, *US Healthcare Labor Market* (Mercer, 2021),
mercer.com/content/dam/mercer/assets/content-images/north-america/
united-states/us-healthcare-news/us-2021-healthcare-labor-market-
whitepaper.pdf.

p. 19   *As of 2024, nearly half of all:* Chris Testa, "The Graying Utility Workforce,"
Energy Central, 2020, energycentral.com/c/um/graying-utility-workforce.

p. 19   *The US trucking industry is projected:* International Road Transport Union,
"Global Truck Driver Shortage to Double by 2028, Says New IRU Report,"
November 20, 2023, iru.org/news-resources/newsroom/global-truck
-driver-shortage-double-2028-says-new-iru-report.

p. 20   *According to McKinsey, by 2030:* James Manyika, Jaana Remes, and
Richard Dobbs, "The Productivity Challenge of an Aging Global
Workforce," *Harvard Business Review*, January 20, 2015, hbr.org/2015/01/
the-productivity-challenge-of-an-aging-global-workforce.

p. 20   *The Organisation for Economic Co-operation and Development (OECD)
reports:* Christophe André, Peter Gal, Álvaro Pereira, and Matthias
Schief, "Demographic Challenges to Productivity: How to Reconcile
Population Ageing with Economic Growth?" *OECD Ecoscope* (blog), June
17, 2024, oecdecoscope.blog/2024/06/17/demographic-challenges-to-
productivity-how-to-reconcile-population-ageing-with-economic-growth.

p. 20   *In Canada, by 2030, wage growth:* Conference Board of Canada, *Skills
and Productivity: Which Skills Shortages Are Impacting Canadian
Productivity?* August 15, 2024, fsc-ccf.ca/wp-content/uploads/2024/
08/skills-shortages-impacting-productivity_aug2024.pdf.

p. 20   *OECD countries could lose $5.4 trillion:* Karen Harris, Austin Kimson, and
Andrew Schwedel, *Labor 2030: The Collision of Demographics, Automation
and Inequality*, Bain & Company, February 2018, bain.com/insights/
labor-2030-the-collision-of-demographics-automation-and-inequality.

p. 20   *According to BCG, companies with:* Rocío Lorenzo, Nicole Voigt, Karin
Schetelig, Annika Zawadzki, Isabelle Welpe, and Prisca Brosi, "The
Mix That Matters," BCG, April 26, 2017, bcg.com/publications/2017/
people-organization-leadership-talent-innovation-through-diversity-mix-
that-matters.

p. 21   *Researchers discovered that sectors facing:* Kevin Kinsella and David R.
Phillips, "Global Aging: The Challenge of Success," *Population Bulletin*
60, no. 1 (March 2005), Population Reference Bureau, prb.org/resources/
global-aging-the-challenge-of-success.

p. 21   *In my home province of British Columbia:* Akshay Kulkarni, "Emergency
Rooms in Rural BC Were Closed for Equivalent of Around Four Months in
2022, Data Shows," CBC News, December 27, 2022, cbc.ca/news/canada/
british-columbia/bc-er-closures-2022-1.6689970.

p. 21   *For example, in April 2025:* Martin Müller, "Economic Downturn Causes
Skills Shortage to Ease Further," *KfW-ifo Skilled Labour Barometer*, KfW
Research, June 2025, kfw.de/PDF/Download-Center/Konzernthemen/
Research/ PDF-Dokumente-KfW-ifo-Fachkr%C3%A4ftebarometer/
KfW-ifo -Fachkraeftebarometer_2025-06_EN.pdf.

Track 2: The Demographic Tidal Wave

p. 31   *Zurich's head of talent and learning:* Bill Kerr, host, *Managing the Future of
Work*, podcast, "Workforce Coverage: How Zurich Insurance Protects
Its Skills Base," Harvard Business School, May 3, 2023, hbs.edu/managing
-the-future-of-work/podcast/Pages/podcast-details.aspx?episode=
2734980271.

p. 31   *Steve Collinson, chief HR officer:* Jane Hamilton, "Golden Years: Career
Opportunities for Over 50s," *The Sun*, November 15, 2023, thesun.co.uk/
money/24765181/golden-years-career-opportunities-for-over-50s.

p. 34   *Today, across the globe:* Charles Goodhart and Manoj Pradhan, *The Great
Demographic Reversal: Ageing Societies, Waning Inequality, and an Inflation
Revival* (Palgrave Macmillan, 2020).

p. 37   *There, the shift is so dramatic:* Sasha Rogelberg, "Japan's Population So
Old That a Diaper Manufacturer Is Only Making Products for Adults,
Not Babies," *Fortune,* March 28, 2024, fortune.com/2024/03/28/
japans-population-old-diaper-manufacturer-oji-holdings-adults-babies.

p. 37   *Even more pronounced, Japanese workers:* James Root, Andrew Schwedel,
Mike Haslett, and Nicole Bitler, "Better with Age: The Rising Importance
of Older Workers," Bain and Company, July 2023, bain.com/insights/
better-with-age-the-rising-importance-of-older-workers.

p. 37   *In 2025, the country's:* Nippon.com, "Births in Japan Fall Below 700,000
for the First Time in 2024," June 5, 2025, nippon.com/en/japan-data/
h02429.

p. 37   *Remarkably, by 2030, South Korea's:* Claire Lee, "South Korea's Working
Age Population Expected to Fall by 3.2 Million in 2030," HRM Asia,
February 7, 2022, hrmasia.com/south-koreas-working-age-population-
expected-to-fall-by-3-2-million-in-2030.

p. 37   *The US birth rate:* Organisation for Economic Co-operation and
Development, "Fertility Rates," 2023, oecd.org/en/data/indicators/
fertility-rates.html.

p. 38   *According to the US Census Bureau:* US Census Bureau, "US Population
Projected to Begin Declining in Second Half of Century," November 9,
2023, census.gov/newsroom/press-releases/2023/population
-projections.html.

p. 38   *This is without President Trump's:* Rachel Treisman, "5 Things to Know
About the Alien Enemies Act and Trump's Efforts to Use It," NPR,

March 18, 2025, npr.org/2025/03/18/nx-s1-5331857/alien-enemies
-act-trump-deportations.

p. 40   *Louis Hodge, the associate director:* Laura Hendry, "London Primary School Numbers to Drop by 52,000," BBC News, September 16, 2024, bbc.com/news/articles/cly559jnd2zo.

p. 41   *We don't have enough ink:* Enrico Colombatto, "State Pension Programs Feel the Strain of Aging Populations," GIS Reports Online, September 26, 2024, gisreportsonline.com/r/demographic-shifts-pensions.

p. 42   *According to the World Economic Forum:* Andrew Schwedel, "3 Ways Organizations Can Empower Older Workers amid an Ageing Global Workforce," World Economic Forum, September 13, 2023, weforum.org/stories/2023/09/how-organizations-can-embrace-older-workers-amid-an-ageing-workforce.

p. 42   *For example, in the United States:* Center for Workforce Inclusion, "The Changing Face of the Labor Force: Mid-Career and Older Workers on the Rise," 2023, centerforworkforceinclusion.org/the-changing-face-of-the-labor-force-mid-career-and-older-workers-on-the-rise.

p. 42   *Consulting firm Capterra discovered:* Brian Westfall, "How HR Can Help the Overworked, Underappreciated Middle Manager," Capterra, February 13, 2024, capterra.com/resources/middle-manager-burnout-strategies.

p. 43   *A 2023 study by the UKG Workforce Institute:* Workforce Institute at UKG, *Mental Health at Work: Managers and Money,* UKG, 2023, ukg.com.

p. 43   *After repeated quality issues:* Amanda Maile, Mark Osborne, and Meredith Deliso, "New Details Emerge in Case of Alaska Airlines Plane Where Door Plug Blew Out," ABC News, March 13, 2024, abcnews.go.com/US/boeing-overwrote-surveillance-footage-door-plug-repair-ntsb/story?id=108084196.

p. 43   *"We heard repeatedly from experienced employees:* Sharon Terlep, "Boeing's Urgent Mission to Train Thousands of Rookies How to Build an Airplane," *The Wall Street Journal,* June 10, 2024, wsj.com/business/airlines/boeing-planes-safety-jobs-training-ef6873e6.

p. 45   *A 2023 survey found:* The Canadian Press, "Most Canadian Businesses Lack Mentorship Programs, Losing Institutional Knowledge of Retiring Workers," December 13, 2023, thecanadianpressnews.ca/globenewswire_press_releases/most-canadian-businesses-lack-mentorship-programs-losing-institutional-knowledge-of-retiring-workers/article_f3077da3-0a4a-5a5c-af2d-762e7cd000cc.html.

p. 46   *An aging workforce:* Talen Energy Corporation, "Prospectus Supplement No. 8 (Registration no. 333280341)" (SEC filing), July 1, 2024, ir.talenenergy.com/node/7531/html.

p. 47   *For example, in Vienna:* Vollpension, "Our Vision," n.d., vollpension.wien/
en/vision.

p. 47   *And repair cafés around the world:* Repair Café International Foundation,
"About," n.d., repaircafe.org/en/about.

p. 47   *In the United Kingdom:* I'm Not Done Yet, "About," n.d., imnotdoneyet
.co.uk/about.

p. 47   *And at Eldera:* Dan Pontefract, "Eldera.ai Connects Young Children with
the Elderly, and It's Awesome," *Forbes*, April 28, 2024, forbes.com/sites/
danpontefract/2024/04/28/elderaai-connects-young-children-with
-the-elderly-and-its-awesome.

p. 48   *Research conducted by the authors:* Nicola Bianchi and Matteo Paradisi,
"Countries for Old Men: An Analysis of the Age Pay Gap," NBER Working
Paper No. 32340, National Bureau of Economic Research, April 2024,
doi.org/10.3386/w32340.

Track 3: The Experience Conundrum

p. 56   *The United Nations projects Turkey:* AARP International, *Turkey: Aging
Readiness and Competitiveness*, n.d., aarpinternational.org/initiatives/
aging-readiness-competitiveness-arc/turkey.

p. 57   *Gallup estimates that the range:* Shane McFeely and Ben Wigert, "This
Fixable Problem Costs US Businesses $1 Trillion," Gallup, March 13,
2019, gallup.com/workplace/247391/fixable-problem-costs-businesses
-trillion.aspx.

p. 57   *The David Aplin Group reckons:* Mark Swartz, "Why People Leave
Their Jobs," Monster.ca, n.d., hiring.monster.ca/resources/workforce
-management/employee-retention-strategies/why-people-leave-their
-jobs-ca.

p. 58   *Dr. Michael Polanyi likely provided:* Michael Polanyi, *The Tacit Dimension*
(Doubleday & Company, 1966).

p. 58   *Research published in 2020:* Carol P. Huie, Tameka Cassaberry, and Amari
K. Rivera, "The Impact of Tacit Knowledge Sharing on Job Performance,"
International Journal on Social and Education Sciences 2, no. 1 (2020):
34–40, ijonses.net/index.php/ijonses/article/view/1954.

p. 58   *Research conducted in 2023:* Nataliya Galan, "Knowledge Loss Induced
by Organizational Member Turnover: A Review of Empirical Literature,
Synthesis, and Future Research Directions (Part 1)," *The Learning
Organization* 30, no. 2 (March 2023): 117–36, doi.org/10.1108/
TLO-09-2022-0107.

p. 59   *A notable example is NASA's:* NASA APPEL Knowledge Services, "PM
Bridges Mentoring Program," n.d., appel.nasa.gov/career-development/
pm-bridges-mentoring-program.

p. 59   *Longitudinal research by Peter Rex Massingham:* Peter Rex Massingham, "Measuring the Impact of Knowledge Loss: A Longitudinal Study," *Journal of Knowledge Management* 22, no. 4 (2018): 721–58, doi.org/10.1108/JKM-08-2016-0338.

p. 60   *In 2024, the leadership advisory firm:* Robert Voth, "CEO Succession Planning: A Strategic Imperative for US Bank Boards and Their CEOs," Russell Reynolds Associates, November 8, 2024, russellreynolds.com/en/insights/reports-surveys/ceo-succession-planning-a-strategic-imperative-for-us-regional-bank-boards-and-their-ceos.

p. 60   *Perhaps unsurprisingly, 2021 research:* Claudio Fernández-Aráoz, Gregory Nagel, and Carrie Green, "The High Cost of Poor Succession Planning," *Harvard Business Review*, May–June 2021, hbr.org/2021/05/the-high-cost-of-poor-succession-planning.

p. 62   *Christian Jerusalem, an age management leader:* Christian Jersualem, in conversation with the author, February 2025.

p. 66   *By mid-2024, the US Federal Reserve:* Office of the Comptroller of the Currency, "OCC Amends Enforcement Action Against Citibank, Assesses $75 Million Civil Money Penalty," July 10, 2024, occ.gov/news-issuances/news-releases/2024/nr-occ-2024-76.html.

p. 66   *Indications unearthed by Reuters:* Lananh Nguyen and Tatiana Bautzer, "A Key to Citi's Regulatory Woes: Staff Need Skills 'Enhancement,'" Reuters, October 15, 2024, reuters.com/business/finance/key-citis-regulatory-woes-staff-need-skills-enhancement-2024-10-15.

p. 68   *The company unwisely decided: Moffatt v. Air Canada*, Decision No. 525448, February 14, 2024, decisions.civilresolutionbc.ca/crt/crtd/en/item/525448/index.do.

p. 68   *Research from 2022 suggests:* Martin Sonntag, Jens Mehmann, and Frank Teuteberg, "Trust-Supporting Design Elements as Signals for AI-Based Chatbots in Customer Service," *International Journal of Service Science, Management, Engineering, and Technology* 14, no. 1 (January 2023): 1–16, doi.org/10.4018/IJSSMET.329963.

p. 68   *Ethan Mollick's* Co-Intelligence: Ethan Mollick, *Co-Intelligence: Living and Working with AI* (Portfolio/Penguin, 2024).

p. 70   *According to the World Economic Forum's:* World Economic Forum, *The Future of Jobs Report 2025*, January 7, 2025, weforum.org/publications/the-future-of-jobs-report-2025.

Track 4: The Pressure Points of Longevity

p. 73   *For example, the 2024:* Natalie Iciaszczyk, Gabrielle Gallant, Talia Bronstein, Alyssa Brierley, and Samir Sinha, *Perspectives on Growing Older in Canada: The 2024 NIA Ageing in Canada Survey*, National Institute on Ageing, January 28, 2025, niageing.ca/2024-annual-survey.

p. 75   *In cities like London:* Richard Donnell, "House Price Index: June 2025— North–South Divide to Remain over 2025," Zoopla, June 2025, zoopla .co.uk/discover/property-news/house-price-index/#north-south- divide-to -remain-over-2025.

p. 75   *If you wish to own a home:* Ashley Howard, "How Long Does It Take to Save Up for a Down Payment in Each Province?" Nesto, January 9, 2025, nesto.ca/home-buying/how-long-save-down-payment-canada-provinces.

p. 76   *The Institute for Fiscal Studies:* Jonathan Cribb and Laurence O'Brien, *Recent Trends in Public Sector Pay*, Institute for Fiscal Studies, March 2024, ifs.org.uk/sites/default/files/2024-03/Recent-trends-in-public-sector- pay-IFS- REPORT.pdf.

p. 76   *The average salary in Canada:* Statistics Canada, "Table 11 10 0239 01: Employees by Industry Sector, Canada, Seasonally Adjusted," 2023, doi.org/10.25318/1110023901-eng.

p. 76   *According to the US Census Bureau:* Gloria Guzman and Melissa Kollar, "Income in the United States: 2022," US Census Bureau, September 12, 2023, census.gov/library/publications/2023/demo/p60-279.html.

p. 76   *According to a 2023 survey:* New York Life, "Cost of Caregiving Burdens Nearly Half of Sandwich Generation, Finds New York Life Wealth Watch Survey," November 1, 2023, newyorklife.com/newsroom/2023/wealth -watch-survey-sandwich-generation-unable-to-meet-expenses-due-to -caregiving.

p. 77   *As the World Economic Forum:* Mahad Zafar and Adam Skali, "Why Society Must Adapt to Our Longer Lives," World Economic Forum, July 4, 2025, weforum.org/stories/2025/07/why-society-must -adapt-to-our-longer-lives.

p. 77   *Worse, according to the:* National Center for Employee Ownership, "The Retirement Savings Crisis and the Role of ESOPs," n.d., nceo.org/ research/the-retirement-savings-crisis-and-the-role-of-esops.

p. 77   *By 2020, Britons aged 55:* Moneyzine, "Savings Statistics in the UK," 2020, moneyzine.com/uk/banking/savings-statistics-uk; Skint Dad, "Average savings in the UK," 2020, skintdad.co.uk/average-savings-uk.

p. 77   *Families in Japan are estimated:* David Rubenstein, "The 20 Million Yen Problem in Japan," Argentum Wealth, n.d., argentumwealth.com/the -20-million-yen-problem-in-japan.

p. 77   *But as of 2020:* Investment Company Institute, *The Japanese Retirement System*, 2021, idc.org/system/files/2021-12/21_bro_ japanese_retirement.pdf.

p. 79   *For example, Denmark's parliament:* Laura Gozzi, "Denmark to Raise Retirement Age to Highest in Europe," BBC News, May 22, 2025, bbc.co.uk/news/articles/cvg71v533q60.

p. 80   *A Journal of Occupational and Environmental Medicine:* Abdulkarim
M. Meraya and Usha Sambamoorthi, "Chronic Condition Combinations
and Productivity Loss Among Employed Nonelderly Adults (18 to 64
Years)," *Journal of Occupational and Environmental Medicine* 58, no. 10
(October 2016): 974–78, doi.org/10.1097/JOM.0000000000000839.

p. 81   *On average, women can expect:* Brandon Russell, "The UK Is Still at
Least 20 Years Away from Closing the Gender Pension Gap—Scottish
Widows Report," IFA *Magazine*, November 13, 2024, ifamagazine.com/
the-uk-is-still-at-least-20-years-away-from-closing-the-gender-pension
-gap-scottish-widows-report.

p. 82   *According to the Chartered Institute:* Chartered Institute of Personnel
and Development, *Menopause in the Workplace: Employee Experiences in
2023*, October 2023, cedrec.com/cedrec_images/2023-menopause
-report -8456_2.pdf.

p. 82   *A 2022 study by the Fawcett Society:* Andrew Bazeley, Catherine Marren,
and Alex Shepherd, *Menopause and the Workplace*, Fawcett Society,
April 2022, fawcettsociety.org.uk/Handlers/Download.ashx?IDMF=
9672cf45-5f13-4b69-8882-1e5e643ac8a6.

p. 83   *A 2021 report from the:* Tyler Bond, *Stark Inequality: Financial Asset Inequality
Undermines Retirement Security*, National Institute on Retirement Security,
September 2021, nirsonline.org/reports/starkinequality.

p. 83   *The NIRS published additional research:* Nari Rhee, *Closing the Gap:
The Role of Public Pensions in Reducing Retirement Inequality*, National
Institute on Retirement Security, September 2023, nirsonline.org/reports/
closingthegap.

p. 86   *He put it this way:* Dan Pontefract, host, *Leadership NOW with Dan
Pontefract*, podcast, "The Workforce Is Shrinking. Now What? With
Author Bradley Schurman," May 16, 2024, danpontefract.com/podcast/
the-workforce-is-shrinking-now-what-with-author-bradley-schurman.

p. 88   *While Italy has made strides:* Francesca Carta and Marta De Philippis,
"Working Horizon and Labour Supply: The Effect of Raising the Full
Retirement Age on Middle-Aged Individuals," Temi di Discussione
No. 1314 (Banca d'Italia, 2021), bancaditalia.it/pubblicazioni/temi
-discussione/2021/2021-1314/en_Tema_1314.pdf.

p. 88   *As a result, Italy's pension system:* Simone Tagliapietra and Francesco
Chiacchio, "Italy's Pension Spending: Implications of an Ageing
Population," *Analysis* (blog), Bruegel, April 26, 2018, bruegel.org/
blog-post/italys-pension-spending-implications-ageing-population.

p. 88   *In late 2024, the government:* Daniel Baksa, Boele Bonthuis, Si Guo, and
Zsuzsa Munkacsi, "Parametric Pension Reform Options in Korea," IMF
Working Paper No. 24/223 (International Monetary Fund, October 11,
2024), elibrary.imf.org/view/journals/001/2024/223/article-A001-en.xml.

p. 88   *The country's social security system:* Alicia H. Munnell, "Social Security's Financial Outlook: The 2023 Update in Perspective," Center for Retirement Research at Boston College, April 25, 2023, crr.bc.edu/ social-securitys-financial-outlook-the-2023-update-in-perspective.

p. 88   *The net effect is that retirees:* Committee for a Responsible Federal Budget, "Analysis of the 2023 Social Security Trustees' Report," March 31, 2023, crfb.org/papers/analysis-2023-social-security-trustees-report.

p. 89   *Fewer than 20 percent:* Julian Pfrombeck, Anne Burmeister, and Gudela Grote, "Older Workers' Knowledge Seeking from Younger Coworkers: Disentangling Countervailing Pathways to Successful Aging at Work," *Journal of Organizational Behavior* 45, no. 1 (January 2024): 1–20, doi.org/10.1002/job.2751.

p. 93   *For example, the Center:* Laura D. Quinby, Gal Wettstein, and James Giles, "Are Older Workers Good for Business?" Working Paper 2023-19, Center for Retirement Research at Boston College, November 2023, crr.bc.edu/ wp-content/uploads/2023/11/wp_2023-19.pdf.

p. 93   *Worse, the World Economic Forum's:* World Economic Forum, *The Future of Jobs Report 2025,* January 7, 2025, weforum.org/publications/the-future -of-jobs-report-2025.

p. 94   *According to a 2023 survey:* Stephanie Neal, Rosey Rhyne, Jazmine Boatman, Bruce Watt, and Mindy Yeh, *Global Leadership Forecast 2023,* Development Dimensions International, 2023, ddiworld.com/global -leadership -forecast-2023.

p. 94   *Moreover, 36 percent of young leaders:* DDI, "DDI Opens Survey for World's Largest Leadership Study; Participating Companies Receive Custom Leadership Benchmarking Report," news release, April 4, 2024, newswire .ca/news-releases/ddi-opens-survey-for-world-s-largest-leadership-study -participating-companies-receive-custom-leadership-benchmarking- report-813186691.html.

p. 94   *A 2023 Harris Poll report:* Express Employment Professionals, "Most Canadian Businesses Lack Mentorship Programs, Losing Institutional Knowledge of Retiring Workers," news release, December 13, 2023, globenewswire.com/news-release/2023/12/13/2795616/0/en/Most -Canadian-Businesses-Lack-Mentorship-Programs-Losing-Institutional -Knowledge-of-Retiring-Workers.html.

p. 95   *Unsurprisingly, according to SHRM:* Kylie Ora Lobell, "Models in Mentoring," SHRM, January 20, 2024, shrm.org/topics-tools/news/ all-things-work/models-in-mentoring.

Track 5: The Silent Saboteur of Ageism

p. 99   *Draped with autonomy, mastery:* Daniel H. Pink, *Drive: The Surprising Truth About What Motivates Us* (Riverhead Books, 2009).

p. 101 *In his seminal 1975 book:* Robert N. Butler, *Why Survive? Being Old in America* (Harper & Row, 1975), 5.

p. 101 *After years in both startups:* Dan Pontefract, host, *Leadership NOW with Dan Pontefract*, podcast, "Your Organization's Age Bias Is Costing You, with Maureen Wiley Clough," April 19, 2025, danpontefract.com/podcast/maureen-wiley-clough.

p. 102 *In an oft-used 2007 example:* Mark Coker, "Startup Advice for Entrepreneurs from Y Combinator," VentureBeat, March 26, 2007, venturebeat.com/2007/03/26/start-up-advice-for-entrepreneurs-from-y-combinator-startup-school.

p. 103 *For example, in 2023:* Ryan Golden, "HR Pros Say IBM Fired Them Due to Their Age, Planned to Replace Them with AI," Legal Dive, September 22, 2023, legaldive.com/news/ibm-hr-professionals-suit-age-discrimination-layoffs/694682.

p. 103 *A 2024 UK Youth study:* UK Youth, "Harmful Stereotypes of Young People Fuelling Record Numbers to Fall Out of Work," November 12, 2024, ukyouth.org/2024/11/harmful-stereotypes-of-young-people-fuelling-record-numbers-to-fall-out-of-work.

p. 103 *AARP surveyed 1,322 American:* Rebecca Perron, "Age Discrimination Continues to Hold Older Workers Back," AARP, May 6, 2021, aarp.org/pri/topics/work-finances-retirement/employers-workforce/older-workers-new-skills-covid-19-pandemic.

p. 104 *The World Health Organization:* World Health Organization, "Ageing: Ageism," WHO Newsroom Questions and Answers, April 28, 2025, who.int/news-room/questions-and-answers/item/ageing-ageism.

p. 104 *As researchers argued in 2021:* World Health Organization, *Global Report on Ageism: Executive Summary*, 2021, who.int/publications/i/item/9789240020504.

p. 104 *Recruit Holdings is a Japanese:* Macrotrends, "Recruit Holdings Revenue 2016–2024," n.d., macrotrends.net/stocks/charts/RCRUY/recruit-holdings/revenue.

p. 106 *As I wrote in 2023's* Work–Life Bloom: Dan Pontefract, *Work–Life Bloom: How to Nurture a Team That Flourishes* (Figure 1 Publishing, 2023).

p. 108 *As author and longevity expert:* Dan Pontefract, host, *Leadership NOW with Dan Pontefract*, podcast, "Why Leaders Must Rethink Longevity with CEO Avivah Wittenberg-Cox," October 2024, danpontefract.com/podcast/avivah-wittenberg-cox.

p. 108 *In a 2023 research paper:* Organisation for Economic Co-operation and Development, *Retaining Talent at All Ages* (OECD Publishing, 2023), doi.org/10.1787/00dbddo6-en.

p. 110 *In June 2024, the AARP Foundation:* Megan Cerullo, "Raytheon Discriminates Against Older Job Applicants, AARP Alleges," CBS News, June 11, 2024, cbsnews.com/news/raytheon-aarp-lawsuit-age-discrimination.

p. 110 *For instance, a 2020 NBER paper:* David Neumark, "Age Discrimination in Hiring: Evidence from Age-Blind Versus Non-Age-Blind Hiring Procedures," Working Paper 26623, National Bureau of Economic Research, January 2020, doi.org/10.3386/w26623.

p. 111 *A 2021 LinkedIn analysis:* George Anders, "Hiring's New Red Line: Why Newcomers Can't Land 35 Percent of 'Entry-Level' Jobs," LinkedIn, August 18, 2021, linkedin.com/pulse/hirings-new-red-line-why -newcomers-cant-land-35-jobs-george-anders.

p. 112 *According to 2024 research:* Resume Builder, "7 in 10 Companies Will Use AI in the Hiring Process in 2025, Despite Most Saying It's Biased," October 22, 2024, resumebuilder.com/7-in-10-companies-will-use-ai-in -the-hiring-process-in-2025-despite-most-saying-its-biased.

p. 112 *In 2014, the company developed:* Jeffrey Dastin, "Amazon Scraps Secret AI Recruiting Tool That Showed Bias Against Women," Reuters, October 10, 2018, reuters.com/article/world/insight-amazon-scraps-secret-ai -recruiting -tool-that-showed-bias-against-women-idUSKCN1MK0AG.

p. 113 *A class-action lawsuit in 2024:* Daniel Wiessner, "Workday Must Face Novel Bias Lawsuit over AI Screening Software," Reuters, July 16, 2024, reuters.com/legal/litigation/workday-must-face-novel-bias-lawsuit-over -ai-screening-software-2024-07-15.

p. 113 *For example, in 2022:* Jasmine Lianalyn Rocha, "AI in the Workplace: The Dangers of Generative AI in Employment Decisions," *Columbia Undergraduate Law Review*, October 2, 2024, culawreview.org/journal/ai -in-the-workplace-the-dangers-of-generative-ai-in-employment-decisions.

p. 116 *OECD research released in 2023:* OECD, *Retaining Talent at All Ages.*

p. 116 *Another OECD study from 2020:* Organisation for Economic Co-operation and Development, *Promoting an Age-Inclusive Workforce: Living, Learning and Earning Longer* (OECD Publishing, 2020), doi.org/10.1787/ 59752153-en.

p. 117 *Research published in 2023:* Vimal Desai, Antonio Hernandez Conte, Vu T. Nguyen, Philip Shin, Neha T. Sudol, Janet Hobbs, and Chunyuan Qiu, "Veiled Harm: Impacts of Microaggressions on Psychological Safety and Physician Burnout," *Permanente Journal* 27, no. 2 (June 2023): 169–78, doi.org/10.7812/TPP/23.017.

p. 117 *In a groundbreaking 2024 study:* Julian Pfrombeck, Anne Burmeister, and Gudela Grote, "Older Workers' Knowledge Seeking from Younger Coworkers: Disentangling Countervailing Pathways to Successful Aging at Work," *Journal of Organizational Behavior* 45, no. 1 (January 2024): 1–20, doi.org/10.1002/job.2751.

p. 119 *In their 2021 study of performance appraisals:* Federica Previtali and Simona Spedale, "Doing Age in the Workplace: Exploring Age

Categorisation in Performance Appraisal," *Journal of Aging Studies* 59 (December 2021): 100981, doi.org/10.1016/j.jaging.2021.100981.

p. 121   *At 67, Lloyd Wright:* Western Pennsylvania Conservancy, "What Is Fallingwater?" Fallingwater, n.d., fallingwater.org/what-is-fallingwater.

p. 121   *A Yale study from 2023:* Becca R. Levy and Martin D. Slade, "Role of Positive Age Beliefs in Recovery from Mild Cognitive Impairment Among Older Persons," *JAMA Network Open* 6, no. 4 (April 2023): e237707, doi.org/10.1001/jamanetworkopen.2023.7707.

p. 121   *And a 2019 Federal Reserve Bank of San Francisco:* David Neumark, Ian Burn, and Patrick Button, "Age Discrimination and Hiring of Older Workers," Federal Reserve Bank of San Francisco, February 27, 2017, frbsf.org/wp-content/uploads/el2017-06.pdf.

p. 124   *Research by the Federal Reserve Bank of San Francisco:* Neumark et al., "Age Discrimination and Hiring of Older Workers."

Track 6: Plot Twist

p. 136   *Recall Meiji University's Dr. Hideaki Tanaka:* Hideaki Tanaka, in conversation with the author, January 2025.

p. 137   *And wouldn't you know:* Kazunori Yutoku, in conversation with the author, January 2025.

Track 7: Career Canvas

p. 142   *According to Gary Officer:* Dan Pontefract, host, *Leadership NOW with Dan Pontefract*, podcast, "Stop Wasting the Wisdom of Your Older Workers with CEO Gary Officer," March 3, 2025, danpontefract.com/podcast/gary_officer.

p. 143   *Michael Clinton, author of:* Dan Pontefract, host, *Leadership NOW with Dan Pontefract*, podcast, "Michael Clinton on Roaring into the 100-Year Life," January 7, 2025, danpontefract.com/podcast/michael-clinton.

p. 143   *In 2024, it reported revenues:* Michael Fossat and Vir Dasmahapatra, "The Senior Talent Program: Powering the Talent and Aspirations of Our Experienced #SEGreatPeople," White Paper, Schneider Electric, 2024, download.schneider-electric.com/files?p_Doc_Ref=SEWPseniorTalentProgram&p_enDocType=White+Paper&p_File_Name=Senior+Talent+Program+White+paper.pdf.

p. 144   *According to 2024 OECD research:* Organisation for Economic Co-operation and Development, *Career Paths and Engagement of Mature Workers* (OECD Publishing, 2024), oecd.org/content/dam/oecd/en/topics/policy-issues/ageing-and-employment/Career-Paths-and-Engagement-of-Mature-Workers.pdf.

p. 145   *In a global employer survey:* AARP, "2020 Global Employer Survey of OECD Countries: Annotated Questionnaire," August 2020, doi.org/10.26419/res.00399.003.

p. 146 *Through its Grand Career System:* Jeff Schwartz, Kelly Monahan, Steve Hatfield, and Siri Anderson, "No Time to Retire: Redesigning Work for Our Aging Workforce," Deloitte Insights, December 7, 2018, deloitte.com/us/en/insights/topics/talent/redesigning-work-for-our-aging-workforce.html.

p. 146 *Over at Aviva:* Centre for Aging Better, *Developing the Mid-Life* MOT, September 2018, ageing-better.org.uk/sites/default/files/2018-10/Developing-the-Mid-life-MOT-report.pdf.

p. 147 *The company states:* L'Oréal Groupe, "For All Generations Program," n.d., loreal.com/en/commitments-and-responsibilities/for-the-people/seniors.

p. 147 *Stephanie Kramer, chief human resources:* Dan Pontefract, "Lessons from L'Oréal on Careers and Longevity," *Forbes*, March 18, 2025, forbes.com/sites/danpontefract/2025/03/18/lessons-from-loral-on-careers-and-longevity.

p. 148 *As I wrote in* Work–Life Bloom: Dan Pontefract, *Work–Life Bloom: How to Nurture a Team That Flourishes* (Figure 1 Publishing, 2023).

p. 150 *Composer Paul Hindemith:* Leela Gandhi, "Utonal Life: A Genealogy for Global Ethics," in *Cosmopolitanisms*, ed. Bruce Robbins and Paolo Lemos Horta (New York University Press, 2017), 65.

p. 158 *The company launched its* LEAD *Connected:* Sarah Gallo, "Case Study: An Inside Look at Houghton Mifflin Harcourt's Job Rotation Program," Training Industry, April 3, 2023, trainingindustry.com/articles/workforce-development/case-study-an-inside-look-at-houghton-mifflin-harcourts-job-rotation-program.

p. 158 BCLC *implemented a version:* Andrea Earle, in conversation with the author, February 2025.

p. 159 *Like* BCLC, *the Mayo Clinic:* Mayo Clinic, "Benefits," n.d., jobs.mayoclinic.org/benefits.

p. 159 *The* UK *Civil Service's:* Equality Hub, "Returner Toolkit: Helping You Back to Work," Gov.UK, March 17, 2023, gov.uk/government/publications/returner-toolkit-helping-you-back-to-work.

p. 159 *France-based Michelin's:* Michelin, "Michelin Signs a New Job and Career Management (GEPP) Agreement," November 22, 2023, michelin.com/en/publications/group/michelin-signs-a-new-job-and-career-management-gepp-agreement.

Track 8: Wisdom Wheel

p. 163 *Their recordings felt less:* Studs Terkel, *Working: People Talk About What They Do All Day and How They Feel About What They Do* (Pantheon Books, 1974), xxix.

p. 164 *I'm reminded of Charles Handy:* Charles B. Handy, *The Hungry Spirit: Beyond Capitalism—A Quest for Purpose in the Modern World* (Broadway Books, 1988), 127.

p. 168 *Read David Gelles's fantastic:* David Gelles, *The Man Who Broke Capitalism: How Jack Welch Gutted the Heartland and Crushed the Soul of Corporate America—and How to Undo His Legacy* (Simon & Schuster, 2022).

p. 169 *Novartis, a Swiss multinational:* University of Basel, "ZOOM@Novartis," n.d., unibas.ch/en/University/Administration-Services/Vice-President-s-Office-for-Education/Academic-Programs/Graduate-Center/ZOOM-Novartis.html.

p. 170 *In France, Sodexo has taken:* Sodexo, "Mentors Are Essential to Workplace Leadership," *Business and Industry* (blog), March 7, 2023, us.sodexo.com/inspired-thinking/business-and-industry/blogs/mentors-workplace-leadership.

p. 170 *Helen Hirsh Spence, founder:* Helen Hirsh Spence, in conversation with the author, December 2024.

p. 172 *As we have just learned:* Alan Mulally, in conversation with the author, March 2024.

p. 172 *"Our management style is to build:* Konstanze Carreras-Solé, in conversation with the author, February 2025.

p. 176 *Guy Wallace, a performance analyst:* Guy Wallace, in conversation with the author, October 2024.

p. 176 *He offered me a similar warning:* Dan Pontefract, host, *Leadership NOW with Dan Pontefract*, podcast, "The Expertise and Knowledge Crisis with Dr. Richard E. Clark," March 13, 2025, danpontefract.com/podcast/the-expertise-crisis-with-dr-richard-e-clark.

p. 176 *Tata Chemicals, an India-based:* Tata Business Excellence Group, "Tata Chemicals Shares How It Captures Tacit Knowledge of Retiring Employees with Tata Steel," February 16, 2022, tatabex.com/best-practices/bp-overview/bp-top-stories/tata-chemicals-shares-how-it-captures-tacit-knowledge-of-retiring-employees-with-tata-steel.

p. 178 *Deutsche Telekom Shared Services Europe:* Thorsten Schurig, "How Performance Support Is Working at Deutsche Telekom Shared Services Europe," TTS Insights, May 10, 2021, insights.tt-s.com/en-us/how-performance-support-is-working-at-dtse.

p. 180 *Simon Chan, founder and CEO:* Dan Pontefract, host, *Leadership NOW with Dan Pontefract*, podcast, "The Longevity Advantage: Rethinking Work with CEO Simon Chan," January 29, 2025, danpontefract.com/podcast/simon-chan.

p. 181 *Jeanette Leardi—a social gerontologist:* Dan Pontefract, host, *Leadership NOW with Dan Pontefract*, podcast, "Aging Sideways with Social Gerontologist Jeanette Leardi," January 14, 2025, danpontefract.com/podcast/jeanette_leardi.

p. 181   *Prudential Singapore is one:* Economist Intelligence Unit, "Skilled for 100? Leveraging an Older Workforce in Singapore," White Paper, Prudential Singapore, n.d., impact.economist.com/projects/ready-for-100/whitepaper-workplace.

p. 181   *In 2021, Paris-based Atos:* James Root, Andrew Schwedel, Mike Haslett, and Nicole Bitler, "Better with Age: The Rising Importance of Older Workers," Bain and Company, July 2023, bain.com/insights/better-with-age-the-rising-importance-of-older-workers.

p. 184   *Chip Conley, author and founder:* Chip Conley, "Why 'Wisdom Work' Is the New 'Knowledge Work,'" *Harvard Business Review*, August 2, 2024, hbr.org/2024/08/why-wisdom-work-is-the-new-knowledge-work.

p. 185   *In 2024, through a landmark:* Angelina R. Sutin, Martina Luchetti, Yannick Stephan, and Antonio Terracciano, "Purpose in Life and Cognitive Health: A 28-Year Prospective Study," *International Psychogeriatrics* 36, no. 10 (October 2024): 956–64, doi.org/10.1017/s1041610224000383.

Track 9: Longevity Lens

p. 192   *Faced with over 20 percent:* Westpac, "Inclusion Across the Generations," n.d., westpac.com.au/about-westpac/inclusion-and-diversity/Inclusion-means-everyone-matters/inclusion-across-the-generations.

p. 192   *The bank's overarching longevity program:* Westpac, "Our Communities," n.d., westpac.com.au/about-westpac/diversity-equity-and-inclusion/our-communities.

p. 192   *The bank also introduced:* Westpac, "Inclusion Across the Generations."

p. 192   *For example, flexible leave arrangements:* Westpac, "Flexible Ways of Working: Inclusion Means Everyone Matters," 2024, westpac.com.au/about-westpac/inclusion-and-diversity/Inclusion-means-everyone-matters/flexible-ways-of-working.

p. 192   *Through the launch of its:* Westpac Group, *Access and Inclusion Plan 2021–2024*, 2021, westpac.com.au/content/dam/public/wbc/documents/pdf/aw/WBC-access_and_inclusion_plan_2021-2024.pdf.

p. 192   *Westpac reported significant improvements:* Westpac, *Westpac Group 2024 Annual Report*, 5, westpac.com.au/content/dam/public/wbc/documents/pdf/aw/ic/wbc-highlights-2024.pdf.

p. 193   *Lynda Gratton and Andrew Scott:* Lynda Gratton and Andrew Scott, "The Corporate Implications of Longer Lives," *MIT Sloan Management Review*, March 2, 2017, sloanreview.mit.edu/article/the-corporate-implications-of-longer-lives.

p. 194   *In Ralph Waldo Emerson's:* Ralph Waldo Emerson, "Circles," in *Essays: First Series* (Houghton, Mifflin and Company, 1886), 298.

p. 196   *Sandra Nunes, head of people:* Centre for Ageing Better, "Imperial London Hotels: Changing Mindsets," n.d., ageing-better.org.uk/imperial-london-hotels-changing-mindsets.

p. 197 *A 2024 study across Belgium:* Laura De Boom and Kim De Meulenaere, "Age-Inclusive Leadership and Intrinsic Work Motivation: The Moderating Role of the Leader–Member Age Difference," *Work, Aging and Retirement* 11, no. 3 (July 2025): 230–248, doi.org/10.1093/workar/waae016.

p. 199 *In one called Being Like Me:* Sylvia Pfeifer, "Rolls-Royce Hardwires Inclusion into Its Systems," *Financial Times*, November 19, 2024, ft.com/content/4bb7911a-d238-4e10-adae-7e8f701a7997.

p. 199 *Management legend Peter Drucker:* Peter F. Drucker, *Management: Tasks, Responsibilities, Practices* (Harper & Row, 1974), 123.

p. 201 *Massachusetts became the first state:* Commonwealth of Massachusetts, "Massachusetts Becomes First State Certified as an Age-Friendly Employer," April 29, 2022, mass.gov/news/massachusetts-becomes-first -state-certified-as-an-age-friendly-employer.

p. 201 *The Commonwealth's Age-Friendly:* Executive Office of Aging and Independence, *ReiMAgine Aging 2030: The Massachusetts Plan*, Commonwealth of Massachusetts, n.d., mass.gov/news/age-friendly-massachusetts-action -plan-progress-report.

p. 207 *Enter Exhibit A via the World Economic Forum:* World Economic Forum, "The Longevity Economy Principles: Igniting 35 Organizations to Build the Foundation for a Financially Secure Future," January 15, 2024, weforum.org/impact/how-the-longevity-principles-have-ignited-xx -organizations-to-commit-to-support-older-workers.

p. 208 *Organizations give themselves:* Bell Canada, "Bell Let's Talk," n.d., letstalk.bell.ca.

p. 209 *Since over 70 percent:* Sarah Findlater, "Talking Menopause at M&S," Marks & Spencer, n.d., corporate.marksandspencer.com/talking -menopause-ms.

p. 209 *Instead, they fostered:* Marks & Spencer, "Diversity, Equity, and Inclusion," n.d., jobs.marksandspencer.com/inclusion-and-diversity; Zoe Wickens, "Marks and Spencer to Change Staff Menopause Policy," Employee Benefits, October 21, 2021, employeebenefits.co.uk/healthcare-and -wellbeing/marks-and-spencer-to-change-staff-menopause-policy/ 245870.article.

p. 210 *Hilton's "Care for All":* Hilton, "Hilton Expands Wellness Platform and Benefits to Launch New Offerings Supporting Team Member Caregiving Responsibilities," June 21, 2022, stories.hilton.com/releases/hilton -expands-wellness-platform-benefits-new-offerings-supporting-team- member-caregiving-responsibilities.

p. 211 *Given that the Menopause Foundation of Canada's:* Menopause Foundation of Canada, *The Silence and the Stigma: Menopause in Canada*, 2022, menopausefoundationcanada.ca/menopause-in-canada-report.

p. 211 *Much like the groundbreaking example:* HSBC UK, "HSBC UK, First Direct, and M&S Bank Are the UK's First Accredited Menopause Friendly Employers," July 19, 2021, about.hsbc.co.uk/news-and-media/hsbc -uk-first-direct-m-and-s-bank-are-the-uks-first-accredited-menopause -friendly-employers.

p. 212 *For instance, at the request:* Chip Cutter, "The Office Therapist Will See You Now," *The Wall Street Journal*, August 27, 2024, wsj.com/articles/ in-office-therapy-benefit-synchrony-financial-83ab814e.

p. 212 *Foreseeing Japan's demographic crisis:* Jun Nagata, "Toyota Improves Engine Assembly," *Assembly*, September 28, 2023, assemblymag.com/ articles/98041-toyota-improves-engine-assembly.

p. 213 *In addition, the company paired: Toyota Times*, "Promoting a Triple 'Friendly' Kaizen Approach at an Engine Plant: For People, Costs and the Environment," July 26, 2021, toyotatimes.jp/en/spotlights/159.html.

p. 214 *German chemicals firm BASF:* BASF, "More Space for Work and Private Life," n.d., basf.com/dk/en/who-we-are/organization/locations/europe/ german-sites/ludwigshafen/working-at-the-site/work-life-management/ Mehr-Spielraum-fur-Beruf--Familie-und-Privatleben.

p. 215 *In a detailed 2023 study:* Natasa Vujica Herzog, Özlem Kaya, and Borut Buchmeister, "Ergonomics and Ageing: Case Study," in *DAAAM International Scientific Book 2023*, ed. B. Katalinic (DAAAM International 2023), doi.org/10.2507/daaam.scibook.2023.02.

p. 216 *In 2024, the OECD:* Organisation for Economic Co-operation and Development, *Promoting Better Career Choices for Longer Working Lives: Stepping Up Not Stepping Out* (OECD Publishing, 2024), doi.org/10.1787/ 1ef9a0d0-en.

Track 10: The Encore

p. 221 *When I sat down with a good friend:* Roger L. Martin, in conversation with the author, November 2024.

p. 223 *Cicero once observed:* Marcus Tullius Cicero, *De Amicitia (On Friendship),* c. 44 BCE.

p. 229 *The tiger team was inspired:* Goldman Sachs, "Goldman Sachs Returnship," n.d., goldmansachs.com/careers/programs-for-professionals/returnship.

p. 230 *Enter MFlex, inspired by:* Hindustan Unilever Limited, "Future Workforce: Reimagining the Future of Work," n.d., hul.co.in/sustainability/future -of-work/future-workforce.

p. 231 *Stanford's program helps seasoned:* Stanford University, "Stanford Distinguished Careers Institute," n.d., dci.stanford.edu.

About Dan

Dan Pontefract is the founder of Pontefract Group, dedicated to elevating leadership and organizational culture. He has collaborated with firms such as Salesforce, BMO, Nutrien, Virgin Media O2, TD Bank, Autodesk, McGill University, and Alberta Blue Cross to transform their culture, employee experience, leadership practices, and operational strategies. Additionally, he serves as an adjunct professor at the University of Victoria's Gustavson School of Business.

Dan is the author of five influential and award-winning books; for details, see the back of this book. His writing has received numerous accolades: *Work-Life Bloom* was named a 2024 Thinkers50 Top New Management Book and Gold Medal Winner of the Axiom Business Book Awards; *Lead. Care. Win.* won the 2022 Nautilus Awards Silver Medal for Leadership; and *Open to Think* won the 2019 getAbstract International Book of the Year and the Axiom Business Book Award Silver Medal.

Recognized as a thought leader, Dan is on the Thinkers50 Radar list, HR *Weekly*'s 100 Most Influential People in HR, peopleHum's Top 200 Thought Leaders, and *Inc. Magazine*'s Top 100 Leadership Speakers.

Dan previously served as chief envisioner and chief learning officer at TELUS, a leading Canadian telecommunications company.

Prior to TELUS, Dan held senior executive positions with SAP, Business Objects, Crystal Decisions, and the British Columbia Institute of Technology. His extensive career blends corporate and academic experience, supported by an MBA, BEd, and multiple industry certifications. He is a sought-after speaker, having delivered over 600 keynotes, including four TED Talks, reaching over 500,000 people in all his engagements. He writes for *Forbes* and *Harvard Business Review*.

Dan resides in Victoria, Canada, with his wife, Denise. They have three children, two dogs, two cats, and too much fun.

Visit danpontefract.com for more information or email speak@danpontefract.com to inquire about his services.

What's Next?

Book Review

If the ideas in this book sparked reflection or added value to your leadership journey, please consider leaving a review. Reviews help others discover the book and reinforce the importance of these conversations.  The most influential place to post is Amazon (QR code), but platforms like Goodreads and your favourite bookseller are helpful as well. It does not need to be long. Just honest. Thank you for taking the time and for being part of the conversation.

Age Awareness Assessments

Don't forget, if you have not taken the Personal and Organizational Age Awareness Assessments, you should. They're helpful for gauging where you and your organization are at with age acumen. Best part— they're free!

Personal

Organizational

Join *Pontefractions*

If this book resonated, you'll want to keep the conversation going. *Pontefractions* is Dan Pontefract's newsletter, offering deeper insights on leadership, culture, purpose, and the future of work. Each edition delivers  practical ideas, research-backed thinking, and real-world stories to help you lead and live with more intention. It's read by thousands of professionals and leaders committed to doing work that matters.

About Dan's Services

Whether it's a keynote, workshop, or strategic consulting, Dan's clients appreciate that he's adaptable yet possesses deep expertise in leadership, purpose, culture, workplace collaboration, thinking, performance, age, and all aspects of the employee experience.

Dan possesses hundreds of stories and tactics to use, along with an array of practical leadership exercises and pragmatic, valuable takeaways. In sum, he listens, curates, and tailors all sessions in any environment.

SERVICE	OVERVIEW
Keynotes & Talks	Tailored to meet your organization's needs Face-to-face or virtual or even hybrid 15 minutes to 90 minutes/myriad tailored topics
Leadership Workshops	A variety of workshops tailored to meet your needs Face-to-face or virtual/up to 50 attendees 90 minutes to one full day in length
Masterclasses	Senior Leader Masterclass Series: Four to eight modules with virtual, F2F & case studies aimed at directors and above Mid-manager & frontline virtual Leadership Masterclass: Five modules in total
Strategic Planning & Consulting	Myriad options from Purpose-Vision-Mission, Leadership Modelling, Organizational Change, Org Design, Talent/Career Frameworks, and more
Annual or Quarterly Retainer	Tailored combination of any or all options Set number of events, hours, and/or access opportunities with Dan and his talents

Email **speak@danpontefract.com** to begin your inquiry.

Other Award-Winning Books by Dan

Work–Life Bloom:
How to Nurture a Team That Flourishes

- Thinkers50 Best Management Books for 2024

- Gold Medal Winner, 2024 Axiom Business
  Book Awards—Leadership Category

Lead. Care. Win.
How to Become a Leader Who Matters

- 2022 Nautilus Awards Silver Medal for Leadership

- Short-listed for the 2022 getAbstract
  International Book of the Year

- Finalist for the 2022 Page Turner Awards—
  Leadership Book of the Year

Open to Think: Slow Down,
Think Creatively, and Make Better Decisions

- 2019 getAbstract International Book of the Year

- Silver Medal Winner, 2019 Axiom Business Book
  Awards—Leadership Category

The Purpose Effect: Building Meaning in Yourself,
Your Role, and Your Organization

Flat Army: Creating a Connected and Engaged Organization

Visit **danpontefract.com/booksbydan** for more details on all books.